GROWING A SEMINARY IN ETHIOPIA:

A Triumph of Faith in an Uneasy Odyssey, 1994-2024

CARL E. HANSEN

WESTBOW
PRESS®
A DIVISION OF THOMAS NELSON
& ZONDERVAN

This book is a work of non-fiction. Unless otherwise noted, the author and the publisher make no explicit guarantees as to the accuracy of the information contained in this book and in some cases, names of people and places have been altered to protect their privacy.

WestBow Press books may be ordered through booksellers or by contacting:

WestBow Press
A Division of Thomas Nelson & Zondervan
1663 Liberty Drive
Bloomington, IN 47403
www.westbowpress.com
844-714-3454

Because of the dynamic nature of the Internet, any web addresses or links contained in this book may have changed since publication and may no longer be valid. The views expressed in this work are solely those of the author and do not necessarily reflect the views of the publisher, and the publisher hereby disclaims any responsibility for them.

Any people depicted in stock imagery provided by Getty Images are models, and such images are being used for illustrative purposes only.
Certain stock imagery © Getty Images.

ISBN: 979-8-3850-3861-9 (sc)
ISBN: 979-8-3850-3863-3 (hc)
ISBN: 979-8-3850-3862-6 (e)

Library of Congress Control Number: 2024924870

Print information available on the last page.

WestBow Press rev. date: 01/24/2025

REVIEWS

This fascinating, eye-witness account of the birth and development of the 30-year-old Meserete Kristos College/Seminary had me both laughing and crying! I flashed back to my own memories as a child of pioneer missionaries Chester and Sara Jane Wenger.

Now to have this priceless first-hand account of the birth pangs, the clashing visions, the pressing needs and marvelous provisions, the misunderstandings, course corrections, and irksome delays is both agonizing and exhilarating. I could not help but think of T.S. Eliot's line of poetry, "a hundred visions and revisions..." But that is what following the Spirit looks like. "The wind blows where it will..." Sometimes it feels like a hurricane. But God is building his church!

–Jewel (Wenger) Showalter, Communications & Development,
Rosedale Bible College

In his honest and vulnerable memoir about the building of the Meserete Kristos Seminary, Carl E. Hansen describes a thirty-year tempest of financial challenges, competing priorities, political roadblocks, and the slow but steady growth of a fledgling seminary that leaves the reader breathless. Building the Meserete Kristos Seminary has been the work of imperfect, visionary people who walked by faith toward an improbable goal. As one who has had the privilege of teaching students on the MKS campus, I can attest firsthand that this impressive institution produces leaders well-equipped to form the faith and strengthen the Anabaptist identity of their fast-growing churches. In his telling of this story, Hansen demonstrates that prayer, persistence, spiritual discernment, and reliance on God's provision are the *only* reliable resources Christians have in realizing dreams that require us to reach beyond what we have grasped. Thanks be to God for the faithful stewards of the vision for this seminary despite endless potential for distraction!

–Dr. David Boshart, president of Anabaptist
Mennonite Biblical Seminary

The remarkable story of the Ethiopian Meserete Kristos College (now Seminary), that has helped shape the theological formation of several thousand church leaders in the fastest-growing Anabaptist church in the world. Told from the perspective of Carl E. Hansen, a long-term North American teacher, administrator, and advocate for the school, this narrative testifies to the patience, tenacity, and generosity that led to the formation of the Meserete Kristos Church's seminary without flinching from the many conflicts, misunderstandings, and disappointments that were also part of the story. A welcome contribution to the growing field of global Anabaptist historiography.

–Dr. John D. Roth, project director, Anabaptism at 500
Professor of history emeritus, Goshen College

This thirty-year story of the Meserete Kristos College records how its faculty, staff, and students overcame painful conflict, tedious bureaucracy, and lack of resources to grow from a thirteen-student institute in a small, rented house to a sprawling campus housing hundreds of students. With a preacher's conviction and a historian's eye for detail, Hansen has written an illuminating record of a crucial period in the history of the modern mission movement.

–Dr. Peter Dula, professor of religion and culture
Eastern Mennonite University

This autobiography, thoughtfully and carefully written, is clear, concise, and coherent. Above all it is written with honesty and integrity. I cannot hide that there were tearful nights as I read this work, grappling with the past in which I shared. In bringing my buried wounds to the surface, I found this reflection therapeutic.

–Dr. Hailu Cherenet Biru, pastor of Ethiopian
Christian Fellowship Church
Los Angeles, CA

Stories of the phenomenal growth of the Meserete Kristos Church in Ethiopia over recent decades inspire many of us with awe. The story of Meserete Kristos College (Seminary), however, is one of conflicting visions, leadership challenges, broken contracts, cost escalations, destabilizing decisions, demoralized faculty/staff, and a string of relational heartaches. Yet remarkably, it is also a story worthy of awe—for the gritty determination against great odds, and the unbelievably hard work and unflagging faith of coworkers who persisted despite no end of reasons to give up.

Carl Hansen has accompanied the school since its birth and nearly every painstaking inch of growth since. He tells the story with gritty honesty, from his perspective. He does so with resilient love, acknowledging profound disappointments, yes, but also the extraordinary triumphs. The story relays the joy of seeing the wondrous gifts and ministries of the college's many graduates who have become champions for the Gospel. It is a triumph of faith in an uneasy odyssey.

I highly recommend this well-told memoir. It illustrates the immense human cost required to bring an educational vision to reality, and the incredible rewards when vision, leadership, teamwork, and resources coalesce. As a sobering account, it will require much soul searching about how best to build a mission-driven, sustainable institution, but it will also provide cause for great rejoicing as the faithfulness of God and God's people is on full display.

–Dr. Sara Wenger Shenk, Anabaptist Mennonite Biblical Seminary
President emerita

Burdened with Ethiopia's chronic political unrest, tribal warring, and abject poverty, the Meserete Kristos Church (Mennonite) emerged from the oppression of a failed communistic military dictatorship to find itself flooded with newcomers seeking answers to questions that Communism and the political Dergue had failed to satisfy. Rising to provide trained leaders to shepherd the masses, the church opened a tiny Bible Institute in 1994. Today, that institute has become a seminary with hundreds of students enrolled in its undergraduate and graduate programs.

In this well-written memoir, the author recounts from his own experiences the thirty-year struggles and successes that resulted in establishing a seminary in Bishoftu, Ethiopia. This is a compelling story about Christian faith-in-action, which, against great odds, has already produced 2,357 seminary graduates who are making a positive difference in Ethiopia's society.

–T. Ralph Syre, Ph.D., professor, James Madison University (retired)

What a story, a heroic saga to establish a school of higher learning in Ethiopia by the Meserete Kristos Church. Planted with little more than a vision, a desperate need to train leaders, and courageous pioneers, thirty years later the school has a main campus, a couple of extension sites, and dozens of affiliated learning centers across the nation. But the story is not pretty. Bumps and bruises, delays and disappointments litter the ground. The original dream of an accredited college of the arts and sciences remains unrealized. Nonetheless, this is a story of unfailing hope and unlikely success. There at the planting, Carl E. Hansen tells a comprehensive and moving first-hand account over the years. Countless partners joined the pioneers to water, cultivate, fertilize, and prune the planting with creativity and faithfulness. No doubt about it: God has produced the resulting growth and a bountiful harvest for his kingdom.

–Dr. Mark R. Wenger, LMC bishop, and
faculty mentor, Kairos University

REFLECTION

I reflect on the time when, at age sixteen, I made a life-changing decision. I had dropped out of school after completing grade nine, thinking I had enough education to be a farmer, as that was what I aspired to become. My father encouraged me by inviting me to farm with him. We rented another 160 acres of land and worked together. During the many long days of solitude, plowing, seeding, irrigating, and harvesting, I had a lot of time to think, contemplating the future. I had big dreams, plans for a grand and successful career, building up the finest farm in the community with modern buildings and equipment.

Then, as I pushed my dream further into the future, the disturbing question came, "And then what?" Well, logically, the years would pass, the paint would peal, fences would rot, roofs would leak, metal would rust, trees would age, and shrubs would die. One would find his senior years burdened with repairs and maintenance. Such labor would reveal the slow but steady diminishing of one's physical powers. And after that, then what?

Well, when aches and pains or disease sufficiently diminished one's abilities, one would be forced into retirement and, eventually, death. The farm would fall into the hands of the next generation. The young ambitious purchaser would demolish the decaying, outdated buildings and fences and start afresh with his dreams of a fine farm. What was the use of devoting my whole life to building a fine farm that would only decay and be replaced when, if not before, I am gone?

Disturbed by these thoughts, day after day, I finally came to the point that I prayed, "God, I want to be a farmer. But what do you want me to be?" The inaudible answer came to me as clear as a bell. "Instead of investing your life in temporal things that fade away, it would be better to invest your life in helping humans whose eternal value never fades. Now is the time to prepare yourself for greater things. Go back and finish high school! You are still an ignorant kid. There is so much to learn!"

That was it, the turning point. I obeyed, finished high school, went on to college and seminary, and gave my life to the service of promoting God's kingdom in its various human aspects.

Now, sixty-six years later, in writing this memoir, I am reflecting on what has been my ultimate life motivation. It is quite simple. My life prayer is eloquently spoken in the words of the song by Michael Frye, "Jesus, be the center." This is the prayer of my soul, the prayer of my life, but the prayer that I often forget to pray.

> Jesus, be the center.
> Be my source, be my light, Jesus.
> Jesus, be the center.
> Be my hope, be my song, Jesus.
> Be the fire in my heart,
> Be the wind in these sails.
> Be the reason that I live, Jesus, Jesus.
> Be my path, be my guide, Jesus.

Written by: Michael Frye, CCLI#2650429 ©1999 Vineyard Songs (UK/Eire). Added: 1999-09-07

CHALLENGE

In my dream, I watched seven of my best friends and leaders in our church, dressed in their business suits and carrying their briefcases, walk out through the airport gate and climb into the little airplane parked on the runway. I was following them. I was to be their pilot.

Suddenly, I realized that I had never flown a plane before! I had never even sat in a pilot's seat. I knew nothing about all those dials, buttons, and levers. Yet, these men all trusted me, and were entrusting their lives into my hands, believing I would bring them safely to our intended destination.

This awful thought gripped me, and I began to have a "Gethsemane experience" (Mathew 26:36 – 42). Two things I knew: I needed to pray, and I had to urinate!

Then I woke up. I began to think. Truly, Meserete Kristos College is like an airplane, carrying a precious cargo of leaders forward into the church's future. The Meserete Kristos Church is entrusting its leadership and its future into the hands of the college. The college can assist it directly toward its desired destination, or wander off course into some lifeless desert, or it can crash on the way. Whatever the college does, it will have a lasting and eternal effect on the church. Its success or failure depends on how it is "piloted." And the one chosen to be the principal acts as that pilot.

Yet, the college is new and the principal inexperienced. We have never flown this "plane" before. We do not really know how to make it "take off" and guide it through uncharted future time and space. We are not sure we can bring it down safely at its proper destination. It is time we had a "Gethsemane experience." It is time to pray, to prepare, to "urinate," to put aside all unnecessary "waste," every sin that holds us back, all foolish pride, and every self-exalting opinion that might lead us astray or interfere with our journey. We must seek the Lord, the "auto-pilot" who alone knows best how to pilot our plane through unknown space and time.

Then I thought further. Each of our students is a "pilot" who will be entrusted with an important organization of God's people. Into his/her hands will be entrusted the lives of hundreds or thousands of people. Each is being trained, enabled, prepared. Each must bring his/her people safely through the distractions and storms of life to their true destination, their eternal home. Each will always need the help of the "auto pilot." We the administrators and the teachers, as well as our students, must never forget to pray, to seek the Lord, to depend upon him to undergird and direct our "flying" and our "landing." Only he can bring our "plane" safely to its desired destination!

DEDICATION

I wish to dedicate this work to the memory of those pioneer Mennonite missionaries who went to Ethiopia before us. While recognizing the fraternity of other missionaries of various persuasions who pioneered before them, these felt called to add to Ethiopia, an Anabaptist witness. These pioneers went, preparing the way, laying the foundation upon which a mighty movement, the Meserete Kristos Church (MKC), literally "Foundation Christ Church" (I Corinthians 3:11) is being built.

Starting in 1946 and continuing throughout a thirty-year period, 196 Mennonite adults served, for short terms, or extended periods, in this challenging task. The earliest arrivals represented the Mennonite Relief and Service Committee (MRS), a branch of the Mennonite Central Committee (MCC). They administered relief to victims of WWII, organized medical work, trained staff, and operated the Haile Mariam Mamo Memorial Hospital in Nazareth.

In 1948, their foundational work was handed over to the Eastern Mennonite Board of Missions and Charities (EMBMC). To continue the service, others came as builders and educators, building schools and teaching children, and establishing a school for the blind. They built a campus, establishing the Nazareth Bible Academy, a first-class boarding high school. Others operated premium Christian bookstores in four locations, built the first permanent houses of worship for emerging churches, managed a guesthouse, and wrote and published Christian literature.

Growing a Seminary in Ethiopia: A Triumph of Faith in an Uneasy Odyssey, 1994-2024

By Carl E. Hansen

With Foreword by Pastor Hailu Cherenet Biru (PhD)

CONTENTS

FOREWORD

Although this book is a memoir, it encompasses content that would be considered as a historical document. It is written by an eyewitness who played a vital part in this journey of Meserete Kristos College. The vision was ambitious: "to become a full Christian University." However, the leaders in those days trusted the big God who specializes in things which are impossible.

Through the pages of this memoir, the faithfulness of our God is demonstrated repeatedly. Implementing this vision was not a dinner party. There were high and low moments. Despite challenges, the faculty and college campus were developed successfully. This remarkable progress is clearly outlined in this memoir. As a person who has walked on this journey, I am grateful to the Lord for what he has accomplished in these thirty years. Since history is His story, we see the invisible hand of God in each step of the way.

Though there were joyous moments in this odyssey, there were times of lament and brokenness that left physical scars on some of the pilgrims. Carl explicitly outlines those moments in this memoir. Since I shared some of the pain that the writer included, I struggled a lot in remembering those painful circumstances. However, I cannot hide that the good Lord transformed those pains into gains for the writer and his fellow pilgrims who shared the vision and mission of Meserete Kristos College.

Although the vision and mission are not fully realized, the foundation is laid, the baton is passed to those who will carry it on to become the envisioned full-fledged university sometime soon. As sociologists say, "it takes a village to raise a child," and I would say it takes generations to build institutions. To that end the seminary wing is realized at this point. However, it gives us a heartache that the liberal arts wing is lagging. In fact, I concur with the dissatisfaction of the writer that we do not see the liberal arts wing of the college realized at this time of writing.

In my assessment, the culture of avoidance and suppression in conflict management has contributed to the anguish, confusion, and physical harm of the pilgrims who labored in this journey. Openness and transparency were foreign in interpersonal relationships in our culture. As a result, the building project was slowed, institutional development was delayed, and key leaders of the college were exposed to multi-faceted emotional and physical pain.

As I said earlier, the memoir has high and low points. Because of different leadership styles, the project suffered lots of setbacks; however, the Lord repeatedly transformed the stumbling blocks into steppingstones in this journey. Therefore, the college building flourished, and multitudes graduated from the seminary wing.

Finally, I would like to use an illustration to summarize my readings of thirty-five chapters of this memoir in the following fashion: I see life as a show, and, in this show, we see different characters. Our God is the script writer and the producer in this difficult show. He played his part beyond our expectations. Carl and Vera took the leading actor roles in this show, and they played their roles effectively and successfully. I am certain the Lord would smile and respond positively with my assessment of this journey. The twenty-eight-year show was not a one family show. Multitudes of saints from the USA, Canada, Europe, Australia, Hong Kong, and Ethiopia played their part as well. Through the assigned role of the script writer and producer, i.e., the triune God Almighty, each played their given part. Visible on the stage at MK College were the leading actors, Carl and Vera, and their fellow actors. Just as important were those indispensable invisible players all over the world, who gave financial support anonymously. However, the main characters in retrospect still ask the question, "Was this vision of having a liberal arts college an illusion or a reality?" Though I cannot answer for God, as an actor with a decisive role in this show, I conclude that the leading characters, Carl and Vera, played the God-given script well.

I am sure God would say *'Well done, good and faithful servant! You have been faithful with a few things; I will put you in charge of many things. Come and share your master's happiness!' (Matthew 25:23 NIV)*

—Pastor Hailu Cherenet Biru (PhD), Ethiopian
Christian Fellowship Church,
Los Angeles, CA

PREFACE

Friends and colleagues have pressed upon me that I must write a history of the Meserete Kristos College, now called *Meserete Kristos Seminary*. Responding to that challenge upon officially retiring some years ago, I began drafting the story, not as an objective historian, but as a memoir, my story as I remembered it.

I accepted this challenge humbly, as an amateur storyteller, for the sake of future generations, most not yet born. They may be curious as to how their school was founded. January 1, 2024, marked the thirtieth anniversary of the founding of Meserete Kristos College. It seems that this is the right time to finalize this book.

While trying to be as objective as possible, I recognize that for twenty-eight of those thirty years, I have invested heavily of my time and energy in the development of this institution. During the first fifteen years, I was intimately involved, and upon my retirement continued supporting the college as a volunteer fund-raiser and promoter. Although I am a *ferrengi*, an outsider to the Ethiopian culture and context, I have been deeply involved and therefore am, to a degree, limited by the subjectivity of an insider.

From the beginning, I felt a divine call to the work of developing this college. As I write this, reflecting on my earlier life, long-buried memories surface. Back in 1958, in my teenage years, while attending a five-week *Winter Bible School* in Kalispel, Montana, I was intrigued by the older church leaders and teachers discussing the possibility of our Alberta-Saskatchewan Conference establishing a Bible institute. I followed with interest in the years immediately after, but no steps were taken. Four years later, upon entering Eastern Mennonite College, I chose to enroll in Bible as my major, with history as a minor emphasis, in the liberal arts program. Again, one of the motivating factors in choosing such a major, besides preparing for a pastoral ministry, was the possibility of being a teacher in our conference's proposed Bible institute.

By the time I graduated years later, I realized that the concept of a Bible institute was out of sync with the times, as the demand of young people was for more advanced studies offered by the colleges, universities, and seminaries that were proliferating in the North American society. Our tiny conference would never have its own Bible institute. Our interested young people would be encouraged to join the larger institutes already existing in faraway places.

Somehow, it seemed providential that upon leaving seminary in 1967, my first job assignment was to be a Bible teacher at the Nazareth Bible Academy, a full boarding high school operated by Eastern Mennonite Missions (EMM) in Ethiopia. Later, during my stay there, I thought prophetically, that someday, this high school would develop to become a full Christian college or university. At the time, I did not see myself involved in that vision.

However, after a busy life of directing a development project in Ethiopia, pastoring a Canadian church, engaging in rural development among the Maasai, and teaching in a Christian liberal arts college in Kenya, here I was back in Ethiopia. I was invited to teach in and to serve as a consultant with the Meserete Kristos Church (MKC), in establishing its infant Meserete Kristos Church Bible Institute. In looking back, although not a trained "pilot," I could see the hand of God through all my varied life experiences, preparing me for this huge challenge.

Throughout these last twenty-eight years, I have been driven by a vision that has been a part of my waking and my sleeping hours, a constant driving force that will not let me rest.

I expect many of my observations will be challenged by others who see things or remember things differently. I would like to be fair to them and give them a hearing as much as possible. However, this is my version of the story.

–Carl E. Hansen

ACKNOWLEDGMENTS

This book is intended as a memoir of the twenty-eight years my wife, Vera, and I have been involved in the life and growth of Meserete Kristos College. As such, our witness is a primary source. During the years covered in this memoir, I kept a diary which has been of great assistance to me in recalling much of the detailed content and dating.

I am deeply indebted to Vera, my beloved life partner, who has stood with me in all the struggles and achievements chronicled in this book. This is the story of MK College, but it is also our story. Having been a participant and witness, she has examined my manuscript, verified the facts, and offered multitudinous suggestions for its improvement.

Further, I owe a debt of gratitude to our eldest daughter, Cindy Kreider, who has meticulously assisted in editing the manuscript. While battling cancer, holding down a full-time counseling job, and maintaining her household, this grandmother of eight still persistently found time to diligently go over each sentence and paragraph again and again to improve my rough draft. This is also her work.

Also, I have deep appreciation for a colleague and friend, Kebede Bekere, lecturer and counselor, who carefully read my manuscript and contributed helpful insights from an Ethiopian point of view.

I must also acknowledge the loving support of our second daughter, Karen Hansen, a seasoned high school English teacher, who sacrificed her precious hours of needed rest to give this manuscript its final editorial polish, eliminating my many overlooked punctuation and grammatical errors. I think she caught most of them.

–Carl E. Hansen

ACRONYMS

AMBS	Anabaptist Mennonite Biblical Seminary
CDC	Campus Development Committee
CMF	Christian Missionary Fellowship
CRA	Canada Revenue Agency
EGST	Evangelical Graduate School of Theology
EMBMC	Eastern Mennonite Board of Missions and Charities
EMM	Eastern Mennonite Missions
EMC	Eastern Mennonite College
EMS	Eastern Mennonite Seminary
EMU	Eastern Mennonite University
EPRDF	Ethiopian People's Revolutionary Democratic Front
ETS	Equipping the Saints
ETC	Evangelical Theological College
FPU	Fresno Pacific University
ICMT	Institute of Christian Ministries Training
MBBS	Mennonite Brethren Biblical Seminary
MCC	Mennonite Central Committee
MRC	Mennonite Relief Committee
MKC	Meserete Kristos Church
MKC-DC	Meserete Kristos Church Development Commission
MST	Missionary Support Team
NGO	Non-Government Organization
NWMC	Northwest Mennonite Conference
OCI	Overseas Council International

SACS   Southern Association of Colleges and Schools
SIM   Society of International Missions
TOEFL   Test of English as a Foreign Language
WV   World Vision

CHAPTER 1

Background

Early Strategies for Leadership Training

From the very beginning, education was heavy on the minds of the pioneer missionaries. With their two hospitals and clinic work at Deder and Nazareth (now renamed *Adama*), they established two dresser Bible schools to train nursing assistants or "dressers," as they were called in those days. They also opened a school for the blind in Addis Ababa and about a dozen elementary schools in Hararge and Shoa provinces, where there were no schools. Additionally, they established a boarding high school, the Bible Academy at Nazareth, while they also planted churches in those locations. By the mid 1970's, the Meserete Kristos Church (MKC) operated these flourishing institutions.

In the mid-1960's, a spiritual movement, *Heavenly Sunshine*, broke out among some public high school students in Nazareth and spread to colleges in Bahar Dar, Harar, and other places. Young students sought God in persistent prayer, and as promised in Acts 1:8, God poured out his Spirit.

This outpouring of the Holy Spirit brought dramatic changes in the lives of the students, characterized by transformed lifestyles, including a deeper level of victory over sin, a contagious prayer life, and evidence of the fruit of the Spirit. They were bonded together in love and fellowship. They had a deep hunger for the Word of God. They exercised the gifts of the Spirit expressed by boldness in witness, miracles, healings, exorcisms, and speaking in tongues. This resulted in transformed worship, divine guidance in life, and growth in numbers.

As this movement spread among the youth, it provoked a stern reaction among the parents and their traditional Orthodox or Muslim religious leaders. Their united opposition encouraged persecution by the imperial government and local authorities. When the persecution became severe, these young people eventually affiliated with the more established evangelical churches, including MKC. Their enthusiastic involvement transformed the essence of MKC.

When the Provisional Military Government (the *Dergue*) came to power in 1974 and moved toward adopting the Marxist path to development, Christians studied how the church survived in the Soviet Union and anticipated that possible eventuality. The time came in January 1982 when government officials imprisoned the MKC leaders and confiscated all church properties and institutions. The Meserete Kristos Church officially ceased to exist.

However, the church morphed into its underground mode, small groups meeting clandestinely in homes. Such cell groups were not a new idea. Jesus started with a small group, and the persecuted church in Jerusalem met in homes. The cell is more effective than the larger congregation for teaching and discipling believers. People are taught more intensely and personally. They get to know each other better. They know the problems and goals of the church. They grow spiritually and socially. They are more accountable. They are more honest in paying their tithes.

Pastor Kassa Agafari reported that in 1984, at a secret all-night meeting, fifteen elders drafted a strategy for ministry under the restricted conditions. They formed an education committee that prepared training materials, trained cell leaders, and organized the cell groups consisting of six to ten people. He described how a few elders organized themselves.

> We prayed day and night until we got some instruction
> from God. We felt led to go out and visit the people in
> their homes to encourage them.... We divided the city
> into six areas; each of us was responsible for one area.

We identified possible leaders in each of our regions. We trained them and called them "watchmen." There were both male and female leaders. The training had to be on a one-to-one basis. The watchmen conducted secret services in the home "chapels" …. All who became Christians were instructed in soul winning, and they then reached out to others ….

To avoid detection, they met in groups of six to ten people. When a group grew too big, it was time to split and form another cell group. The people arrived at meetings in one and twos but never in a group or at the same time. They also left at different intervals. When they came in, they knelt and prayed. When the leader felt that enough people had gathered, he started the service.

The singing had to be very soft. Most of the time was spent on studying the scriptures, sharing, encouraging each other, and praying.

When the groups became better organized and established, the church started collecting tithes to help with the administration. All information was kept in the leader's head. There were no written documents. (MWC News Service)

Evangelism was done with great care. New converts were carefully taught and then baptized before being brought to a cell group. Preachers travelled to each cell group on Sundays, some starting as early as 6:00 a.m., and moved all day until late at night. Pastor Paulos Gulilat spoke of ministering in up to seven meetings in one day.

Weddings and funerals became occasions for celebration and encouragement in larger assemblies. However, the real growth in discipleship took place in the small secret groups. Even among the Ethiopian diaspora, in Nairobi, in 1995, Paulos reported there were forty-four cell groups.

Women played an especially significant role in the cell church movement. They served as leaders in the home cell groups, provided hospitality in their homes, led Bible studies, led in fasting and prayer activities, and did pastoral work in preaching, teaching, and discipling new believers. Women ministered by comforting and encouraging those who suffered illness, persecution, temptation, discouragement, or physical need. They did neighborhood evangelism through visiting, hosting, or attending coffee ceremonies, and attending and assisting funerals and wedding ceremonies.

During that dark decade, men were watched by the secret police for any sign of possible "subversive" activity, so they had to keep a low profile. Women were assumed by the Marxist government to be less of a threat and could move about incurring less suspicion.

This revival movement flourished and spread. God's church does not consist of human-made organizations, buildings, or budgets. It is more than an organization. It is an organism, a body enlivened by the indwelling of God's life-giving Holy Spirit. Yet God's church, being made up of social beings, thrives best when it takes on organizational forms, traditions, and budgets.

In 1984, the elders started a *One Year for Christ* program. This was a six-week "boot camp" or training program for twenty to forty volunteers who wanted to serve the church. It was an orientation program conducted by the church's Evangelism/Missions Department. They were taught using the Amharic language.

After six weeks of training, these volunteers were assigned to churches or to church planting settings. They were "God's shock troops," sent out to assess their calling, to evangelize, to heal the sick, to cast out demons, to invade the devil's territory, and to plant churches where there had never been churches before. If they were fruitful, they would be employed as full-time evangelists, missionaries, or pastors. If not, they would go on to other careers upon completion of their assignment. Most of MKC's evangelists came through this program.

The Marxist ideologues failed to understand the church. They did not understand that the church is the "body of Christ," and its head is Christ. Merely imprisoning its leaders and confiscating its properties did not kill the church. Where they closed one church, fifty clandestine churches sprang up in its place. When official leaders were imprisoned, unofficial leaders sprang up to take their places. Where male leaders were stalked and watched, less suspected females assumed the leadership. And where its schools were closed, a "seminary without walls" was developed and operated in secret.

In fact, unknown to themselves, the Marxists became, by far, the best "missionary sending agency" that anyone could have devised. The dictatorial Dergue government took upon itself to assign all high school and university graduates to their places of employment, usually without considering the individual's choice. Among those being sent were hundreds, then thousands, of strong underground church believers with experience in leading cell groups. These were sent all over Ethiopia. Wherever they were sent, they worked at their assigned jobs, but also, while off duty, shared their faith one on one, and formed new converts into underground cell churches. Thus, the Marxists unwittingly facilitated the sending out of thousands of church planters, and best of all, the government paid their support!

As in the early history of the Anabaptist movement, rapid growth with persecution propelled recent converts to positions of leadership without the advantages of training and experience. There was danger of absorbing and passing on the confusing, distorted, and sometimes false teachings of many ministries and cults that proliferated in the troubled milieu. Books, pamphlets, tracts, cassettes, and videos from every possible source were copied and circulated widely. Visions, dreams, and "prophecies" were shared and gossiped, each adding its unique flavor to the theological soup from which these recent converts indiscriminately found their spiritual and theological nourishment.

To counteract wrong, confusing influences, and to give clear direction in matters of doctrine and Christian practice, church leaders developed curricula and duplicated training materials. This subversive illegal activity was performed with an old Gestetner in a secret office, hidden in the labyrinthine back streets of Addis Ababa. The clandestine venue was a shipping container converted to "guesthouse" on the MCC compound. Materials were discretely distributed to the cell congregations to guide them in their Bible study.

The clandestine MKC leadership established an education department. Its purpose was to help members and ministers to grow in the character of Christ and in a thorough knowledge of the Word of God, to train them in the skills necessary for ministry in their churches. To accomplish this purpose, the department administered a Key Teachers Training Program that provided training twice per year for ministers in training centers positioned throughout the country. These were often held in church buildings of other denominations that were still open.

The training covered four topics each year based on biblical and theological issues. Teaching on Marxism and relevant issues was included.

The education department also held different workshops, symposiums, and seminars dealing with specialized topics for ministers (evangelists, elders, pastors, Sunday school teachers, and Bible study leaders) and congregations which faced doctrinal problems.

Realizing the need for key leaders more deeply trained in biblical studies and theology, the education department also administered a very limited scholarship program that made it possible for a few to study in local Bible colleges or seminaries abroad. In collaboration with Eastern Mennonite Missions (EMM), they sent a few selected leaders to study in Mennonite colleges and seminaries in the USA and Canada. However, these did not return to serve after their graduations.

Disappointed, the church sent selected leaders as students to the Evangelical Theological Seminary in Osijek, Croatia, to the Mennonite College and Seminary of East Africa in Musoma, Tanzania, to Daystar University in Nairobi, Kenya, to Mekane Yesus (Lutheran) Seminary and Evangelical Theological College (SIM) in Addis Ababa. This was more effective, as these graduated and returned to serve their church and its people. However, this was also disappointing, as some of those trained locally, espoused theological viewpoints alien to the Meserete Kristos Church doctrinal distinctives and practical norms.

The Need for Leadership Training

It may seem a bit ironical that Ethiopia, sometimes listed as one of the poorest nations on earth, was known to be among the richest in matters of the Spirit. In a country torn by protracted wars, recurring famines, and endemic poverty, there was a spiritual hunger and turning to God on a scale seldom witnessed anywhere. Since the fall of the Dergue government and the official restoration of freedom of religion, the Orthodox churches, the various kinds of mosques, the evangelical churches, and a host of imported cults were all doing a brisk business in religion. MKC was no exception.

Today, the church in Ethiopia survives and thrives in the context of continuing opposition, stifling poverty, pervading ignorance, ethnic bigotry, and proliferating heresies. However, the most urgent challenge is that brought on by rapid growth. How can it provide solid, trained leadership for its mushrooming congregations, regional offices, and emerging institutions?

Such significant church growth means that half of the members have been in the church for less than ten years. This means that in terms of nurture, most members are still spiritual adolescents. New members with keen spiritual appetites are eager to eat at every spiritual "junk food" outlet they find on the way. How can they be protected against preying international evangelists or prophets who manipulate them for shameful gain? They challenge the poor to "test the Lord" through sacrificial giving, promising amazing prosperity in return. Then, shamelessly filling their suitcases with the people's offerings, they fly away in first class comfort, leaving behind a flood of confusion for the pastors to straighten out.

The challenge continues with the local, smooth, self-styled "prophets" and "apostles" with their loud dogmatic preaching and predicting. One is reminded of Hitler's technique, who said, "If you shout loud enough and often enough, people will believe whatever you say!" Jesus warns us to be aware of these "wolves in sheep's clothing."

How are untrained leaders to deal with these smooth con artists? What can they offer to the crowds, ever eager for miracles, instant healings, direct words from God, or to hear that God really wants them to be rich and prosperous? The best defense against error is to know the truth. The need to train congregational leaders is urgent.

At the same time, anointed local evangelists, without training, labor selflessly, night and day. They put their whole lives into sharing the Good News, giving hope to the hopeless and depressed and minister grace and forgiveness to those burdened with their failures and sins. They bring release to those captivated by superstition and ignorance, and minister deliverance to those possessed by or in bondage to evil spirits. They plant these trophies of grace into thriving churches.

After a few years, these leaders are burned out, having given their people all they had. However, the people are maturing. They have had enough "milk." Who will give them "meat"? The leaders need time to rest, to be refreshed, to be updated, to be re-tooled. Leaders need to be nourished if they are to nourish those under their care.

Shaping Vision for a Church-owned College

Besides being a dispenser of information and a sharpener of skills, a college is a shaper of the minds and characters of its students. Education, in shaping the understandings, viewpoints, and guiding vision of church leaders, will determine the theological direction any church of today and tomorrow will take. To be specific, a college established by MKC would have a tremendous impact upon the congregations of that church, as well as of other churches, society, and the nation, in the years, decades, and centuries ahead.

When the Dergue government collapsed, and religious freedom was restored, MKC was found to have grown from 5,000 members in 1982 to over 35,000 in 1991. With freedom, that number grew almost immediately to 50,000. By 1994, that number had swelled to about 78,000.

Although some of its houses of worship were restored to it, the rapidly growing church had to find temporary shelters in which most of its growing crowds could worship. Despite its increase in numbers, it had no elementary or secondary school. And until 1994, it had no college or seminary in which to train leaders.

In that period, between 1991 and 1993, the church leaders strategized how they could best establish an institution of higher learning that would meet the needs of their burgeoning congregations. They concluded they must establish a Christian college to ground their own leaders in their own theological perspectives, and to provide tertiary level educational opportunities for their own young people.

In their deliberations, the leaders decided they did not want "just another theological college." Pastor Siyoum stated their vision to me in the words, "We need a Daystar in Ethiopia." They envisioned establishing a tertiary-level biblical seminary and college that would grow to become a full Christian university, offering a selected range of undergraduate and graduate programs relevant to impacting the Ethiopian societies and beyond towards a more honest, just, compassionate, and prosperous future. Instruction would be approached from a Christian, charismatic, Anabaptist perspective. It would have a wholistic emphasis, integrating the spiritual and the mundane, linking knowledge with ethical and moral values. It would equip men and women to serve the churches, institutions, businesses, and societies of Ethiopia and Africa with integrity.

The college would also have a strong continuing education program, offering evening classes, practical short courses, seminars, and workshops as in-service training in various fields of interest to the public.

Graduates would serve as evangelists, pastors, teachers, and administrators in the churches. They could also serve Christ as "tent-making ministers" by serving society according to their gifts and callings as Christian professionals, employees, or entrepreneurs who establish their own businesses and provide jobs and training for others.

In the background of that era, in a desperate effort to mobilize resources as quickly as possible to educate the masses of Ethiopia's population, the Ethiopian People's Revolutionary Democratic Front (EPRDF) government was encouraging private investors to join in the national effort by opening for-profit elementary and high schools and colleges. Private non-profit institutions such as churches were also encouraged to join. It was an ideal time for MKC to accept this challenge to the best of her ability.

In response to this challenge, many private investors rushed to develop colleges. It was a time when thousands of high school graduates found there was no room for them in the limited government universities. Parents were willing to pay fees to have their youth educated. The first colleges found their temporary rented campuses packed, and the profits rolled in. The downside of this was the disappointment that set in when greed undermined the quality of many of these private ventures. Their outcomes were substandard, and the citizens felt cheated. The government had to order many of them to be closed.

While this was going on, the government filled the need by establishing thirty new universities, upgrading the academic requirements of private ventures, and making it more difficult for new ones to emerge. The new government universities took "the cream of the crop" of new high school graduates, attracted by free education with a modest cost- sharing obligation after graduation. This forced the private colleges to compete with greater disadvantages.

CHAPTER 2

A Humble Beginning at Haya Hulet Mazoria

In January 1994, the church leaders opened the *Meserete Kristos Church Bible Institute* in a small compound near Haya Hulet Mazoria in Addis Ababa. The leaders had little experience with developing and running a sophisticated higher educational institution. Among them, they had no one qualified with post-graduate academic credentials in theology. Although they had extremely limited financial resources, they started with what they had in their hands.

The facility consisted of a small house of five rooms, and a second building with two larger rooms, which served as a classroom and an office, and two Asian-style squat toilets. Later, a steel and plastic tent was constructed in the center of the compound, which served as a chapel, study hall, and dining hall.

There were no typewriters, computers, or copiers, only a few shelves with library books and a few textbooks. The male students all slept in one room, and for the first year, they did not even have mattresses. Some visitors saw their plight and donated funds for mattresses. Blankets and pillows were borrowed from the church.

Pastor Siyum Gebretsadik was the first principal and teacher. Evangelist Hailu Cherenet was a part-time teacher. Ann King-Grosh, a missionary, taught the English courses. Other church officers and pastors volunteered to teach selected courses. A few missionaries from other missions filled in as they were able. Emebet Mekonnen served as dean of students, registrar, business manager, general service manager, and librarian.

Two single women, Chewanesh Berka and Asnakech Gebre Selassie, purchased the groceries, prepared the meals, and kept the compound tidy. They worked seven days a week and slept on campus. Three guards, sent from the MKC Head Office, rotated their shifts.

Thirteen evangelists were selected for a diploma program taught in English. Of these, all were males except one. A female evangelist from an Orthodox renewal group was included as a special case. These students studied for a three-month term, after which they went home to serve for two months. While they were working at home, another seventeen students came for two months to study in a certificate program taught in Amharic.

Stephen Penner, a pastor and visitor from Fresno, California, was impressed and wrote this poem published in the June 1994 issue of Missionary Messenger:

At the MKC Bible School
By Stephen Penner

In this lion's land
> source of the Blue Nile
> twelve men lie on mattresses
> to await a new day
> of Old Testament study.

They have left
> farm and family,
> the laughter of children,
> the taste and touch of village,
> for this temporary Addis Ababa home.

Here they find
> a library
> with one shelf,
> a classroom
> with a single light.

12

Their faces beam
    remembering Abraham
    traveling with his tent
    southward, to the green Negeb,
    and sister Ruth,
    leaving her Moabite home
    to cling to Naomi
    among golden barley fields of Judah.

To finance and resource the growth of this infant institution, the church allocated 55,000 Ethiopian birr or US $5,500 as seed money. The owners of the compound donated it rent-free for the first two years. A grant of $15,000 was received from Canada. Another grant from TEAR FUND, UK. made it possible to move ahead for the moment.

Haya Hulet Mazoria campus: office and
classroom with tent - 1994-98

The first diploma class – 1994

Search for Assistance from Outside

In the meantime, the leaders met some brothers representing the Shiloh Bible School, a Pentecostal-related Bible college based in California. These brothers invited MKC to send representatives to explore the possibility of establishing a partnership with their church in California. They wanted to assist MKC with its leadership training and educational needs. In March 1994, at Shiloh's expense, they welcomed the chairperson of MKC, Solomon Kebede, and the general secretary, Bedru Hussein, to visit their church and college in California. However, the brothers were uneasy about what they found there.

At that opportune moment, they met Tesfatsion Dalellew, a former teacher and general secretary of MKC, who was working with World Vision in California. Tesfatsion strongly urged them to investigate an educational relationship with Mennonites, especially with Eastern Mennonite University (EMU). They agreed to do so.

In Harrisonburg Virginia, EMU officials warmly received the exploring Ethiopians. The Ethiopians requested the establishment of a formal relationship with EMU that would include assistance with curriculum development, teaching personnel, and assistance in meeting accreditation criteria. This began a conversation between MKC and

EMU that stretched from April 1994 to November 1995 and developed into a formal partnership agreement.

While EMU and MKC were working out the details of this agreement, MKC approached EMM to provide a teacher couple. Somehow, our names were suggested to be considered for this post. Twenty years had passed since we left Ethiopia. During that time, the nation, including the church, had gone through revolutionary changes.

Back in February 1995, before negotiations between EMU and MKC had progressed to this stage, I attended the bi-annual meeting of the Council of Eastern Africa Mennonite Churches in Kenya. The assembly included about thirty delegates from churches in Ethiopia, Somalia, Djibouti, Tanzania, and Kenya, and representatives from MCC and EMM. This council was really my boss, in the sense that it was they who requested EMM to place me as a teacher at Daystar University.

One of the items of business was our future appointment since our contract with Daystar was up for renewal. While we had an open invitation from Daystar and the Kenyan church to continue for another term, the Ethiopian church had been asking EMM for a teacher to be placed in their new Bible institute. Unofficially, they had been suggesting that I be that teacher.

The question was brought before this council. They debated over us. The Ethiopians pulled hard for us to be released to go to Addis Ababa; the Kenyans pulled just as hard to keep us there. It was a tug-of-war. I suggested an auction. We could go to the highest bidder!

In the end, the council took action to allow us to make the final decision ourselves. Therefore, once again, we faced one of those testing transitional decisions. One thing was clear. It felt a lot better to be fought over than to be rejected because nobody wanted us!

It was a hard decision. We were enjoying our work at Daystar, a growing, dynamic, Christian, liberal arts university. We had developed many friends among the staff and in the Kenyan church. Did we need to leave it all? On the other hand, things in Ethiopia had drastically changed politically, economically, socially, and spiritually. We really did not know how we would fit in.

To help us decide, we agreed to accept an invitation to go to Addis Ababa to teach in the Bible Institute for three weeks. We would have time to ask a lot of questions, make observations, and get a feel for the situation. We would have time to pray and seek God's clear direction and then make the decision when we returned at the end of the month.

On March 4, 1995, I was warmly welcomed at Bole International Airport by Pastor Siyum Gebretsadik, principal of the MKC Bible Institute, and Million Belete, a veteran founding father of MKC. Vera followed on March 16th. I taught a block course on the book of Romans for two weeks. There were eleven diploma students, all evangelists and church leaders. Their English was not as good as that of my Kenyan students, but they were very eager to learn. The contrast with the well-established Daystar campus could not have been greater.

What impressed me most, though, was the dedication and vision these people had. They were successful with evangelism and church planting. There were more than 110 congregations and about 350 outreach points which would become congregations within five years. It was almost an instant church, and it desperately needed trained leaders. Leadership development was their number one priority. They already had an informal training program that trained about 700 persons a year in short seminars, had forty-three young leaders in the *One Year for Christ* program, and then these eleven in the institute. Now they were envisioning a degree-granting university, a "Daystar in Ethiopia"!

What a colossal dream! I knew it would take a lot of miracles and hard work to be fully realized, but with God, it could be possible. It was desperately needed. What a challenge!

In our interview, I quizzed the church leaders, Solomon Kebede, Siyum Gebretsadik, and Bedru Hussein, about their vision. I asked them what kind of church they wanted MKC to become. Their reply was clear; they wanted a biblically-based, Christ-centered, charismatic church shaped by Anabaptist/Mennonite theological understandings that were culturally relevant to the Ethiopian setting. Knowing that the proposed college would influence the shape of the future church, we felt theirs was a vision with which we could work.

These leaders took pains to press us to accept the role of "teacher/

administrative consultant." They offered no clear assignment for Vera, which was too typical, but we knew there would be plenty for her to do.

We returned to Nairobi with the conviction that this invitation was from God. We informed Harold Reed of EMM that we would be willing to accept the invitation to transfer to Ethiopia if EMM were of the same mind. We would have to resign from our commitments to Daystar and relocate back to Ethiopia.

To expedite that decision, EMM agreed to our transfer from Daystar. MCC agreed to assist with funding our support to the tune of $10,000 per year.

EMU appointed me to serve as an adjunct faculty member, to be liaison between them and MKC in planning the development of an accredited Bible institute program. This included advising MKC regarding the requirements for meeting North American accreditation standards and advising EMU as to the ongoing progress made by MKC to meet those accreditation standards. It also included encouraging the further education of Ethiopians, so that MKC would eventually have educationally credentialed faculty for their Bible Institute.

On June 1, 1995, Siyum Gebretsadik, as principal of the fledgling Bible Institute, was quick to send me a letter of welcome, a copy of their curriculum, and a list of courses I should teach the next January. Clearly, they were eager for our arrival.

First, we resigned from Daystar, effective at the end of June. In preparation for this transition, EMM allowed me to attend a two-week consultation in Oxford, UK, on "Institutional Development for Theological Education in the Two-thirds World," on our way home. We were allowed five months of home leave, most of which was spent in Harrisonburg, in the environs of EMU, where we had fruitful consultations.

CHAPTER 3

Laying Foundations

Developing a Teaching Faculty

In accordance with the agreement and with the support of EMM, Vera and I arrived in Addis on January 7, 1996. We settled into a nice house one km from Haya Hulet Mazoria.

As expatriates, Vera and I were allowed access to the internet right away. This amazing innovation was not yet available to the Ethiopian citizenry. The United Nations had its own system called PADIS. With special permission, they allowed us to subscribe. This email prototype revolutionized the way we communicated with the outside world.

During that first semester, I only taught one course, "The Church and Development" while brushing up on Amharic. Vera enrolled in a six-month Amharic language program offered by the Society of International Missionaries (SIM).

When I came to teach, I found the original thirteen students had been reduced in number to ten. Pastor Siyum had departed in August, taking a study leave to earn his master's degree in Nairobi, and Hailu Cherenet had assumed his place as Acting Coordinator.

The first graduation ceremony of the new Bible Institute took place on April 5th, 1996. The class of ten graduated with a two-year diploma. Vera and I missed this first historic celebration because we had to go to Nairobi to apply for a work permit from outside Ethiopia.

The ten, with their diplomas, returned to their home districts to work in the urgent business of evangelism and disciple-making. Meanwhile, I thought they were so few, only one for each of MKC's ten districts. Since the time they enrolled three years earlier, fifty new congregations had formed, each needing trained teachers and pastors. Even taking in twenty new students for the next round would not begin to meet the growing need. What could we do to speed up the slow process of training leaders? Rent bigger facilities? Hire more teachers? Yes, but with what?

Being in Ethiopia, the second poorest country on this earth, the Christians' resources were limited. Yet, they gave their tithes to their congregations. What they gave in their Sunday offerings were above their tithes. They were also challenged with special fundraising drives for church buildings above tithes and offerings. At such times, Christians might pledge a month's wages, or take off their jewelry, even their wedding bands, and put them in the offering. I could see that persuading the church members to take up the challenge of expanding the Bible Institute could take decades. We did not have decades to wait.

After the April graduation had emptied the facility, seventeen certificate students returned for the next two months. Vera taught an English-language course. Since the certificate-level courses were taught in the Amharic language, I was free to draft a preliminary curriculum and catalogue and prepare to teach hermeneutics and Bible doctrine to the next intake of students.

We changed the diploma curriculum to a three-year associate in arts degree in Christian ministries to meet the standards expected for accreditation through EMU. We had some reservations as to whether it would work or not. The students' level of English was very low and might take additional remedial work.

We were prepared to test this curriculum on the coming group. It would take three years for them to do two years' worth of work since they were coming to school for three-month terms, then going to work in their churches for two months, then returning for the next three months. This staggered approach kept the minister close to his home church and his family. However, it stretched his time of learning over a three-year period rather than a two-year period.

On June 17, 1996, a new batch of fourteen evangelists arrived to begin the new experimental associate in arts (AA) degree in Christian Ministries. Dr. Calvin and Marie Shenk arrived at the same time to teach Old Testament Survey in a three-week block format. In those years, the Shenks were teaching in Israel for six months each year, then they would come to Ethiopia to teach in a three-week seminar, then return to EMU where Calvin taught in the Bible Department for the rest of the year.

On the same day the Shenks departed, Dennis and Effie McAdams arrived from Tanzania to teach Theology of Missions for three weeks. Dennis was an American, and Effie was a Solomon Islander. They were missionaries with EMM, teaching at the Mennonite Theological College in Musoma, Tanzania.

Prior to my appointment, Eastern Mennonite Seminary (EMS) had offered a scholarship to MKC, suggesting that Siyum Gebretsadik, as principal of the Bible Institute, should be the recipient. However, since Siyum had already enrolled in the master's program at NEGST in Nairobi, the offer was dropped for the moment. Realizing this and cognizant of the need for properly credentialed teaching faculty, I encouraged Hailu Cherenet to apply for this scholarship opportunity. Hailu applied and was accepted.

Being ignorant of MKC's established protocols, I had made the first of the many blunders that provoked the disapproval of the top leaders of the MKC Executive Committee. I was unaware of any MKC guidelines/policies for recruiting and sending candidates on international scholarships. They had a priority list of who would be next in line to benefit from such opportunities. Hailu had jumped the line, and by failing to consult the leadership first, I was to blame.

However, considering the urgency of the need, the appropriateness of the choice, and benefit of the positive outcome, in retrospect, the decision was right. Sometimes, when you know a move is right, "it is easier to ask forgiveness than it is to get permission!" After an appropriate scolding, the fact on the ground was accepted and the leaders got behind the move.

An interesting sideline that was not known to many: Hailu had been offered a teaching position by the Evangelical Theological College (ETC) which included a full scholarship to study in the Dallas Theological Seminary in Texas. This was a very tempting offer to Hailu, but he was committed to his own church and felt the call of God to give himself to develop the MKC Bible Institute. With considerable pain and self-sacrifice, he had rejected the tempting offer.

One evening in July, several of us leaders were having dinner at a local restaurant. At a nearby table, a group of leaders from ETC were having a farewell banquet for Hailu's best friend, Simon Mulat, who was leaving to do MTh studies at Dallas Theological Seminary, the same kind of scholarship which Hailu had painfully declined. It was an emotional experience for Hailu, a test, seeing his friend going and knowing that he was not going along. Two days later, Hailu received notice that his own application to EMS was accepted!

So, in September, Hailu left on a three-year, full scholarship to study at EMS, with the clear understanding that he was to return to join our teaching faculty upon completion. With Hailu's departure, the executive committee appointed me as *Acting Coordinator*.

Developing a Governing Structure

During the summer and fall of our first year, in 1996, I worked with Bedru Hussein, Solomon Kebede, and Million Belete in drafting a *Constitution* for Meserete Kristos College, a *Memorandum of Organization for a Board of Trustees, Administrative Bylaws,* and a list of *Procedures*. After being thoroughly examined, revised, and polished, these instruments were adopted by the MKC Executive Committee in May and August 1997 as official foundational documents shaping the newly formed Meserete Kristos College.

When they decided on naming the new school *Meserete Kristos College*, some suggested a more attractive, inclusive name, other than that of the denomination. They suggested the name should be inviting to members of other denominations. However, while the college was to be open to all Christians of all denominations, MKC leadership felt very strongly that the name should remain as it now stands in its constitution.

Upon approval of the Constitution and the Memorandum of Organization for a Board of Trustees, the executive committee appointed nine board members.

It was a great relief to me when the board held its first meeting on May 3rd, 1997. We had been drifting leaderless for the past year. Finally, we had a system in place that enabled us to make concrete decisions and move ahead.

The First Meeting of the Board of Trustees

True to his character as a visionary leader, Chairperson Million Belete led in a meditation based on Hosea 4:1–14 (NIV).

> "My people are destroyed from a lack of knowledge.... A people without understanding will come to ruin (vs. 6, 14)." He emphasized that education is vital to the health and growth of the church. The prophets of the OT and the rabbis of Jesus' day often led peripatetic "schools" of disciples who in turn became prophets or rabbis. Paul started the first Christian "Bible college" in "the lecture hall of Tyrannus" (Acts 19:9).
>
> Jesus (Eph. 4:11-13) gave "apostles, prophets, evangelists, pastors, and teachers" to the church for the purpose of nurture and evangelism, to build up the body. These "gifts" are people with potential whom God gives to the church. It is the church's challenge to develop that God-given potential. Schools are good places to develop that potential. Our church is good at promoting bigness, but we are in danger of being destroyed for lack of knowledge. We need this college to train quality servant leaders who can do proper exposition of the

Word and build up the body in knowledge. (Minutes of the Board of Trustees, May 3, 1997)

The board decided to change the three-month cycle to a four-month semester system, and the new curriculum, offering an associate degree instead of a diploma, was approved. The associate degree and the certificate programs should run simultaneously. This increased the enrollment, and a second house needed to be rented as an additional dormitory.

Developing the library

Already in the summer of 1995, Arlene Leatherman, a retired teacher, and Clara Landis, a retired librarian of Telford, Pennsylvania, had visited the campus and devoted a few weeks to show Emebet Mekonen how to catalogue books that had been donated. They set up an arrangement whereby Emebet would record the relevant data from each book and send it to Arlene and Clara in Pennsylvania. They would print out library cards, book labels, and send them back to Ethiopia. Thus, through those early years, they built up a card catalogue of many thousands of volumes. This process continued until the library was computerized in 2006.

That first summer, Vera was appointed as English teacher. She was also assigned to be the librarian to continue what Emebet had started. More wooden shelves were made for the library. With the assistance of two university students, they did an impressive job of getting the 4,000 labeled books into working order on the shelves.

A young woman, Tigist Alamirew, was assigned by the church as a library assistant. She took advantage of a six-week training at the British Council Library. She was also appointed to help as a cashier and typist.

Vital to the development of the library, we must recognize the major contribution of Books *at Home and Abroad* organization. This USA-based organization had depots managed by volunteers in seven Mennonite communities. They collected used books from local donors, mostly retired pastors and university professors, and sorted them into mail bags or packages. These were mailed out, free of charge, to needy institutions, churches, or individuals in the third world. The college was required to pay customs on these free used books at that time. Later, the government removed the customs charge on educational books.

Developing International Academic Support

Other guest lecturers came in 1997. Dr. Mel Loewen taught *Church and Development* for two weeks in February. He was a 71-year-old retired missionary-teacher-banker from Maryland, USA. Together with his wife, Elfrieda, they served as missionaries in the bush of Eastern Zaire for thirteen years. He became a teacher and founder-president of the Protestant University in Zaire. Then, for twenty years, he worked as a consultant in the World Bank. Mel's wealth of experience and knowledge in the world of missions and development made him an interesting teacher and a great resource as a consultant in the development of our school. He gave me a lot of creative ideas, and a lot of encouragement to go ahead with our proposed college.

Dennis McAdams returned to teach Bible Doctrine again for three weeks at the end of March 1997. Calvin and Marie Shenk returned for three weeks during which he taught a course on Islam. He was followed by Dr. Neil Lettinga, a history professor from the Baptist Bethel College in St. Paul, Minnesota, who came for six weeks to teach Church History. He was a very helpful and stimulating teacher. Being from the Christian Reformed Church, he added a pietistic touch.

Dr. James and Peg Engle came in late July 1997. Jim, a professor of Old Testament at Eastern Mennonite Seminary, devoted his sabbatical year. Peg had served in Ethiopia as a missionary nurse for over twenty years before she met and married Jim. She taught pastoral care and counseling and study skills.

In June 1997, the first seventeen students in the certificate program graduated. Bedru Hussein was granted a full scholarship to study in the Master of Divinity (MDiv) degree program at EMS. He left his role as general secretary of MKC at the beginning of September 1997, with the understanding that, upon completion of the three-year program, he would return to be a full-time teacher in the college.

In October 1997, the board of trustees appointed me to serve as principal. They appointed officers who made up a management committee to help administer the college. They also approved of our proposals to make the college financially autonomous by opening a bank account, setting up our own bookkeeping and accounting system.

In January 1998, the board approved a budget and plans to include twenty certificate students along with the fourteen associate degree students. This meant we needed more money to provide more food and to rent more bedroom space. Since one of the official responsibilities of the principal is to see that adequate funding is in place, the burden of fundraising fell on me. I was to be the servant *beggar*, and God the provider; indeed, a promising combination!

Developing a Support Base

In an environment of extreme poverty, growing and operating church institutions has its challenges. While the college should look to its mother church for support, its head office was facing a crisis near the end of 1997. Many of the congregations failed to remit their required 15% needed to run the church-wide programs. In my diary, I expressed this frustration:

> It may be that some programs will be cut, and staff may lose their jobs. Jesus made 'tax collectors' into disciples. Perhaps we need to convert some 'disciples' into 'tax collectors' for the church?

As I meditated on this situation, I came to realize that one possibility was to turn to our much more affluent brothers and sisters in the west for external support. While aware of the dangers of creating dependency, this was an emergency, just as real and demanding outside relief assistance as a natural disaster such as a tsunami or famine. Training leaders in this fast-growing church could not wait for another generation. This was the formative generation! Something had to be done immediately. Now was the time for foundation-laying, for sorting out the correct theology, and setting the course which would determine the kind of church MKC would become in the generations to follow. This was a God moment.

With this emergency in mind, I wrote an urgent appeal to former missionaries, personal friends, and some congregations back in the USA and Canada. However, the response was very slow. It was a test of faith. We knew the need for training leaders was urgent. We were available, and our staff members were available to do more, but it costs money to feed and house students.

I must confess, I was one of God's worst fundraisers. I never saw myself as a fundraiser. I did not like fundraising. My policy of operation was that it was my responsibility to make the needs known, and it was God's responsibility to do the asking. If God did not motivate the potential donor's heart to support this cause, then we did not really want that person's gift. God loves cheerful givers, not resentful givers who felt conned into giving by clever manipulation or emotional appeals. I know that policy is not rated very highly as a key to successful fundraising!

Those provisions came slowly, one by one. Responding to Bedru's application, the DeMoss Foundation gave us a new Gestetner duplicating machine, a new TV, and a video player. World Vision Ethiopia gave us a new computer and printer, our first, as well as a computer desk, chair, and a filing cabinet. We received a grant of 200 British pounds for library books from Evangelical Literature Trust in England. The German Evangelical Mission gave the college a set of excellent reference books. About 900 volumes of donated used books were added to the library in 1997, increasing our holdings to about 5,900. These came to us from various organizations and individuals, mostly in the USA. A good quality steel card catalogue file was ordered, manufactured, and delivered to the library. Bit by bit things came together.

By October 1997, we were already receiving encouraging reports from the congregations where our students and graduates were serving, positive reports about the effects of the training given. One of our first graduates, Getahun Assefa, was serving as the principal of *Abyssinia Mission*, a small pentecostal institute dedicated to the specialized training of local missionaries to penetrate the Somali Muslim Horn of Africa. Some became teachers. Others were serving as pastors and evangelists. Pastor Tefera Gonfa Kano, upon graduating, went home to Agamsa in Wollega and started a tiny Bible school teaching eleven students in his church building of mud and sticks, using the Oromo language.

In November, we were still hoping to take in a new batch of twenty certificate students in mid-January, but we did not receive the money needed. Would we have to delay the plan? We could only pray. *Unless the Lord builds, we labor in vain!*

As the time approached, I wrote in my diary:

> We are hoping to take in twenty more students for the certificate program this weekend. We really do not have enough money to rent the proper space, so we will be piling the students into the present quarters for a while. It will be a bit like sleeping in prison, I am afraid. I hope they do not get some kind of epidemic.

Then, in mid-January 1998, in faith, we rented another house nearby to keep the eighteen new students who came for the certificate program. The fourteen associate degree students spent their final semester sleeping in the original house. We also started evening extension classes for the working public who wanted to upgrade themselves on a part-time basis. Thirteen signed up. These were employed, and therefore, paying students.

Responses to our international appeal came slowly at first. The first two gifts were given in May 1998: a $5,000 gift from Chester and Sara Jane Wenger and a $25 gift from Neil and Virginia Lettinga. Both supporters became faithful regular partners for many years. In June, another $6,635 came in from five supporters, and in July, $6,882 came in from fifteen partners. And support has continued, something every month. In September 1998, we became courageous enough to rent another compound and enlarge our intake of students when we received $33,466.

EMU Accreditation Setback

In the spring of 1998, the administration received a letter from EMU expressing their regrets that they are unable to give their degree to our students because of the Southern Association of Colleges and Schools (SACS) accreditation requirements that extension campuses must have the same high quality of library and technological learning resources as the mother campus, and that the students be able to pass the TOEFL (Test of English as a Foreign Language) exam.

This disappointing news was not surprising. In response, under the board's direction, we wrote a letter to EMU, expressing our regrets that our graduates would not be able to receive EMU degrees for their work. We understood their fears of facing the stringent requirements of SACS as it reviewed their accreditation status. We also expressed our thanks for all the ways they supported and encouraged us. We asked them if they would permit us to use the words, "Meserete Kristos College, in association with Eastern Mennonite University, Harrisonburg, Virginia, USA, have granted this degree..." on our diplomas. Permission was granted.

Searching in Vain for a Permanent Home

Because of the large vision to establish a Christian university, we began to search for a suitable site upon which to build the campus. The trustees suggested we keep in mind seeking a space large enough to include a conference/training center, although that should not be included in the official description. A large enough plot of land in downtown Addis was prohibitively expensive, and I was bothered about the concept of soliciting foreign donors to purchase land in Ethiopia. We followed a lot of leads, most of them inadequate for the size of the vision. A few suggestions merited serious consideration.

One such possibility raised considerable interest and motivated us to launch a fundraising campaign. In November 1997, we negotiated on a plot of six-and-one-half acres located off Jimma Road on the western edge of the city, serviced with water and electricity, for only $150,000. The big challenge was to find funding for it, keeping in mind the high cost of erecting suitable buildings.

Later, in the summer of 1998, we presented this possibility at a meeting of interested *Friends of MKC* which met in Goshen, Indiana. The participants pledged to raise $150,000 to purchase the land. Over the next two years, they did raise $80,000 of what was pledged. Then, the lawyer on our board informed us that the seller did not have legal proof of ownership and could not legally sell the land to us. So that dream turned out to be a "rabbit trail," leading nowhere. The $80,000 that was raised was added to our building fund instead.

Question of Sustainability

When the Bible Institute was first launched in 1994, the church chose the first batches of students and found support for them, largely through grants from two philanthropists, an individual in Canada and from Tearfund in the UK. That set a precedent; students did not pay.

In April 1998, the Board of Trustees wrestled with the question of financial sustainability. It was felt that, while foreign assistance would be needed for building and equipping a campus, the congregations sending their full-time ministers should cover the costs of tuition, food, and accommodation. Those wishing to attend, who were not full-time ministers, should raise their own funds to cover their expenses. Accordingly, a letter was drafted for the Education Committee to send out to all the congregations notifying them that it was time for them to submit applications for their students, and that it was their responsibility to sponsor the ones they sent to the college.

This letter was sent. However, it was later nullified by another letter which invited students to come without the mentioned congregational support. This action was justified with the comment, "If we would have followed through, we would have no students in our college." It was obvious that poverty on the congregational level was such that they felt they were unable to sponsor their leaders for training at this time.

This pushed the problem back to the college and its board: "Who is to pay the costs of educating leaders?" If the head office thinks the cost should be borne by the congregations, yet the congregations expect it to be given to them free, then the whole burden falls on the college. Is it a burden the college can or should bear?

The board tended to be sympathetic to the congregations' dilemma. With such rapid growth, most of the congregations were new and were dealing with the costs of paying high rents for their places of worship and were in various stages of purchasing or seeking to build permanent houses of worship. At the same time, their tithes and offerings were supporting their pastors and evangelists full-time, as well as sending the required percent to support the denominational office.

To make it more difficult, whenever a congregation sent one of their leaders for training, they were paying three quarters of his or her salary for family support, while hiring another person to do the work in his or her absence. Adding to that burden, the cost of tuition and room and board for their minister in school was too much for most congregations to consider. An alternate argument also considered was: "Our congregation is doing well without our leaders being trained, so is it really important to train our leaders?"

With the stark reality of congregational poverty in mind, the board left the burden to the college administration. We continued to supply one hundred percent of the costs of food, room, tuition, and textbooks for our students. Our capacity to do fundraising put limits on the number of students we could admit.

When the possibility of launching a four-year degree in Bible and Christian Ministries program was proposed to the board, the question came up again. Serious objections were raised. Most congregations, while paying 75% of his or her salary for family support and hiring a substitute felt it would be difficult to release a leader to be a student for four years. The church cannot continue to be so generous. Where will the money come from?

The board was divided. How negative should we be about things we do not know for sure? Where does moving ahead by faith come in? If we take the side of caution, when, if ever, will we be ready to move ahead with a four-year degree? Will these above-stated conditions ever change? The board was torn between faith and reason.

Finally, a compromise was reached. It was decided that we follow the two-year associate degree curriculum with the present intake of students, with the possibility of extending to a four-year degree two years later, depending upon facilities, availability of funds, and the willingness of local churches to send their candidates.

Our Paraguayan Daughter

One Monday morning in mid-February 1998, we received a phone call. A woman's voice in very broken English asked to speak to Carl Hansen. Assured that I was he, she introduced herself as Hedwig Unrah from Paraguay. Immediately, by her name and strong German/Plautdietsch accent, I recognized that she was of the Dutch German Russian Mennonites, a sister in my tribe.

She said she was a Mennonite, a missionary, and that she just arrived in Addis the day before, with only $20 and our phone number, which a pastor in Nairobi had given her. She had tried to call us from the airport, but we were not home. Then she contacted an SIM missionary, working with the Somali refugees living in Addis, and spent the night with her. But there was no room for another night. She really needed a place to stay.

She seemed tremendously relieved when I offered her a place in our guest room. I went and picked her up at a service station. She had come to Kenya with a faith mission from South America, hoping to work with the Somali people. While she was in Nairobi learning the language, she lived with a Kenyan family. She had entered on a tourist visa and had it renewed after three months. At the end of six months, while waiting for a work permit to be processed, she went to renew the visa again. The authorities refused and ordered her to leave the country at once. Since she had only enough money for a one-way ticket to Ethiopia, plus twenty dollars, she did not have any other options. She decided in one hour's time to come.

Hedwig was an interesting person. She was twenty-seven years old. In her teen years, sensing a deep call of God to be a missionary, she prepared herself with nurses' training and social work. In the meantime, she got involved in evangelism and ministry in her country, then did three years mission work in Uruguay and three years in Brazil. During that time, she felt called to a ministry to Somalia. With her church's blessing, but without a solid support base, she departed for Kenya, alone. Now she was in Ethiopia, in our home, searching for a way to get involved in learning the Somali language and culture and finding a ministry among them.

Thus began a fascinating story of interacting with Hedwig for over a decade or more. She found in us a second set of parents, and in our home, a place of refuge, a place to relax, to heal, to rejuvenate, to process her many decisions, and a place to pray. We enjoyed her presence as our "Paraguayan daughter." Her story would fill a very captivating page-turner book.

A Fundraising Furlough

In the spring of 1998, the board asked Vera and me to shorten our term by two weeks to enable me to do fundraising for one month while on home leave. Therefore, squeezing our work into the shortened time limit, Vera and I left Ethiopia on May 1st to begin a three-and one-half-month furlough. We began by meeting our mother, Elizabeth Hansen, in Germany for a six-day visit with about forty relatives who recently moved from Russia to Germany and whom we had never met. We spent one month in Virginia visiting our children and grandchildren.

The next two-months were spent on a visiting and fundraising tour that took us 18,000 kms (11,000 miles) by car to many places in

Pennsylvania, Ohio, Indiana, Ontario, New York, Minnesota, Iowa, Manitoba, and Alberta.

In upstate New York, we gave our presentation at a district Mission Board meeting and at the Pleasant Valley Mennonite Church at Hammondsport. In Goshen, Indiana, we attended the weekend Ethiopian conference with about one hundred Ethiopians from the diaspora and former missionaries who formed an "Association of Friends of Meserete Kristos Church" and pledged themselves to raise the $150,000 mentioned above for the purchase of land for the college within the next two years.

While sharing with a Sunday School class at the Goshen College Church, Dr. Howard Charles (my former teacher at Associated Mennonite Biblical Seminary) offered to donate his personal library to our college. It contained approximately 2,000 volumes. Getting those books to Addis was a new challenge. Eventually, Books at Home and Abroad accepted the challenge and mailed them to us, bag by bag, at their expense.

Our summer was very exciting and challenging. We attended all the right meetings, covered all the bases, met so many people, did so many things, but we felt we did not do justice to our nearest of kin, especially our children and grandchildren.

Also, our fundraising efforts were not a stunning success. Although we did receive enough that enabled us to keep going, we were not able to expand as we had hoped. After meeting many old friends and making new acquaintances and speaking in different churches on Sundays in many different places, our lengthy tour came to an end.

In October, our spirits were encouraged with news that our friend, John Yost, a retired farmer from Red Hill, Pennsylvania, had donated $20,000 to our school. Also, he had put $110,000 into an account to be used for a matching grant for anything we could raise after September 1st. Another donor couple in eastern Pennsylvania promised they would be giving us between $50,000 and $100,000 over a two-year period. They kept their promise.

In Growth Mode

Vera and I returned to Ethiopia just in time for a night's rest before getting ready for a graduation exercise the following day. Twelve diploma students graduated. The thirteenth one, Seyoum Tesfaye, could not get back from Eritrea for the final two months of his program because war had broken out between his country and Ethiopia. The border was closed.

That fall, at the annual MKC General Church Council meeting, it was announced that 19,000 people were added to the church's membership rolls from the previous year. That brought the count to 133,000 people, which included children. These were fellowshipping in 212 congregations and about 500 church planting centers. This kind of growth made our program of leadership training most urgent.

College enrollment in the fall of 1998 climbed to thirty-two full-time students crowded into the two little compounds. Among them, eighteen new students were admitted into a new intensive English program in preparation to enter the new associate in arts (AA) degree program, and fourteen students returned for the final semester of their certificate program. Besides this, twelve students continued in the evening extension program on the degree level.

Another milestone was reached on November 1, 1998, when Vera took over the bookkeeping of the college with the helpful assistance and coaching of Belayneh and Daniel from the head office. She accepted this challenge on a temporary basis until a permanent, qualified person could be hired. This was in addition to her role as librarian and part-time English teacher.

Emebet was given the responsibility of managing the cash. Up to that time, the college's finances had been handled like another department under the head office of the church. It caused a lot of frustration. Finally, the college had its own bank account, its own bookkeeping, and its own source of funding. Although the college was still on the denomination's budget, it did not receive any more funds from the head office of the church.

I continued as a teacher, principal, academic dean, development officer, fund-raiser, consultant, and public relations officer. Emebet Mekonnen continued performing the roles of registrar, dean of students, business manager, secretary, and cashier. Besides those roles, she was an amazing support and confidant to me in my manyfold responsibilities. The teachers were Ethiopians who assisted on a volunteer, part-time basis. Vera taught English. By the fall of 1998, the little college was a remarkably busy place. I described the scene:

> The routine activities at Meserete Kristos College seem to go on about the same from day to day. Students come and go; teachers arrive and leave; the guard opens and closes the gate and answers the phone; kitchen workers cut onions and bake injera; the librarians arrange their books. The crowded little compound, with its modest house, outbuilding, and green tent, still does not look much like a college campus. The casual observer might conclude that it is just another sleepy, little school, where nothing ever changes, and where, whatever hopes and visions there might have been, have long since died.
>
> But all is not as it seems. Taking a closer look, one would notice that the thirteen-member student body has mushroomed to thirty-two since early February, when eighteen new students joined the certificate program. Their arrival precipitated a flurry of activity, as a larger house had to be rented to serve as a dorm. Additional beds, chairs, and desks had to be purchased. The dining room needed to be modified into a classroom, and the tent reinforced to serve a multi-purpose function as dining hall, chapel, and study hall. Now 230% more students come and go; 100% more teachers arrive and leave; the gate opens and closes 2.3 times as often; workers cut and bake 2.3 times as many onions and injeras as they did; and the phone rings more often.
>
> Further, the astute observer might notice an additional eighteen ambitious adults arriving every

Monday, Wednesday, and Thursday evening at exactly
5:30 p.m. They head for the classroom, anxious to
discover what new insights they will learn. So, with the
new extension program, this little college is touching
the lives of fifty eager learners each week.

No, this little college is certainly not sleeping.
Meserete Kristos College has made a good start, and
with God's grace and a lot of human effort, it stands a
good chance of achieving its goals.

First Fundraising Banquet

On Saturday evening, January 9, 1999, the board of trustees sponsored
its first fundraising banquet for the building project at the Addis Ababa
Ras Hotel. In hope, we invited about 200 potential supporters. In
what we felt was realistic optimism, we asked the hotel management to
cater for 125 meals. In fact, eighty men and women attended, leaving
much food wasted. After an interesting program, people made cash
contributions of about $5,500, plus an equal amount in pledges. We
had hoped to raise much more. However, it was our first attempt, not
bad considering the adverse conditions in which most people lived and
the fact that the college was in its infancy and had not yet proved itself.

CHAPTER 4

Enlarging the Space

After Christmas, fourteen evangelists graduated from the certificate program. Two days later, the *One Year for Christ* training program was launched with twenty-nine students for the month of January 1999. Since we were not involved in that program, we had time to celebrate Ethiopian Christmas (January 7), facilitate the move from Haya Hulet Mazoria campus to a new campus in Kotebe, and prepare for the next semester of teaching.

At that time, the college was working out of congested rented quarters in two separate compounds. It had completely outgrown its first home of five years. The students slept in one small house, where toilet and shower conditions were totally inadequate, pathetic, and disgusting. Lectures were given in two small classrooms in the other compound, where the kitchen, library, dining area, and office were also located. Kitchen work was done, mostly outside in the rain and sun. The library had room for only one small table, and 30% of the books were stored in cartons due to lack of shelf space. The dining room was simply a leaking tent. All the teaching and administrative staff crowded into one office. The conditions were fast becoming intolerable. We had to find a larger place for this growing college.

With more funding, came more confidence. We began looking for bigger property to rent while we continued the search for a suitable property to purchase or upon which to build a permanent campus.

Move to Kotebe, January 1999

On November 9, Mulugeta Zewdie, general secretary of MKC, Siyum Gebretsadik, Million Belete, and I went to see the property of Wezero Senait, widow of the late General Bekele, in Kotebe in eastern Addis Ababa and decided to rent it. It was a large property, about 800 meters downhill from the main Dessie Road. It was divided into two compounds of 2,000 m² each.

We decided to rent the compound that had the main house with many service rooms beside and behind. It had twenty rooms altogether. It would have room for about seventy students with adequate classroom and office space. We thought this facility would be suitable for the next two years, after which we hoped we would have acquired our own facility. We signed a contract, renting it for two years at $650 per month.

The owner agreed to clean, paint, and get it ready for occupancy by the first of January 1999. However, to adapt this facility for our purpose, we had to make some necessary repairs and changes at our expense. For example, we installed four more sinks and toilets and showers and cleaned and repaired leaking plumbing and lights that did not work.

Moving a whole college is not a simple thing. Even though our college was small, it was a logistical challenge, complicated by the fact that we were running the *One Year for Christ* program at the old campus while we were making the necessary modifications at the new site. Each time we went to the new campus, we loaded our Hilux pickup with non-essentials and library books.

The most exciting day of the year dawned on January 26th, 1999. That was the day we moved the whole college into this new larger campus seven kilometers east of us. We began the day with a graduation exercise for twenty-nine students in the *One Year for Christ* program. Then, we spent the afternoon moving the remaining furniture, including kitchen equipment, beds, and desks. We hired a big truck which made two trips to do that.

No one was sorry to leave the two little dilapidated compounds with all the memories of sleeping twenty men to a room, of eating in the dark, of studying in a leaking tent, of squeezing into congested classrooms, of queuing before the only toilet that sort of worked, of sharing one office with all the staff, of cooking supper for thirty in the rain, or of playing volleyball over Pastor Siyum's car.

At first, the new campus seemed extravagant, elegant, and spacious. It had been built about ten years earlier. It was surrounded by a high stone wall on the outside with young trees and flowering shrubs set behind an attractive low stone barrier that outlined the asphalt driveway. The eight rooms in the main house were apportioned as the library, two classrooms, three offices, and two dorm rooms. Outside, along two compound walls were twelve rooms that served as dorm rooms, kitchen, and a dining facility.

New students started to arrive at the new campus that evening, and the new semester classes started the next day. The students were incredibly happy about everything, and the morale of the staff was much better.

To complete the transfer, we were obliged to clean, repair, and re-paint the two former compounds before vacating them. According to custom, house owners expected the renter to vacate their house in mint condition when they leave, even if it was in disrepair when the rental agreement was signed.

Faculty and administrative staff at the Kotebe campus, 2002

Kotebe campus - Some of the 110 students & thirty staff, 2004

Guest Lecturers Enliven Summer Classes

The summer term of 1999 not only brought twenty-four new students for the intensive English program, but it also introduced new teachers. Loretta Wideman, an Assemblies of God missionary from Oklahoma, USA, volunteered to teach Public Speaking for the month of June. Mary Zehr, from Pennsylvania, joined in July, teaching reading comprehension. Old standbys, Alemu Checole, Vera Hansen, and Teku Kebede completed the English teaching team.

Old timers Calvin and Marie Shenk were back again teaching in the degree program for three weeks in June. While Calvin taught OT Survey, Marie bravely launched a popular new course called "A Christian Response to Modern Israel." She also taught this course in the evening extension. Students received her challenging views with great interest, many questions, and some skepticism.

Paul Zehr, a bishop and seminary professor from Pennsylvania, challenged the degree students, as well as the evening extension students, with his lectures on the book of Romans. Students were also impressed with the way Paul and Mary, in the two months they were present, fit in with the Ethiopian way of life, eating their food, riding in the "blue donkeys" (the blue and white mini-bus taxis), and attending the Amharic services.

Daniel Abebe, from the Equatorial Business Group and a new member of our board of trustees, volunteered to teach Introduction to Psychology for five weeks.

Rapid Growth

In the spring of 1999, Hailu Cherenet completed his MDiv degree at Eastern Mennonite Seminary. At his graduation, Hailu was honored for his outstanding academic achievements as well as his contribution to the spiritual environment of that campus.

Upon his return to Ethiopia in the fall, Hailu was assigned the duties of academic dean as well as to teach four courses right away. His outstanding commitment and exceptional service set a high standard for his fellow teachers and staff.

When Hailu moved into the dean's office in early August, things began to change around the college. First the dean of students, Emebet Mekonnen, found herself vacating her spacious office to accept humbler quarters in the staff room. A new desk and office furniture moved in for the dean. Out of the dean's office issued newly designed course evaluation forms for students to criticize their teachers, fresh teaching schedules for the new semester, a school calendar, and new standards for the course syllabi.

Students soon found that this new teacher was not a slouch and had little sympathy for their complaints about work overload. This was a college, not a baby-sitting institution or even a high school, and we expected students to maintain high standards of academic performance.

What Hailu expected from students, he also expected from himself. He set an exemplary standard of commitment by teaching a full load plus one guided independent study, along with the regular duties of the dean's office. He was punctual and prepared. One could find him at his desk half an hour before the starting time and often working late and on weekends.

Hailu Cherenet, lecturer, academic dean, and later, president

The curriculum was revised and expanded to provide for a complete four-year Bachelor of Arts degree in Bible with a minor in Christian ministries.

With Hailu, the fall semester was off to a good start with fifty-one full-time students. These were in three different programs: four-year degree, two-year diploma, and one-year certificate programs. In addition, there were eleven part-time students in the evening extension program. Our new campus was full. There was harmony among the staff and an optimistic, happy spirit among the students as well.

The college's freshest teacher was Woudeneh Endaylalu. After serving as an evangelist in Adama for several years, his church had released him to attend the Evangelical Theological College in Addis. He graduated with a Bachelor of Theology (BTh) degree in June 1999 and joined the teaching staff on a full-time basis in mid-October.

The new campus, with its increase in enrollment, required the purchase of furniture, including eighty-three chairs, eleven bookshelves, six dining tables, five library tables, thirty desks, eight bunk beds, twenty-seven mattresses, a photocopier, a computer, two computer tables, an office desk, two filing cabinets, and other office supplies.

The 2,000 m² compound was well utilized. The main house had a large living room, which was divided into a library on one side and a chapel/classroom on the other. There were three bedrooms. The master bedroom was the largest, so it became the staff room with a table where teachers could come for tea or to eat their lunches. We put the photocopier on a board straddling the bathtub in the general's marble-lined bathroom. The two other bedrooms became the offices of the principal and the academic dean.

After Bedru Hussein returned with his MDiv degree from Eastern Mennonite Seminary in the fall of 2000, he occupied my office as associate principal. Vera and I moved our desks into the staff room and shared the space with the staff. The large kitchen became a classroom. We blocked off a space at the end of the hall to make a small cubical for the secretary/receptionist.

The general's den became the business and finance office. It had been his private brewery and still exuded a permanent smell peculiar to that trade. Beneath the house was a half basement with one room which became another classroom. It was all cozy, warm, close, and adequate.

We cut down several small trees and installed two twenty-foot freight containers that were donated by MCC. One was used as a secure storage shed for food and other valuable supplies, and the other was converted into two offices for staff. We set them thirty feet apart and built a roof between them giving a sheltered space that was used for table tennis and sometimes as a dining hall. Wezero Senait, the land lady, was not too pleased about the trees. We had failed to ask permission.

*This shelter served as the college's gymnasium
from 1999 through 2006*

*Lecturer, Girma Teklu, in the basement classroom,
introducing eager students to the mysteries
of the Biblical koine Greek language*

Sustainability

Apart from the qualified success of that first fundraising banquet at the Ras Hotel in January 1999, we were not able to stimulate meaningful participation among the congregations to raise a portion of the costs of maintaining their students in the college.

We began by asking each scholarship recipient to bring at least one offering from his/her congregation. The church leadership also asked each congregation to take at least one offering per year to support their college.

Even those measures were disappointing. If local leaders were aware of the colleges' existence at all (most of them were not), they would be more committed to the needs of their rapidly growing congregations. In the prevailing condition of poverty, it was hard for them to add the burden of supporting a college far away. That was a burden they could easily ignore or leave for God and his foreign supportive community.

It seemed like, when the local churches heard that the *ferrengis* were sending money, and that they could send their full-time ministers for free theological education, they felt no obligation to support their college financially. Even the head office of MKC showed the same attitude by removing the token 15,000 birr allotted for the college from their budget. They did not apply the principle of self-reliance to the newly established college.

One of the college's main weaknesses was the lack of a public relations department to publicize and promote it. College administration and leadership were too overstretched to motivate the constituency in any meaningful way. Financially, the foreign donor community supplied at least 95% of the funds needed to support daily operations and to grow the building fund.

Fundraising efforts abroad continued to yield results throughout the year. From the time the campaign began in May 1998 to the end of September 1999, about $382,000 was received from 158 different people or organizations.

First Exchange Student Adds Perspective

Aaron Kauffman, from Lancaster, Pennsylvania, arrived in Ethiopia in mid-July 1999, as our first exchange student. He was a third-year EMU student, filling his year abroad requirement by doing an internship in missions. He earned credit for cross-cultural studies and for courses he took while with the college. He also fulfilled requirements by doing his practicum in TESL (Teaching English as a Second Language) for a full year.

Upon arrival, Aaron took a crash course in Amharic for six weeks. This enabled him to engage in simple conversation, enough to give him confidence in interacting with fellow students with whom he lived in the dormitory. His presence on campus was unique, being a teacher of English, and, at the same time, a student in regular classes. Besides sleeping in the dormitory, he could be found eating with students in the dining hall or sitting in the classroom with the degree students. Also, he could be found working on his laptop or drinking tea in the staff room or teaching English to the diploma students.

Someone informed Aaron that the key to learning Amharic was to eat lots of enjera. This must be true because Aaron was perfectly healthy on that diet, and the language came accordingly.

His presence outside of campus was even more unique. People who happened to be out on the street on any early morning may have spotted this rather short, young man with *ferrengi* features, jogging along the cobblestone streets of Kotebe, dodging between cars, donkeys, pedestrians, and beggars.

Developing a Teaching Faculty

Since the leaders' vision was that their Meserete Kristos Church should be a charismatic Anabaptist church and that its college should teach theology from that perspective, it was important that our teaching staff should receive some training in one of the known Anabaptist seminaries. To move toward that end in the first year, as already noted,

Eastern Mennonite Seminary (EMS) granted a three-year scholarship to Hailu Cherenet for an MDiv degree. This was followed in the second year by granting Bedru Hussein a similar scholarship.

With these scholarships granted, I challenged the president of Associated Mennonite Biblical Seminaries (AMBS), (now named "Anabaptist Mennonite Biblical Seminary") in Elkhart Indiana, to match EMS in assisting in developing our teaching faculty. They responded by granting one scholarship to Girma Teklu.

Then, at the Mennonite World Conference in Calcutta, India, in 1997, I met Henry Schmidt, the president of the Mennonite Brethren Biblical Seminary (MBBS) based in Fresno, California. I inquired whether they would also join EMS and AMBS to assist in the training of our teaching staff. There was a delay, but they also granted a scholarship which went to Girma Kelecha. This began a trend in which twenty-one Ethiopian church leaders have benefited from scholarships to study in North American Anabaptist seminaries.

Most of these, upon completing their studies, joined our faculty on a full-time basis for at least a few years. Some of them were given posts with the church, but taught, or are still teaching courses on a part-time basis from time to time. Others taught for a brief time, then went on to more lucrative posts in other para-church organizations. Of course, these were a disappointment to us as administrators since they were sent by us with high expectations of loyalty and a sense of calling that they would contribute to a quality teaching faculty. However, we recognized that, just as the college and church belonged to God, so each of these belonged to God, so we had no hard feelings. Let Him call his people as he wishes.

Graduations

At the end of the first year on the Kotebe campus, on December 18th, 1999, a graduation ceremony honored thirty-one certificate students. Seven of these were from our college, and twenty-four from the Semien MKC congregation which had started its own training program. Theirs was one of the first emerging local Bible schools, which adopted our curriculum and used the same teachers we were using. The ceremony was held in our dining hall. The decorated car port served as the stage, and a tent was set up as the audience hall for about 150 guests. The rest of our students had gone home to their families and congregations.

The next day, thirty-two new students arrived for the six-week *One Year for Christ* special orientation program. Then, two days after they graduated, a new academic year opened with a total of sixty-two full-time students enrolled for the spring semester. The campus was reaching its capacity.

At about this time, we began to encourage congregations or regions to run their own certificate programs as the college would discontinue offering one-year certificate programs on our full-time boarding campus. Local efforts have made this service much more accessible and much cheaper to operate. Several local and regional Bible schools emerged around this time.

A Divine Appointment: God's Call to Fundraising

It is amazing how God works through ordinary people in unexpected ways and unique circumstances, like Mary getting pregnant without knowing that the outcome would change the history of humankind.

I had been a friend of Darrell Jantzi of Elmira, Ontario, since childhood. His family and our family were friends. We parted ways when my family moved back to Alberta when I was fourteen years old.

Later, we renewed our friendship when we both attended Eastern Mennonite College in Virginia. Darrell came with Florence, his young wife, in 1962. Our friendship circle expanded when I enticed Vera to join me in holy matrimony in 1964.

Again, Darrell and I parted ways when Vera and I went to Ethiopia as missionaries in 1967. Darrell and Florence eventually moved back to Ontario where he worked as a pastor for thirty-five years. We had stayed connected through the years with Christmas letters and occasional visits to Ontario.

Then, for the first time, on December 19, 1999, Darrell and Florence came to visit us in Ethiopia. We entertained them, showing them the sights, sounds, smells, and tastes of Ethiopia for twelve days. Then we flew with them to Nairobi, Kenya. There, we took the night train to Mombasa on December 31st. The four of us occupied a private compartment where we played *Rook* until past midnight.

Being the last day of the 20th century and the second millennium, exactly at midnight, our train stopped at a railroad siding somewhere in the vast empty darkness of the Tsavo desert. The engineer turned off the diesel engine. There was complete silence as the old millennium passed and a new millennium began.

We looked out the window into the darkness. Up the line was a small single light bulb. Someone read a scripture, and a group sang a hymn. Then the train started up and we moved on through the Kenyan desert night into a new millennium. We reminded each other that the "Y2K" bug did not bite the train system, or, as many worried, we could have faced an uncertain calamity stranded out there for who knows how long. We enjoyed another ten days with this couple in Kenya.

Unknown to us, God was putting in their hearts a special love and calling for the church and the people of Ethiopia. It would later have a major impact on the development of the college and the church. By that time, Darrell had retired from pastoral work and had taken up the challenge of fundraising for the Mennonite Central Committee. Florence was still working at the Rockway Mennonite Collegiate.

It was not until August of 2003 that the couple returned to Ethiopia. This time they were leading a Tour Imagination group to attend the Mennonite World Conference in Bulawayo, Zimbabwe, with a side trip to Ethiopia.

By 2005, Darrell had resigned from his MCC assignment, and Florence retired from her job at Rockway. They were now free to organize and lead an *Experience Ethiopia Tour* in February 2006. By this time, they felt called and were committed to becoming involved in the development of MK College as fund raisers.

CHAPTER 5

Finding a Permanent Home

Searching for Land

The search for a permanent home took a lot of time and emotional energy. When rumors hit the informal communication channels that we were searching for land, hungry, would-be brokers emerged from everywhere, offering their advice and services. We checked out a lot of leads, some of them promising, that turned out to be rabbit trails that went nowhere. Most of the properties in the city were either too small, too expensive, poorly located, or had political or legal issues connected.

At the beginning, we had a spark of hope that the government would return, to the church, the former Nazareth Bible Academy, which had been illegally confiscated by the former Marxist government. That ten-hectare (twenty-two-acre) campus, with its many well-established and well-maintained buildings, would make an ideal home for our envisioned Christian liberal arts university.

Two attempts were initiated. MKC leaders submitted their application to the government with all supporting documents. Their lawyer oversaw the follow up, but his efforts led nowhere.

A second approach was made in 1998 when Million Belete and Negash Kebede, accompanied by the missionary founders of the Bible Academy, Chester and Sara Jane Wenger and their children, Sara Wenger Shenk and Mark Wenger, met with the president of Ethiopia, Negasso Gidada Solon. He had been a student during their time at the Bible Academy. They presented an appeal on behalf of MKC for the return of the Bible Academy as well as other properties formerly held by the Church. President Negasso welcomed his old friends and promised to do what he could. He said other properties could probably be returned soon, but the Bible Academy property would take longer.

Knowing how political promises work in that country, we could not wait for that vague promise to happen. We had to work with the realities at hand. Acquiring access to that prize property remained a distant and fading dream.

The current Kotebe compound was a vast improvement over the previous campus. Wezero Senait, the owner, now wanted to sell the whole compound to us, 4200 square meters with about twenty-eight rooms plus a big warehouse, for 6,000,000 birr (US $600,000). In negotiating, the Board made a final offer of 3,700,000 birr ($370,000). Her last offer was for 4,200,000 birr. She would not sell for less. With room to build upward, it would have been large enough for a compact seminary, but we were still thinking of a liberal arts college that would need more room in the years ahead.

The board decided not to pursue this option any further. They would concentrate on two other options simultaneously: to initiate a fresh effort to secure the return of the former Nazareth Bible Academy by an application through the Prime Minister's Office, and to prepare an application to be submitted to the Addis Ababa City Council requesting free land for our college.

Daniel Abebe prepared and submitted another application for the return of the Nazareth Bible Academy property. It led nowhere.

While waiting for a response to that application, I developed an application for free land for the future home of the college. This became a sixty-six-page document entitled: *A Project Proposal for the Establishment of the Meserete Kristos College as a Multi-Disciplined Institution of Tertiary Level Education in the Liberal Arts Tradition.*

This was signed by Mulugeta Zewdie, the general secretary of the Meserete Kristos Church. It was dated March 14, 2000. We submitted it to the Municipality of Addis Ababa, Minister of Urban Development. It included a complete fifteen-year plan. We were assured by others that, if our feasibility study was impressive enough, free land should be forthcoming.

However, we proceeded with some skepticism since the privately-owned Unity College, which had over 8,000 students, was still operating in rented quarters, waiting for its free land. We submitted our sixty-six-page document in March. Our follow-up with several visits to the Municipality building led us into a labyrinth of rabbit trails. We followed our document from office to office, but it led us nowhere.

Acquiring the "Promised Land"

Accordingly, after several years of praying and searching and following many trails to dead ends, we finally found an answer to prayer in an unusual situation.

One Sunday afternoon at the Gihon Hotel, Vera and I were standing in a long line with over 1,000 invitees attending a lavish wedding reception of someone we did not know. The wait in the hot sun was long and tedious. We began a conversation with a lady in line. We shared something about our work and vision for the college. When she heard we were searching for land for the future campus, she said, "Do you want land? I know someone who can get you land." She took our name and phone number and promised to call us. Then, we sort of forgot about it.

One evening about ten days later, the woman phoned and said that she was bringing the wife of the president of Oromiya Region to our house in a few minutes! (Oromiya was the largest region in Ethiopia, with more than 20,000,000 Oromo inhabitants). A little later she came with the young wife of the president, her twenty-four-year-old brother, and the wife of the first secretary of the Oromiya government. We welcomed them into our simple abode. They said that their government would give free land to churches and schools in their region, and that they would be glad to set up an appointment for me to see the president. They would call me when the appointment was made. Then they took their leave.

It was intriguing: not every home gets a visit after dark from the wife of the president of Oromiya. Not every aspiring college principal has the president's wife and entourage knock on the door and say, "Hey, I just came by to say I want to help you get some land for your college!" It was a kind of unique experience.

I waited a few weeks; nothing happened. In the meantime, I quickly adapted our sixty-six-page *Proposal* to fit the Oromiya Region rather than the Addis Ababa Region. Then I got a call from the young man. He wanted to meet me at a nearby cafe on Saturday afternoon. On Saturday morning, he called again and changed the appointment to Tuesday at 4:30 p.m. I got two board members to go with me, thinking he might bring the president himself. We waited for more than an hour, but he did not come. So, we went home. About ten days later, he called again and made another appointment for the next Monday at 4:00 p.m. This time he came after I waited at the cafe for another full hour and was ready to go home.

He told me that he had rushed back from a big political celebration in Adama just to keep this appointment. I gave him our proposal, and he agreed to meet me at 9:00 a.m. the next day to take the proposal to the Oromiya Region Investment Office to start the process.

Tuesday morning, I met the brother waiting for me at the café, this time ahead of schedule. He took me to the office and submitted the document. He told the man in charge that this project must be processed "from the top down," not the usual "bottom up," meaning that the president was interested that it be approved without a lot of hassle and waiting for bribes. The man said, "Okay" and told us it would be brought to the board "this week for approval."

To us, this was an extremely exciting development, almost too good to be true. The next few days were filled with excitement tempered with a bit of skepticism. Could this be the answer to our prayers? Or another rabbit trail? The saying goes: "If it's too good to be true, it probably is!"

When I went back on Monday to hear their decision, I found that the proposal had been accepted! We had asked for 200,000 m² (forty-four acres) near Addis. But we were to be given 100,000 m² (twenty-two acres) of land about thirty-five kms southeast of the city between

Dukum and Debre Zeit (recently re-named *Bishoftu*). This meant there would be transportation challenges. Distance from the city has its disadvantages. It was located two kms off the main road in an open teff field close to an East Africa Industries factory. Also, it had deep black cotton soil, the worst kind of soil upon which to build. It was not an ideal location, but the government would give it to us at $3.50 (thirty-five birr) per square meter. After searching for land for four years, what could we say?

The Board assigned Fikru Zeleke to follow up with the legal processes to obtain the final documents. It turned out that when we went out to the site with the surveyors, the 100,000 m² was nonexistent. That is, it had not been expropriated by the government from the farmers' association, so it was not available.

Instead, they offered us a lovely plot of 60,000 m² (thirteen acres) of land at the north-east edge of the town of Bishoftu. It was a nice sloping plot between the seasonal Lake Chelekleka at the bottom and the crater Lake Hora, just over the tree-covered hilltop. It had sandy volcanic soil, ideal for a campus. We were pleased with the location but disappointed with the reduction of size.

While Fikru was working out the legalities, the young man invited me to his favorite café for a talk. He finally revealed his expectations: $20,000 (200,000 birr) for his services! He said he needed it "to open doors in high places." I protested that it looked like a bribe and would be unacceptable to our trustees, but I would present the request to them for a decision.

After hearing this, the board members were disappointed, but not surprised. After much deliberation, they decided we could only give the young man $2,500 (25,000 birr) for his transport and other expenses for his kind services as a land broker. We do not bribe. I was given the task to present the check. Surprisingly, the young man took it graciously and offered to be of future service, if needed. A short time later, the president of Oromiya was replaced on charges of corruption. Not surprising.

Considering the long search for land, we were happy to acquire the empty plot at Bishoftu. It was an attractive site. Yet, it was far removed from the center of Addis Ababa. Some of the faculty and staff could not leave their homes and move their families from the city. There would have to be a service bus for some time. That would mean long hours every day stuck in traffic, and it would mean added expenses operating the bus. Further, it was far for adjunct teachers to drive out of Addis to teach one class. Also, day students would find it difficult to come from such a distance, and more of the students would need a boarding facility.

In securing this land, we were very happy, feeling this was a gift of God in answering our prayers. However, there was one major flaw in the whole transaction. Due to my inexperience in transacting such a legal matter in an unfamiliar land, I trusted others to investigate the details. I had clearly requested free land for educational purposes in our application. I just assumed that the officials concerned had read our application and were implementing the same. In ignorance, I did not question why the young man took me and our application to the investment office, nor why they were charging a small fee per square meter for the land. Also, the Board did not raise the issue when they appointed Fikru to take care of the legal work.

It was only years later, after my official retirement, that I learned that we had been allocated the land as an investment, a lease that requires payment of an annual rent, not a rent-free charity. Getting this mistake rectified has caused a lot of pain for the church leadership and is still not settled. Getting free land for a seminary is not yet possible. The college/seminary pays rent every year for what was assumed to have been "free" land.

Securing the Ground

The transfer of the 60,000 m² plot by the regional government to MK College was finalized by June 2000. Immediately, the plot was surveyed and marked out. A topographical survey producing contour maps followed, costing $1,200. With the land secured, and the topographical survey in hand, the Board appointed a Campus Development Committee (CDC) to proceed with the building of the campus.

Initially, we naively hoped to get started with the construction of the first building by December 2000. After all, the municipality, in giving us the land, had stipulated that construction "should commence within six months." We had no idea how complicated the process of building could be, especially when collaborating with committees and with an inexperienced church being the owner, and, of course, a shortage of funds.

Later, when I told an architect of this six-month stipulation imposed by the municipality officials, he laughed and commented: "Obviously, they know nothing about building." In retrospect, it took four years from the date we were given the land to the time of actual commencement of construction.

The CDC had its first meeting on September 27th. It was decided that while we worked on the architectural designs and the fund-raising, we would start by constructing a high fence around the plot and drilling a water well.

As soon as the farmers got their crops harvested in November, we took possession of the land. Tibebu, a committee member, was given a contract and built a formidable perimeter fence around the plot. It was made with reinforced concrete posts 2.4 meters above ground and 2.3 meters apart, carrying thirteen strands of barbed wire. It looked like a concentration camp until the shrubbery grew up to camouflage it. Workers planted 5,000 kai apple seedlings to reinforce the wires all around. These thorny plants made an excellent fence.

While the fence was being constructed, the CDC contracted the Mekane Yesus Church Water Development Department which drilled a fifty-six meter deep well at cost, minus 10% as their donation. The twenty-four-hour pump test yielded five liters per second, and the water level dropped only seven centimeters. This gave us confidence in having an adequate supply of water for the college. They also installed a pump and connected it to a 4,000-gallon holding tank on the top southwest corner of the campus in May 2001. We purchased a diesel generator to power the electric pump.

*The "Promised Land," an empty open field with a beautiful
view of Yerer Mountain in the distance – 2000*

Planning the Campus: Collaborating with the Architects

We advertised and received bids from architectural firms to draw up
a campus masterplan and building designs. An architectural firm,
Associated Engineering Consultants (AEC), won the bid. However,
before signing a contract, we needed to try one other option. Could
we get someone from America to do this work for us gratis? The CDC
encouraged me to try.

I contacted Leroy Troyer of Southbend, Indiana, to see if he would
be interested in assisting us. Leroy was famous in Mennonite circles
as a congenial, careful, creative, sympathetic architect. He understood
Anabaptist/Mennonite values, was sensitive to environmental issues,
and incorporated those into his designs. He was also well known for his
many generous works of charity. Our inquiry generated positive interest.
Being a busy person, it took a few months to arrange a visit. We delayed
signing any contract with our Ethiopian architectural firm.

Leroy Troyer arrived in Ethiopia on Friday morning, March 9,
2001, and was taken immediately to study the Bishoftu site, where he

took a lot of pictures and measurements. After a night's rest in his hotel, he spent the next three days sorting out ideas with college staff and members of the CDC, which chose to include Mersha Sahle. He was an engineer and the owner of the reputed and successful architectural firm, AEC, which had won the bid for our project.

Leroy Troyer committed his firm, the "Troyer Group," to prepare the Campus Master Plan at their expense. He would also consider if their Group would find the time to do the schematic designs of the buildings. They would depend on AEC to do the preliminary construction drawings and provide the professional certification needed. As the design architect, the Troyer Group would review these drawings. Leroy took the Tuesday morning flight back to his home. We were very happy and optimistic about the decisions we had made.

However, we were still very ignorant and naïve about the work of architects and the time it would take to complete the designs of a project. Nine months after Leroy Troyer's visit, by early November, we had only received drafts of the campus master plan, the library design, and the first draft of the dining complex.

The work was going way too slowly. I was really stressed. The government, in giving us the land, stipulated the condition that we start construction within six months or risk forfeiting it. That was seventeen months ago. Yet, the architectural work was only beginning. We were impatient to get started.

We sensed that, while the Troyer Group was committed to giving us a free service, it was preoccupied with the pressures of earning the salaries of its one hundred employees during an economic recession. We felt that their commitment to assisting us was becoming a worrisome burden to them. So, on November 15, 2001, we gave the contract to AEC to complete the preliminary designs and all the necessary detailed drawings as well. They were to complete all their work within six months.

I had to write a difficult letter to Leroy Troyer, thanking him for his efforts and at the same time informing him that our committee decided to shorten the process by giving the whole contract to the AEC. Leroy's response was not a happy one. The Troyer Group had invested a lot in the preliminary work they had already done. Now it was all wasted.

Personally, I mourned the loss of the expertise and care the Troyer Group would have put into these designs. In hindsight, I still feel our CDC made the wrong decision. Our ignorance and impatience did us a disservice. I was not greatly impressed with the results of what our chosen architects eventually did.

Our romance with the AEC was not an easy one either. They had promised to complete the work within six months. However, it took another year to get all the drawings done.

Another change was the removal of the sports field from the scene in favor of more generous spacing of the other buildings. The rational for that was that a campus should not be congested with buildings, and we wanted to use the need for a sports field as a bargaining chip with the government to request more land.

Unrealistic Ambitions

The CDC, working with the architects, produced rather ambitious plans that called for building the campus in three phases of five years each. The respective phases would end in 2005, 2010, and 2015. The engineers estimated the cost to build the whole campus was about $15,000,000. With the whole campus completed, the college would have the capacity to accommodate about 2,000 students.

Phase I of the Campus Development Plan envisioned, unrealistically, supplying the buildings and equipment necessary to accommodate 500 students in a dormitory setting within two years. The total cost of Phase I would be about US $2,350,000. At that time, fundraising efforts had only gathered $600,000. I sent out a special appeal along with our newsletters to about 400 addresses in the USA and Canada.

Unfulfilled Vision: A Retreat Center

Leroy Troyer's Campus Master Plan included a retreat center on land extending up the hill from our plot. It reached the crest and looked down into Hora Lake, the water-filled crater above the campus. It was an ideal location, but the reality of raising enough money pushed the dream into the distant future.

At the beginning of March 2001, we went to the municipality in Bishoftu and asked them to extend our plot a bit. We must have talked with the wrong people, for they offhandedly promised to add another five acres up the hill from the campus. However, we would have to apply.

Accordingly, we took our application to the Investment Bureau where we started the original process. The official in charge firmly informed us that there was no way they would give more than 60,000 square meters for universities or colleges. However, he suggested, if we have a legitimate request, we must first at least lay the foundations of the present campus before we ask for more land. In fact, he sternly reminded us that the generous allotment of land was given with the stipulation that construction was to begin within six months. He warned us that nine months had already lapsed. We were in mortal danger of losing the land. We had better keep quiet and hurry with the construction.

Working with the Campus Development Committee, AEC prepared the master plan which squeezed everything, including the retreat center idea, within the existing 60,000 m² campus plot. College dormitories, dining hall, and chapel would serve a dual purpose, used jointly by the students and conference guests.

Stress in Planning

We should not have been surprised to learn that it can be difficult for architects to work with a committee. Every time they presented their updated plan, we committee members pointed out weaknesses, and asked for some changes. It is to be expected; plans evolve by the selection of the fittest.

For me, these complications and prolonged delays with building caused a lot of stress. I sometimes wistfully reflected on the good old days when the missionary drew up the plans in his home office in the evening after the assignments were corrected and the kids were in bed. With these sketches in hand, he went out and hired some local help, and, following his sketches, constructed the building himself. In a few months, the building was completed, done well, and done cheaply.

I recognized that times had changed, and government inspections were now mandatory, and educational buildings must be built to a high standard to get accreditation as a tertiary-level training institution. Therefore, we were trying to do it right, so it will last for a hundred years. We could no longer get by with Bible Academy quality construction. I was confident the final product would be a lasting monument worthy of the extra effort and expense if it ever got built!

CHAPTER 6

Launching a New Millennium with Vigor

After six years of experimental growth, the year 2000 was one of the better years in the college's history. During that millennial year, it reached several important milestones.

The board of trustees approved plans to implement a full four-year degree program which would double the enrollment. Doubling the student population was alarming news for the support staff. Had it not been a major achievement to care for sixty-two the previous semester? How could we manage double that many? Where would they sleep? What about classrooms or dining facilities? How could they all fit into the library? How could the mini kitchen with its skeleton staff feed all the hungry mouths three times a day? Was this not a bit too ambitious?

With about two weeks between the summer term and the fall semester, the staff got busy. Another nearby compound was rented for $300 per month. It had two houses with sixteen additional rooms for dormitory. A local welding shop was contracted to make thirty more bunk beds, and sixty mattresses were purchased.

Room for two offices and library space in Wezero Senait's adjacent compound was sub-rented for an additional $200 per month. All the library furniture, shelves, and 9,000 books were carried and installed into the new place. The old library morphed into a classroom, which doubled as a chapel. Extra kitchen staff were hired. A larger wood stove, dishes, and food were purchased. Three new computers and tables, four office desks, three more bookshelves for the library, three filing cabinets, thirty student desks, and eighty chairs were also purchased.

When the students arrived, there was food and lodging for all! Classes started on time. Semester enrollment reached one hundred and sixteen full-time and ten part-time students. Nine were females who lived off campus. There were eight full-time and seven part-time teachers.

Doubling enrollment meant we needed two sections of preparatory intensive English. MCC supplied a full salary for one Ethiopian English teacher. We employed two. Growth put new demands upon teaching and support staff. Bedru Hussein and Girma Teklu had completed their studies abroad and returned, eager to teach. Aklilu Abebe, a recent graduate with a BTh degree from ETC, was hired as a Bible teacher.

We had to say "Goodbye!" to Emebet Mekonnen, our dean of students and business manager. She was given a scholarship to do graduate studies in an MEd program at Fresno Pacific University in Fresno, California. She left her office for Vera and me, her work to Bedru, Woudeneh, and Girma, and her children to the care of her husband, Fikru Zeleke. Bedru took on her business manager role, Woudeneh her registrar role, Girma her dean of students' role, and Aboma Byessa was hired to take over much of the detailed work of Emebet in the new post of storekeeper and general service officer. He was also assigned to teach one course. Aboma was a recent graduate with a BTh from Nazarene University in Nairobi, Kenya.

Mattias Lemma was contracted to assist Vera in re-organizing the accounting system on the computer using the Peach Tree #7 program. By May, Vera succeeded in getting all the college's accounts into the computer.

Since our first secretary quit one month after starting her job, we hired Wolansa Yisahak to be our receptionist and secretary. This cheerful, cooperative young lady proved to be a long-term faithful worker, later assuming the role of registrar as well.

Pastor Teku Kebede enrolled at AMBS on a scholarship. Kebede Bekere and Gemechu Gebre had scholarships to EMS. All these were committed to strengthening our teaching faculty in the next two or three years.

Students agonize over a tough exam

Challenges Along the Way

For several months every spring, the citizenry of Addis Ababa faced the rationing of electricity. Koka Lake, the main reservoir that supplied hydro power, lacked capacity to supply the growing city through the long dry season. The limited flow of electricity had to be rationed. For about six days in a month the electricity was shut off from 7:00 a.m. until 8:00 p.m. Different parts of the city were affected on differing days. Besides the negative effect on the economy, this inconvenience affected the efficiency of our work, especially when one needed to use a computer or other electrical devices. This was the pattern until July, when the rainy season began to replenish the water supply in Koka Lake.

On this millennial year, the government-owned Ethio Telecom introduced its first internet service. This was limited to about 5,000 subscribers. Our college applied, but we were told to wait. A year later, Ethio Telecom installed new equipment, and then there was room for us.

On the news, we heard that 8,000,000 Ethiopians were facing starvation. The UN World Food Program was appealing for emergency help. Accordingly, food prices were escalating.

The Growing Challenge of Supplying Textbooks

One of the challenges that taxed our ingenuity was the matter of supplying textbooks for the growing body of students. When the student body was small, we felt it would be helpful to supply our evangelists and pastors, not only with free tuition, room and board, but also with free textbooks. That way, they would be able to build up a "pastor's library" as a resource for when they returned to full time ministry. It was a kind idea and was deeply appreciated by the students.

However, this generosity was detrimental in that it added to our financial burden, especially as the student body increased in number, and perpetuated a dependency mentality among the recipients. Finding the books in Ethiopia was impossible. We had to shop in the outside world, collect the books, and carry or ship them months in advance of when they were to be used. New teachers sometimes decided to use different textbooks than those previous teachers had selected. Expensive unused books remained on the shelves in our book storage room.

One of my activities back home during our summer break in the year 2000 was to purchase and deliver the year's supply of textbooks. As we prepared to return, we had collected twenty boxes and four suitcases full of new textbooks. We could not carry all of them with our luggage, so we arranged to ship them by air from Washington to Addis.

We arrived on August 22nd. The semester started a few days later. The book shipment arrived at Bole International Airport a week later. However, the customs authority took possession of our shipment. They could not release them to us immediately due to congestion at the customs warehouse. An extensive line of customers was waiting ahead of us. Fairness required us to wait our turn. There would be the matter of shipping charges, customs charges, taxes, handling fees, and storage fees. In fact, the shipment was "stored" on pallets out on the tarmac outside the warehouse for several weeks. It being the rainy season, the books on the tarmac were "protected" by leaky plastic sheets.

The teachers and students needed the books. We kept checking as the weeks passed. We were told to wait our turn. So, we waited and waited.

Having had a previous experience a few years earlier in getting our computer and printer out of customs, I faced this ordeal with trepidation. At that time, it took three days and visits to twenty-seven different "offices" to get a stamp or a signature or something from each office before we could pay our tax and have the goods released. It amazed me that they did not consider that if they simplified the process of getting things out, there would be no backlog. Why should it take three days to clear a simple item? Why twenty-seven different stations in the drawn-out process? Were there no organizational geniuses in the government? More than likely, it was a mental carryover from the Communist era when the government was obligated to provide jobs for as many of its citizens as possible.

Finally, at the very end of September, Bedru and I got our twenty boxes and four suitcases out of customs. It took us only two full days, a considerable improvement over my earlier experience. Like usual, it was frustrating, almost maddening. At the end of the first day, they decided that we owed the government about $7,000 in taxes and fees. We were shocked. Even though we were a non-profit college offering almost free educational services, and these items were all gifts with no cost to the Ethiopian economy, their tax came to about 50% of the original value!

So, I wrote a letter of objection, asking for mercy and presented it on the second day. They looked at the documents and admitted there had been a "miscalculation." The adjusted charge was about $4,000. Sometimes it pays to write a letter.

We had also prepaid Ethiopian Airlines almost $2,800 for air cargo so the books would "get there on time." However, customs kept the shipment in "storage" for a full month for which they charged us daily storage fees, while the students and teachers were waiting.

Because of their storage facility, water managed to access about eight of the twenty-four boxes, and some of the books were seriously damaged. For the next three weeks, our staff-room tables and desks served as drying racks for the many soggy books. They looked ugly but were useable.

Personal Reflection: Motivation

Sometimes when I felt exhausted, I questioned my motivation, "Why do I keep driving myself to campaign for this college, raising funds for building the campus and for scholarship support?"

The answer became clear. My motivation was my deep admiration of the quality and potential of the students. These were very highly motivated, gifted, committed, and deserving young people. These were God's "storm troopers," invading enemy territory. Most of them had been working in the countryside, preaching the gospel where it had never been heard and planting churches where there had never been any. They had been working for many years with little or no support, ten to thirty dollars per month. Their main means of transportation was on foot. Many of them worked in areas where there were no roads, or they could not afford public transportation. Many of them owned no other book than one Bible.

A scholarship was a well-deserved, precious gift. With it, they were enabled to take a much-needed break. It provided them with the opportunity to learn, to access books, and to find answers to some of the many questions that troubled them or their people. Many were married and had families back home. It was painful to be away from them, but they were happy and appreciative of this opportunity.

They had the most amazing stories. One of them planted a church that took over a mosque because all the Muslims became Christians. That is rather unusual. Another worked among an ethnic group on the western fringe of the country who did not wear clothing at all. Try to imagine a church full of naked people! He had to get used to it. Of course, the new believers (there were about 2,000 of them when he told me this) soon learned to put on clothes. They also started schools, so their children could learn to read and write. The gospel was changing their lifestyle.

It was a most amazing privilege to teach these young leaders. Most of them were under thirty-five years of age. When they started their ministries, they were mere adolescents. When they came to college, many of them were still quite ignorant, unpolished, and sometimes foolish.

Yet, they had already planted and nurtured growing congregations and ministered to the deep needs of their people. When I learned about what they had already done, I marveled and remembered St. Paul's advice to Timothy: *"Let no one despise your youth!"*

The task of elders is to recognize and unleash the gifts, enthusiasm, and energy of their young people. If leaders encourage them and give them freedom and power to do the work of God in the church and community, they will find that they have pastors to export.

This was my motivating drive. The least I could do, besides share a fraction of the knowledge God had allowed me to accumulate, was to find scholarships for them and support for building a campus. My unique position as an expat, a foreigner, was to be a bridge person, connecting my brothers and sisters in the resource-rich west with the need of these faithful evangelists.

Alum Publishes History

Pastor Tefera Gonfa Kano is a respected pioneer and father of the Meserete Kristos Church in the regions of Wollega and Gojam. He was born in Bora in Eastern Wollega.

Before the gospel was known, his people worshipped idols and spirits in the trees and mountains. Furthermore, they lived in bondage to demons who kept them under a curse. Even though they plowed their land thoroughly, their crop production was extraordinarily little. Since they were under the control of demons, wild animals such as pigs, apes, monkeys, and baboons came out to destroy their crops. As a result, farmers were on the verge of starvation throughout most of the year.

Tefera came to faith in Jesus Christ at age sixteen through the witness of his elementary school teacher, Mekuria Mulugeta, who preached the gospel in his hometown back in 1968. At age eighteen, Tefera, compelled by the call of God to evangelize, left his fifth-grade school and joined Mekuria and another evangelist, Tadesse Negawo, on an itinerant ministry of evangelizing and disciple-making among the towns and villages of Wollega and Gojam. They preached the good news of deliverance from the bondages of sin and the curse of demonic spirit domination in their lives and the resultant joy and peace that freedom in Christ brings. Their ministry was accompanied by miracles, casting out demons, and healings. All three of them experienced great persecution including four months in prison.

When Mekuria and Tadessa, both government-employed teachers, were transferred to other places, Tefera continued alone. Imagine this scarcely twenty-year-old, poorly educated boy, traveling from village to village, usually on foot and alone, preaching to skeptical, hostile crowds. He did not know about *Pentecostals*, *Baptists*, *Mennonites*, or *Presbyterians*. He only knew about Jesus, and, like Jesus, his preaching was in the power of the Holy Spirit, accompanied by miracles, healing of the sick, and casting out of demons. Such activities brought mixed results. On the one hand, like with Jesus, the established Orthodox clergy, the authorities, and community leaders stirred up opposition. On the other hand, the poor, the sick, and the weak listened. In time, many became his disciples and were formed into congregations.

In the early years, the persecution was mostly at the hands of the Orthodox communities they visited. After the ending of Emperor Haile Selassie's reign, severe persecution continued under the Dergue government. Tefera continued traveling from place to place, without any regular support, often hungry, often hiding in the forests, sometimes sleeping in trees surrounded by hungry hyenas, and often imprisoned. Like Menno Simons, he persisted in travelling, teaching, encouraging, and shaping the infant congregations into an association. After sixteen years, in 1986, Tefera led his region of congregations, with over 2,500 members as an underground movement, to join MKC.

As persecution got so intense that Tefera could not freely move about preaching and teaching, he decided to resume his high school education. In 1985, hoping that the communist cadres would not notice him, he introduced himself as a businessperson and enrolled in Gidda Ayana Abiot Free Secondary School. Students and teachers respected him. Being older than most students, his classmates elected him as their representative. This enabled him to organize an underground Bible study group.

This very secretive group grew to twenty students by the third year. When the communist cadres learned that Tefera was converting students to evangelical Christianity, where they hoped to produce young communist cadres, they ordered the police to arrest him wherever they found him. However, because the government was preoccupied with the re-settlement schemes following the 1984/85 famine, the arrest never took place.

After planting, organizing, and developing the church, Tefera was ready to take a break. He joined the first class of the MKC Bible Institute in 1994 and graduated in 1996.

Immediately upon completion, with his diploma, he went home to Agamsa, and with the cooperation of colleagues, started a small Bible institute. They founded the Wollega Bible Institute under the most basic conditions in the regional office of Wollega MKC. They began by offering a certificate level, basic training taught in the Oromo language. Since this was a pioneering effort in that language, all materials had to be original or translated, a challenging task. The first class had eleven students.

After a few years, in the fall of 2001, the local government gave them thirteen hectares (twenty-eight acres) of land in Nekempte, the capital city of Wollega Region. It was a central location for the establishment of the church's regional office and Bible college. The church in Wollega, although very poor in material goods, sacrificed and persevered, using its own resources, managed to build a simple campus and keep the school growing.

A true leader, Tefera, empowered the next generation by selecting and sending many of his best young leaders to be trained in Meserete Kristos College. He, himself, returned to MK College at Bishoftu in his late fifties and completed a bachelor's degree. Then for a third time, after reaching retirement, he returned to complete a master's degree.

Recently, Pastor Tefera produced a 410-page history of the Oromo church in western Ethiopia, titled *From a Small Spring into an Ocean*. It is written and published in Amharic and translated into the Oromo language. First, Tefera makes history, now he writes history! God bless this true apostle!

CHAPTER 7

Some Ups and Downs in Financing the College

Some letters from supporters are precious, but the letter below, sent to us from a ten-year-old girl, topped them all. She wrote:

> Your college recently received money from the Pleasant Valley Mennonite Church in Bath. Some of that money was mine. While I was watching your video, I noticed how you and God seem to work together. It touched me, what you are doing for all these people. You flew from your family to try and make your own new family in Ethiopia. Your college is a great place for kids and adults to go and learn. I know my money is in good hands."
> Love, Rachel Moore, Bath, New York.

"I know my money is in good hands!" Isn't that a confidence every donor wants and deserves to feel? Even a ten-year old demands accountability!

Over the years, hundreds of generous people have made thousands of contributions with some feeling of confidence, "I know my money is in good hands!"

Local Initiative

Being in one of the poorest countries of the world, the Ethiopian church suffered all the frustrations that go with poverty. The congregations supported themselves as best they could, paying the salaries of their full-time ministers, their office expenses, and rents, or building their worship centers. However, for their institutional development and church-wide programs, they needed help, and they cast their eyes toward the mother lode of western funding.

By the beginning of the year 2000, the college was still giving full scholarships, providing free tuition, room, board, and books to over sixty students, besides collecting money for the building fund, all from outside foreign sources. For its own self-respect and the respect of its foreign donors, the church urgently needed to show evidence of local ownership and involvement in its educational enterprise.

During its annual meeting, the General Church Council solicited the participation of all the local congregations of MKC to help the college with its financial burden. It announced a special fundraising campaign by designating March 12th as "Meserete Kristos College Sunday," a time when each of the 232 congregations would promote Christian education and take an offering for the college. A letter to this effect was sent out to all the congregations.

Disappointingly, most of the congregations failed to follow these instructions. Of the few that did respond, the offerings were a mere pittance. In contrast, MKC believers have a keen sense of ownership of their church, both their local congregations and the national church. In promoting the mission of their church, members are willing to contribute what they have. However, we did not observe that kind of commitment even among some college faculty and staff. Had we done wrong by external fundraising, spoiling them with money, nourishing an easy dependency on outside sources that they were taking for granted?

But there was a deeper problem. This response showed the need for an organized, active public relations department committed to creating awareness and a sense of ownership. A single letter from the head office could not do it. Communications between the denominational center and the scattered congregations out in the periphery were very weak. Most of the members would not have seen that letter. Having a college at all was a new thing, and most of them did not even know they had a college, nor any idea of the value of a college to the church. They were mostly new Christians and knew little about the value of education to improving good leadership.

Failure to Qualify for Duty Free Status

According to the laws of the land, churches were exempt from paying taxes or duty on imported goods. MKC, however, had never been able to take advantage of this government provision, and neither had its college. She always had to pay duty on imported goods. The reason being that it was registered as an "association" rather than as a church. Schools were exempt, but we could not register with the Ministry of Education as a school because the secular government did not register theological schools, and furthermore, we were owned by an "association." Business ventures had duty free status on imported capital goods, but we were not registered with the Investment Bureau as a "business." So, we just paid duty and taxes.

Another Summer Fundraising Furlough

As the number of students increased, the operations budget also grew. By the year 2000, it reached US $151,000. As usual, we proceeded by faith, not knowing how, but believing the money would be provided. Of course, faith must be accompanied by work, that is, my work as a fundraiser!

In that light, plus the fact that we had just received the 60,000 m² plot, the board of trustees asked Vera and me to undertake another fundraising effort during our upcoming home leave. This decision proved to be very timely, as we had something concrete on which to make our appeal for building funds.

After seeking and gaining EMM's approval and permission to extend our furlough by an extra month, we designed and printed appropriate brochures. Then we hired a video producer to create a promotional video. His effort produced a twenty-seven-minute video entitled, *A Christian College in Ethiopia*. It was completed two days before we left. Once in North America, we made twelve VHS copies and distributed them to volunteer promoters in various parts of the continent. We learned a lot about video making, and subsequent versions were much shorter and better focused.

We arrived in Virginia on May 20, and divided the summer between visiting family and meeting supporters. We attended our daughter, Kristina and James Blakely's wedding, reported to EMM, and attended their Black Rock Retreat in July.

For me, venturing into the unfamiliar world of fundraising, I found the situation completely unnerving. I was shocked to discover that our North American Mennonite institutions of higher learning were busy, collectively raising $75,000,000, that year for construction projects on their various, already well-endowed campuses. Each of these institutions had large, well-organized, well-trained, and experienced development teams, committed to full-time fundraising programs, successfully raising that money from our small denominational constituency.

I had just come from one of the poorest countries in the world, in which our fast-growing church thrived. Yet it had only one little Bible college, in rented quarters, training sixty-two leaders, the only Bible school in a denomination that was larger than the whole Mennonite church in the USA.

On this campaign, I was allowed one month to pursue the modest goal of raising $1.9 million, to build phase one of our first, and only permanent campus. We focused our efforts on the North American Mennonite constituency. Yet their total church membership was smaller than ours, and their growth rate was below zero. However, fighting back sentiments of jealousy, undaunted by the competition, and pressed by the tremendous needs in Ethiopia, I felt it my God-given duty to move on with my amateur, one-person, continent-wide, one-month long, fundraising campaign.

First, we drove to Alberta, visiting supporters in Indiana, Illinois,

Minnesota, and Winnipeg along the way. We spoke in numerous churches and showed our video at special meetings, distributed almost 4,000 brochures, and made some individual contacts. We spread the word. The results were in the hands of God. The returns would be seen in the contributions that came in the months ahead. We returned to Ethiopia on August 22nd.

Those results came in very slowly. We were encouraged when a donor from Winnipeg sent Cdn $100,000, but that was the only large contribution. We were looking for $1.9 million for Phase One. I consoled myself in my diary:

> We will start with what we have, and we believe more will come as we move along. The widow had to give away her last pancake before the oil and flour began to multiply (I Kings 17:7-16). The priests had to put their feet in the water before the Jordan stopped flowing (Joshua 3).

CHAPTER 8

Envisioning and Legalizing International Support

The Daystar Model

Drawing from my experience with Daystar University, I was aware that a key factor in its financial viability lay in it having a strong support base through its office in the USA.

The vice chancellor of Daystar University traveled to the USA twice a year, for a month at a time, to promote that school. In advance of his arrival, the Daystar USA office arranged a heavy itinerary of appointments so that his time would be well utilized, visiting churches, interested groups, and individuals. Their school was able to grow to about 2,000 students in 2001, up from 600 in 1993. They built a modern campus, thanks to the support of the USA office and its six full-time employees.

I, on the other hand, while working full time as principal and teacher at the MK College, had no one on the North American side to assist me in that heavy responsibility. I knew that having a full-time professional staff committed to raising financial support and recruiting volunteers was essential to our success if we hoped to become "a Daystar in Ethiopia."

Whether that happened or not, we needed to have a registered charitable not-for-profit corporation, capable of issuing tax deductible receipts. We had never travelled on this road before. Achieving that legal, non-profit status was a long, painful journey.

At first, EMM assisted by acting as a conduit, issuing tax-deductible receipts to donors and forwarding the gifts to the college in Ethiopia. They agreed to do it "for a couple of years" with the stipulation, "until you get your own office organized." They were not ready to assume any of the other functions of support we had envisioned.

Friends of Meserete Kristos Church

Back in 1996, Dr. Zenebe Abebe and Dr. Dagne Assefa, along with other Ethiopians of the diaspora, drafted a proposal for an *Ethiopian Voluntary Service Program* that would be open to support any need in the whole MKC, including the college. This would require the establishment of a legal, non-profit, tax-deductible organization.

The following year, the three brothers in the USA, Zenebe Abebe, Dagne Assefa, and Paul Gingrich, formed a committee with some friends and organized a reunion of friends of MKC that was held at Goshen in June 1998.

At that meeting, the group officially formed an association called *Friends of MKC*. This organization had a larger picture in mind to find ways to assist the whole church, which would include assisting the college.

This group agreed as their first project to try to raise $150,000 for the purchase of land for a permanent home for the college. They made pledges for this purpose.

This led to the question of how to collect the pledged funds and who could provide tax deductible receipts for the contributors? Again, EMM representatives restated their willingness to help receipting and forwarding funds "on a temporary basis."

When funds began to come in, EMM served the college very well in issuing tax-deductible receipts, banking the funds, reporting to the college, and transferring funds as the college requested.

On October 6, 1998, the Board decided that, because of a report that the newly formed Friends of MKC had an intention to incorporate their own non-government, non-profit charitable agency, and since

EMM has agreed to assist us with channeling funds for the time being, we should delay action on incorporating in the USA for a time.

Two years later, by the summer of 2000, that incorporation was still undone. We began feeling guilty that our "one or two years" had become "three years," and that somehow, we as "guests" in EMM's Finance Department had been "overstaying our welcome." Of course, if they did not kick us out, we could stay forever. But we had overgrown our "mother's house" and given them a lot of extra work. It was time to move out on our own, establish our own charitable non-profit organization, open our own bank account, receive donor's funds, issue receipts, and forward funds to the college.

MK College Link, Incorporated

While attending a meeting of Friends of MKC in Harrisonburg in June 2000, Bedru and I noted that the Friends group seemed no nearer to incorporation than they had been. Four and one-half years had passed. So, we contacted Lynn Suter, a Christian lawyer, to explore the possibility of incorporating a USA Office.

At its next meeting on September 23, 2000, the board of trustees decided that we should continue to make the necessary follow-up with the lawyer. They also nominated seven people, in the USA, to be approached to serve as founding members of a newly formed board of directors.

On October 28, 2000, I reported to the board the response from the lawyer. Establishing a USA-based office process would take from six to twelve months. The process would cost $1,500. She wanted the Board to suggest a name.

The Board members decided to call the new corporation *MK College Link* since its basic purpose was to serve as a link between the Ethiopian-based college and the USA-based supporters.

On March 21, 2001, I wrote to Paul T. Yoder a letter outlining some of the significant ways we foresaw MKCollege Link helping us:

1. Information: to be our public relations arm, a voice for the college in the USA; to disseminate information; to receive and answer inquiries; to forward news releases.

2. Promotion: to advertise needs and opportunities to help; to organize group visits of people interested in the college and the Ethiopian Church.

3. Fund-raising: to seek out potential donors and solicit support for the various needs of the college; to receive and channel funds; to issue tax deductible receipts.

4. Funds management: to establish an agreement with Mennonite Foundation whereby they can assist with receiving gifts through estate planning, etc., and investing those gifts as reserves or endowment until needed; to maintain bank savings and current accounts; to forward funds to the college as requested; to supply monthly statements to the finance head of the college.

5. Support: to alert the college to resources that may be of interest to it; to assist in the recruiting of guest lecturers; to assist in facilitation of a student exchange program; to liaison with helping organizations such as "Friends of MKC;" to gather and ship textbooks from time to time.

In July 2001, the Articles of Incorporation were approved, and MK College Link became a legal nonprofit 501(c)(3) stand-alone charity. This is the same category that works for any USA church or congregation. Its operations must fall under the scrutiny and regulation of the Internal Revenue Service (IRS) of the US Government. Its board members must be chosen from within the USA. Foreign control is not allowed. This meant that MK College Link would function legally autonomous from our college and our church but could be "spiritually connected." Its purpose was the same, to promote the interests of the college, but its legal status was separate from the college or its owner, the Meserete Kristos Church.

This was less than ideal, but it seemed the only way possible to link the college and the American donors to provide these necessary services.

Unsettling Distraction

Then something alarming happened at the biannual Mennonite Assembly in Nashville, Tennessee. While the chairperson of MKC and his deputy were present as fraternal guests, they attended a side meeting of the Friends of MKC. At that meeting, someone raised a question about MK College Link and presented a copy of the Articles to the chairperson.

The Ethiopian leaders were caught completely by surprise and embarrassed. They did not know about its formation. How could this important international legal agreement affecting the Ethiopian college and the government of the USA be created without the permission or knowledge of the MKC Executive Committee? The chairperson phoned home to the general secretary to ask him about it. He did not know anything about MK College Link either. Understandably, the chairperson came home quite disturbed, thinking we had done something behind the church's back. Immediately we were accused of going beyond our authority.

I was deeply sorry that the chairperson of MKC went all the way to Tennessee to be confronted with a matter of which he was uninformed. It must have been quite embarrassing for him. However, I did not think we had anything to apologize for, as far as following proper procedures was concerned.

In defense, we pointed out that over the past five years, the idea of registering a USA office to handle MK College interests had been discussed repeatedly. All decisions were recorded in the minutes of the Board of Trustees. Over the years, every one of these minutes was submitted to the executive committee for information and approval. Somehow, inexplicably, the chairperson had been caught unaware. Did he not read the minutes that the committee he chaired had approved? Was not the general secretary sitting as an ex-officio member of the board of trustees? How could they not have been aware?

When that was settled, attention turned to the content of the Articles. The executive committee found them very disturbing. The legal requirements of the US government allowed the Ethiopian church no control over this 501(c)(3) charitable organization that existed solely for the purpose of supporting their college. They would not be able to elect the board members nor control the use of the funds.

The chairperson's concern was not a matter of distrusting the current Link Board, but to close any gap that a future generation could digress from the original intent and purpose for which it was established. This led to a long-drawn-out dialogue between the MKC Executive Committee, the American lawyer, and the newly elected MK College Link Board members. In the meantime, the MKC Executive Committee blocked its use.

As to my role, although I was principal of the college and secretary of the board of trustees, and although I was personally involved in initiating this whole innovation, I found myself completely cut off from communications on this matter. The executive committee tried to renegotiate with Lynn Suter and the Link Board the whole legal structure and stance of the Link.

For the next year, I had to painfully watch the unnecessary drawn-out ordeal from a distance. For me, there was no discussion, no input, no sharing of my vision, just helplessly watching, waiting, and wondering if they were going to destroy what we already had successfully built. I felt that, because they were caught unaware and embarrassed, they could not admit their failure nor forgive me. From that time on, I felt their relationship with me turned sour.

In looking back over this episode, I was unaware of another cultural requirement. I knew that the board of trustees had discussed and mentioned this issue in its minutes repeatedly over a five-year period and that those minutes were scrutinized by the MKC Executive Committee and approved each time. As a westerner, since the minutes were approved, I had assumed we had the green light to proceed. It just made sense to me.

However, Ethiopians are an oral society. They usually do not communicate serious matters by sharing documents only. Important decisions must be made by talking about the matter again and again. Documents such as constitutions, reports, or minutes are easily forgotten or dismissed. They may have little bearing on reaching a decision. If I were an Ethiopian, I should have preceded and followed up the minutes with periodic discussions, a kind of lobbying with the top leaders. If I had been in the executive committee meetings while the minutes were being presented, perhaps the outcome would have been different. As CEO of the college, I should have been included as a non-voting member of that committee, but for some reason unexplained to me, I had been excluded.

While the new MK College Link Board in the USA waited for the impasse to clear, they opened a bank account. Its members met from time to time to assist in the dialogue and do what they could to comply with the wishes of the MKC Executive Committee. They agreed to respect its wishes and delayed commencing their duties until the Ethiopian leaders gave their approval.

It was a year later, near the end of May 2002, that the executive committee gave its reluctant consent. Finally, that contentious issue was settled, and MK College Link was free to do its work on behalf of the college.

Ongoing Need for an Active Fundraiser

Up to that time, whenever I was on home leave in North America, I added extra effort to raise funds. However, I had been doing most of the fundraising by correspondence from Ethiopia, along with all my other responsibilities. I knew that I could not do enough by myself. If the college were to grow, we would need a full-time fundraiser in North America. We needed someone with those unique skills and a sense of calling, someone with time on his/her hands, plus a heart and a vision to help.

In the meantime, would it be possible to find someone or some people willing and able to do some of this work on a voluntary basis? I was willing to continue working at it from Ethiopia for the time being. I had a mailing list of over 500 addresses, and postage was cheaper in Ethiopia compared to that of the USA. But mail has its limits. There is a need for personal contact, to build relationships, to be the right person in the right place at the right time, to reach the big donors. That, I could not do from Ethiopia. My Ethiopian advisors, the board members, were suggesting I travel to the USA and Canada specifically for that purpose. But I was a teacher and college administrator. How could I go and still do justice to my calling in Ethiopia?

Funds from Canada

In the fall of 2002, we ran into a serious problem with receiving the contributions of Canadians who wanted tax-deductible receipts. The normal channel had been a roundabout way. Canadians either sent their contributions through their congregations which issued receipts, or directly through the Mennonite Churches' Canadian office. From there, the funds were sent to the Mennonite Church General Board office in the USA, which forwarded them to Eastern Mennonite Mission. EMM made periodic transfers to the MK College bank account in Ethiopia. I received occasional reports of the names and addresses of the donors and the amounts each gave. I would then write a thank-you letter to each donor.

In that year, the two largest Mennonite denominations in North America, the Mennonite Church and the General Conference Mennonite Church merged into one denomination. But then, that one denomination, the Mennonite Church, split into two national bodies, Mennonite Church USA and Mennonite Church Canada. Now, with all the structural changes in forming two new denominations, the old agreements no longer applied. New legal arrangements for tax-deductible international money transfers had to be worked out.

We received a disturbing letter in September from the General Secretary of Mennonite Church Canada. They no longer had legal agreements for channeling funds from Canada to the USA. Their head office was holding over Cdn $40,000 in contributions for MK College that they could not send until a legal channel was created. Those who made those donations were also waiting for their receipts, so this was an urgent matter.

When I visited the Mennonite Church Canada (MC Canada) office in Winnipeg in October 2002, I was told that new legislation, regulating non-profit charitable organizations in Canada, no longer allowed them to transfer gifts outside the country, unless they had a joint agency agreement that specified a budgeted project, which conformed to a long list of requirements. They also told me they could no longer supply to me the names and addresses or the amounts given by each donor, a major block to our fundraising in Canada.

They suggested the best way to get funds to Ethiopia would be for MC Canada to have a formal agency agreement with the church in Ethiopia. Since they had about Cdn $40,000 waiting to be sent, they were eager to find a legal way to send it. After some months, MC Canada decided to take a risk and sent the money to EMM via the old method, but they warned me that they could not continue to do it that way.

A year later, the problem of getting contributed money out of Canada legally was still not solved. There were no legal channels that offered tax deductible receipts. We knew it would be best if MC Canada could make a direct agency agreement with the MKC or MK College. Bank fees and exchange rates would be simplified. Reports could be sent directly to MC Canada. Besides, it would also foster direct international links between the sister churches that could have beneficial bilateral spin-offs in the years ahead.

We even considered that we should incorporate a non-profit organization in Canada, like the MK College Link in the USA. However, the pain we incurred over the Link issue was still fresh in our memory, and we did not even dare to suggest doing that again. It seemed the best thing would be to have MK College or MKC make a formal agreement with MC Canada. However, my standing with the MKC Executive Committee was so low that, although my job description included that of "consultant," I did not dare offer them any further advice. So, I just kept quiet.

The issue was resolved when the MK College Link Board made a formal agreement with MC Canada to have the Canadian contributions channeled through their Link organization in the USA. The arrangement served well for the next eleven years until the spring of 2015, when an agency agreement was finalized between MC Canada and MKC.

Northwest Mennonite Conference

In 2002, the Northwest Mennonite Conference (NWMC) decided against joining the newly formed MC Canada denomination. The same problem of legally accepting, receipting, and forwarding funds designated for MK College applied. Up to that time they had been forwarding funds through EMM in the USA. They continued for a few more years until the Canadian Revenue Agency (CRA) demanded that they have an agency agreement between them and EMM. EMM found it too difficult and refused. Then, NWMC made an agency agreement with MK College Link.

In January 2007, the NWMC made an agency agreement directly with MK College. Since then, donors from the NWMC constituency can receive tax-deductible receipts, and the funds are sent directly to the college's bank account in Ethiopia.

To Foster Local Ownership – A Public Relations Office

From its beginning, the college belonged to the church. However, the members of the church, scattered widely throughout Ethiopia, had little knowledge that the church had a college, and consequently, the college received little, and in most cases, no support from its members. Something had to be done to create awareness and challenge the members and congregations to support their college with prayers and finances.

To remedy this need, I submitted a proposal to TEAR FUND UK to assist the college in launching a public relations/development office. As a result, TEAR FUND provided a grant of 5,500 pounds sterling in the fall of 2000. Assistance for this office would continue for three years on a reducing scale. It was understood that, after three years, the office's effectiveness in generating income would empower the college to carry this added cost.

The first year they would provide office furniture and a full salary for the college to hire a full-time public relations officer and a secretary. On the second year, they would cut the grant by 1/3rd, and on the third year, by 2/3rds. By then, the college public relations ought to generate enough extra income to cover these ongoing expenses besides supporting the college to run on a self-sustaining basis. Following proper protocols, we advertised this position.

However, the college was not always free to make decisions in the prescribed way. Occasionally, the MKC leadership intervened in the college's decision-making process. Sometimes those intervening decisions were made, more to resolve problems in the church, without thinking about the negative effects on the future of the college.

In this case, the MKC Executive Committee intervened, ignoring the protocols set out in the founding documents, it simply assigned Fikru Zeleke to this position, moving him from the human resources desk at the head office. Procedures spelled out on paper really did not matter. Opportunity for honest, logical, and respectful discussion was bypassed as they imposed their decision.

In June 2001, Bedru Hussein graduated from Eastern Mennonite Seminary and returned home. The church leadership assigned him to join the college staff as a teacher and assistant principal. That was excellent. However, the leadership insisted that Fikru should now work under Bedru's supervision, rather than mine. Fikru was deeply irritated and promptly resigned.

Accepting his resignation, the church promoted Fikru to head up its missions and evangelism department, a position which gave him access to the inner circle of leadership. Consequently, the public relations office was vacant, and we advertised again.

This time, Kebede Sima was hired to work as our new public relations /development officer. He came to the college with a master's degree in education and twenty-two years of experience with the government's Ministry of Education. He left government employment because he was disillusioned with the increasing corruption and politics there. He came to work in the church because he was seeking peace and brotherhood. He was happy and energetic and gave his best to the challenges of developing this college. We saw him as a promising asset.

Kebede Sima represented the college at the MKC Delegates General Assembly in the following January. While he was explaining to the 500 delegates how they could cooperate in the college fund drive, the chairperson of the church quietly ordered the general secretary to silence him. So, he went up to Kebede while he was speaking and told him to stop. When the surprised Kebede persisted hurriedly to wrap up his thoughts, the general secretary switched off Kebede's mike and told him to sit down. Prior to his report, the relief and development spokesperson had been granted seventy-five minutes for his report. Kebede had used thirteen minutes for the college report. Understandably, Kebede was deeply humiliated and offended. He said he was never treated like that in all the years he worked for the Ministry of Education.

This action of public humiliation and rejection by the leadership indicated another problem in the church. Increasingly, the church seemed to be run by a clique of insiders. The insiders wielded all the power and influence. Obviously Kebede was less known, an outsider. No one spoke up in his defense. They would not have done that to him, had he been an insider.

After two months brooding over it, Kebede resigned and went back to a teaching job with the government. He wrote a serious challenging resignation letter in which he questioned, "How can I be paid with the Lord's money, to promote the college, when my church is opposing what we are trying to promote?" His act of integrity challenged the rest of us to re-think our commitment to what we were doing.

In Kebede, we lost a good man. Did that mean the church leaders did not want the congregations to support the college? No one wanted to explain that to us. In one year, we lost two public relations officers, and no one in church leadership nor the college board seemed to care. We decided to stop reacting. It was their college after all. Let them do what they want. God was watching it all.

Hailu and Bedru encouraged me and the rest of the staff, reminding us that it was God who called us to do this great work, not the chairperson of the church. With God's help, we will outlive this opposition, and better days lie ahead. Nevertheless, why is it that those inside the household of faith are the ones who give us the greatest opposition? "Our warfare is not against flesh and blood, but against spiritual forces..." The time of testing had just begun.

I personally was deeply disappointed in the board of trustees' seeming lack of concern about this development and apparent lack of interest in local fundraising. In my thinking, one of the key responsibilities of a college board was to raise support, or see that support was raised for the college to function and grow. Early on, they had initiated a fundraising committee, but when it died, they did not seem to notice. Now, when the officials of the church executive publicly humiliated our PR officer, resulting in his resignation, they did nothing to right the wrong nor to replace him. It did not seem to matter that there was no one to carry on his vital responsibilities.

At that time, the college board members were mainly from Addis Ababa, people loyal to the MKC leaders. Half of them were either on the MKC Executive Committee or were its employees, working in the head office. They did not represent local churches or regions. The decisions the board made were usually not passed on to the local churches.

In contrast, the regional Wollega MK College was mainly supported by the local churches within the region. It received truly little support from outside. Its leadership collaborated with the regions, created awareness, and a sense of ownership.

However, at MK College, the public relations office remained vacant while the grant money was used for other purposes. The position remained empty for the next few years.

CHAPTER 9

Other Developments in 2001

Servant/Saints Under Construction

The year 2001 began with the college hosting another six-week training program for thirty-six volunteers who wanted to serve the church in the *One Year for Christ* program. In the spring semester, we had 115 full-time students. In the fall semester, enrollment rose to 135.

Almost all of these were attending on full room, board, and tuition scholarships. According to our faith, God supplied the need. We had taken a huge leap of faith a year earlier, almost doubling our enrollment and our budget. Now, thanks to the generous contributions of many friends and well-wishers, we were able to complete the fiscal year in the black. Our operating budget for the fiscal year 2000-01 was $170,000.

Some of our students were evangelists who had given up careers in the secular sector, often at great personal sacrifice, responding to the call of God to full-time spiritual ministry. In our student body, we had former schoolteachers, accountants, government employees, medical personnel, military men, Orthodox priests, Muslim sheiks, police officers, businesspeople, as well as many farmers. We even had a few former shamans and wizards. These various backgrounds made classroom discussions interesting.

The training meant a lot to the students. In their ministries, they encountered many tough questions, conflicts, and ethical situations that taxed their creativity and understanding. They also faced a flood of new doctrines and teachings, some of them heretical, and others unbalanced, that troubled the immature Christians. Leaders were challenged to provide answers and guidance. Many of them said that they had longed for and prayed for an opportunity to do in-depth biblical study to equip them for the daunting challenges of active ministry.

On the other hand, not all were faithful. There seemed to have been some "goats" among the "sheep." We had several evangelists who showed no guilt about the fact that they were caught cheating on exams or telling lies. I was amazed. How did they get into leadership posts in the church? What kind of *salt* were they, and what kind of *light* did they produce in the world?

However, we also heard that many evangelicals, including many MKC members, were being hired to work in the Prime Minister's office. It seemed the PM, though seemingly espousing atheism, recognized *salt* in these people and preferred them over others. Also, it was said that Ali Moudhin, the Muslim billionaire, investor, and owner of most of the prominent new businesses in Ethiopia, preferred to hire *pentes* rather than his own kind of people. Obviously, there was at least a little *saltiness* among the eighteen million evangelicals!

Frustrations Along the Way

Developing the campus was taking much more time than we expected. This was partly because we were all terribly busy, giving priority to managing the college and teaching. We found working through committees to be very frustrating if one needed to get things done quickly. This frustration occurred on three levels.

First there was the internal management committee. Believing in teamwork, I consulted the management committee on most decisions. It usually could be convened at short notice and was helpful in making the best decisions.

Then there was the board of trustees which often took months to convene and even longer to get a quorum so decisions could be made.

Further, there was the church's executive committee which met every two months and had to approve major board decisions before we were allowed to implement them. Sometimes it would require waiting up to four or even six months before we were free to implement a major decision. As a result, time passed, and we had little progress to show. Often, we chafed under these inefficient restrictions, longing for a little more autonomy.

Local Funding

Local fundraising efforts began on two levels. First, there was the directive to each congregation to take a special offering annually in support of the college. Of the 248 congregations, seventy responded with an offering in 2001. The grand total received was about US $1,450, only enough to support one student. Did this result express the deep poverty of the people, or a lack of ownership in their college?

Secondly, we held three fundraising banquets. The first, as was already mentioned, was held on January 9, 1999, in response to the $110,000 matching grant challenge. The response brought in about $10,000.

On Sunday, February 11, 2001, we sponsored another banquet at the Ethiopia Hotel in Addis. That evening, about fifty, mostly businesspeople, came to the banquet. In all they contributed about $18,000 in pledges and gifts.

We held a third banquet in May at the Ras Hotel, inviting different people. That one yielded about US $5,000 for the building fund. It was a beginning, but the $1.9 million goal to complete and equip a campus for 400-500 students was far beyond eyesight. These efforts were not encouraging, yet not bad, considering the state of the economy.

External Funding

In the middle of this fiscal year, 2001, we were experiencing another income slump approaching crisis proportions. I commented in my diary:

Sometimes we feel a bit like Elijah, not sure if the "ravens" will arrive on time. The main difference is, Elijah only had himself to worry about. We have the whole "school of prophets" plus the salaries of twenty-four support staff to think about. It is interesting, to say the least!

However, at the end of the year, there was a three-month balance in the operations budget. The Lord's "ravens" came just in time, through the generous support of his people. We were thankful for all the accomplishments and growth we had experienced.

In the building fund, over a two-and one-half-year period, we raised almost $500,000 for Phase One of the development plans. Most of this money, plus the bulk of the operation budget originated from North America.

On September 8, 2001, Tesfatsion Delellew, Co-Director for MCC Africa, and Mekonnen Desalegn, of MCC Ethiopia, hosted representatives of the church and the college with a lovely banquet at the Ararat Hotel. There, Tesfa surprised us with an announcement that MCC had decided to contribute $200,000 towards the college building project. The guests were stunned and delighted. From experience, I knew how hard it was to raise that kind of money. It was a great encouragement to us. When this was delivered, it pushed our building fund total up to $700,000, a third of the projected need for the Phase One buildings.

International Support

It was a great opportunity for our daughter, Cindy, and her husband, John Kreider, when Hailu contacted them with an invitation to come and teach a summer block course on the pastoral epistles. Hailu had become friends with John when they were both in seminary. We were happy, especially when they agreed to bring our eldest grandson, Carlin, along for the three-week visit.

This was a special treat for Vera and me. Not only did it provide John an opportunity to practice his pedagogical skills and broaden his horizons, but it also provided an opportunity for our daughter, Cindy, to come along and re-connect with her childhood home. She had not been back since we left Ethiopia in 1975 when she was ten years old.

Also visiting that summer of 2001 were Mike and Cindy Brislen, leaving their teaching work in sunbaked Djibouti to vacation in a cooler climate. Again, Mike taught a course in July.

The college also welcomed its first international guest lecturer from another African country. Nicodemus Mhana, principal of the Mennonite Theological College, Musoma, Tanzania, came and taught a block course for three weeks. The services of volunteer teachers from outside brought enriching experiences to our students.

Another of our teachers, Woudeneh Endaylalu, was given a full scholarship to do a master's degree program at MBBS in Fresno. As he was about to leave, Sheweye Yalew, his bride of one year, was also given a scholarship to study at Fresno. This was an unexpected blessing.

Earlier that summer, Drs. Stan and Delores Friesen, professors at MBBS, were visiting our campus. We introduced Woudeneh to them as he would be coming to their school in a few weeks. When Delores learned that Woudeneh would be leaving his bride of only one year, Delores said, "That can't be!" She promised to see to it that Sheweye would accompany him. And she did.

On August 10, we received a letter from President Henry Schmidt of MBBS, stating that, if Shewaye Yalew would be acceptable to our MKC leadership as a teacher-in-training, they would grant her a scholarship. This was a pleasant surprise to us all, and especially to Woudeneh, but it did not give us much time to process the issue. She had not applied, she had not been hired as our teacher, and there was the doubtful question of getting a USA visa.

However, the timing was of the Lord. The letter came on the very morning the MKC Executive Committee was to meet. I called the chairperson and the executive secretary and asked them to add the matter to the agenda. They processed the matter that evening.

Considering who the husband and wife were, and their potential as a team, they gave us the green light to proceed.

The matter was also brought to the members of the board of trustees. They unanimously agreed that, if Shewaye signed a written agreement to do the studies and return to teach in our college, we would consider her a "faculty member-in-training".

This unusual decision, made at such short notice, was easier, considering Sheweye was superbly qualified. Not only was she the wife of Woudeneh and they had no children yet, but she had a diploma in secretarial sciences, a bachelor's degree in English, and she had just graduated from Evangelical Theological College with an associate degree in theology the previous month. She did this while working as receptionist and office manager at that school. Not only did she graduate, but she also graduated with distinction and was given the Spiritual Leadership Award. She was also a faithful member of a Meserete Kristos congregation in Addis.

Here we would be getting two master's level teachers for the price of one. Even the air transport, which we would pay, did not cost more because money budgeted for Woudeneh to return for the summer would be used to enable his wife to accompany him instead. Being together, they would not need to come home for the summer. So, it did not increase the burden on the college.

We all felt good about this unexpected arrangement. The final test for this being the will of God would be whether she would be granted a visa from the USA embassy. If they knew her husband was going, the embassy, fearing a migration attempt, normally would block her going. In faith, we simply submitted her application for visa along with another applicant who was going to EMS. The visa was granted without question. Another miraculous confirmation!

Eight days after receiving Dr. Schmidt's letter, on the night of August 18, a farewell party was held for six of our teachers who were going abroad for further studies. Besides Woudeneh Endaylalu and Shewaye Yalew going to MBBS, Emebet Mekonnen was returning to FPU. Tefere Bekere was going to EMS, and Gemechu Gebre was returning there. Also, Aboma Bayessa was leaving on a full private scholarship to Gordon Conwell Seminary.

With these departures leaving the faculty decimated, we were overjoyed to welcome Jerry and Ann King-Grosh, who came on a two-year mission assignment to serve as teachers. They came with fresh enthusiasm, having just completed two years of graduate studies at EMS. They were no strangers to Ethiopia, having provided leadership services to the MCC programs in Ethiopia over a fourteen-year period. Their extensive experience and international perspective enriched their teaching and added a wholesome dimension to campus life. Besides teaching, Jerry introduced the use of computers in the registrar's office, the accounts office, and in the administration. Ann also taught courses and assisted in many other ways.

Kebede Bekere, having just graduated from EMS, returned and joined the teaching faculty that fall. His special interest was in counseling. Besides Kebede, we hired two other full-time teachers on a one-year contract basis.

However, while the college gained much, she also lost some. The MKC Executive Committee moved Girma Teklu from the college and installed him as the executive secretary in place of Mulugeta Zewdie. This was a disappointment to us, as Girma had been granted the scholarship specifically as AMBS's way of assisting MK College in developing its teaching faculty. He was one of our best teachers but taught only one year before the church took him from us.

Besides the teachers we sent abroad for graduate studies, the church also sent Mulugeta Zewdie to join Teku Kebede at AMBS, Simon Badi to EMU, and Kana Dula to EMS. At that time, the church had ten students studying in graduate programs abroad, nine of them in Mennonite/Anabaptist institutions. This would bring some changes to the MKC in the years to come.

MKC owes an ongoing debt of gratitude to EMU, EMS, AMBS, FPU, and MBBS for their significant contribution towards the development of the teaching faculty of Meserete Kristos College and to church leadership.

International Students

The vision of the college included hosting international students. It would enrich the learning environment by bringing a variety of backgrounds, cultures, viewpoints, and friendships. The college's first exchange student was Aaron Kauffman, as was mentioned earlier.

In the fall of 2001, Reverend Jeremiah and Grace Okidi of Shirati, Tanzania, were the first exchange students to come from another African country. This older couple came for a one-year sabbatical. Since we were not registered with the Ministry of Education as an educational institution, they came on tourist visas that had to be renewed every three months. When they went for their second renewal, they were refused and had to return to Tanzania without completing their programs of study. This was a disappointment to all.

Bedru Hussein visited the Mennonite Church in Germany in the summer of 2001. He arranged for the young Armin Otterstater to come as the first volunteer from Germany to do alternative to military service for two years.

His job included keeping the plumbing and electrical systems in working order, fixing broken furniture and equipment, maintaining and keeping the computers in working order, and keeping the grounds neat and tidy. He lived with the students and learned the Amharic language. He also took a few classes.

Armin's stay in the country was problematic. To get him a work permit was impossible, as the government was no longer granting new work permits to churches or mission agencies. Because our college was not registered with the Ministry of Education, we could not get a student visa either. So, Armin came on a tourist visa. When it expired, he discovered it could not be renewed more than once. Sadly, Armin had to return to Germany, assignment uncompleted.

Another volunteer/student, Markus Neufeld, was sent from Germany in the fall of 2002. The same thing happened to him. He had to return home early.

This did not speak well for getting volunteers from Germany or anywhere else. Until the obstacles preventing the college from registering with the Ministry of Education were removed, the door was closed to getting visas for international students. This inability to get student visas remained an ongoing handicap to the college, blocking one of its original goals, to become the number one international Anabaptist Mennonite college in anglophone Africa.

National Student Protests: A Black Day for Ethiopia

On April 19, 2001, I reported in my diary:

> Yesterday was a terrible day for Addis Ababa, and indeed a black day for all of Ethiopia. University students have been conducting peaceful demonstrations over the past week demanding more student rights, like to have a campus free of the loathsome presence of police officers and government informers, and to have their own student union and magazine.
>
> Students on the other campuses and high schools across the land took to striking also, to show their solidarity. The Minister of Education was not amused. She gave them a deadline to get back to classes, or else face expulsion from the campus. The students remained united and steadfast. Therefore, the police harassed and attacked them.
>
> As the students fled, the "hooligans," as the government calls them, (thousands of unemployed youths who loiter on the streets) took this as a golden opportunity to start a riot. They went through the streets stoning government buildings, looting private shops, and burning government cars.
>
> The government called in the troops and ordered them to shoot anyone destroying public property. Yesterday, around 10:30 a.m., rioting started in various places in the city. Soldiers started shooting and the

youths and students ran wild. There was shooting on most campuses, especially the high school campuses. Today's BBC news reported thirty-nine killed and two hundred and fifty wounded.

I remained at home that morning while Vera went to college. At the college, they heard gunfire erupt nearby around eleven o'clock. It sounded like a war and lasted until after twelve o'clock. I did not know about it. I had an appointment at the college at two o'clock, so I came around one-thirty, driving our car. As I got within a kilometer of the college, I noticed that something was not right. Drivers coming from that direction seemed to be disturbed.

Then I noticed rocks scattered all over the road. There were three soldiers with guns motioning me to stop and turn around. I wanted to get to college, so I just ignored them. Then there were four more soldiers in a truck about 200 meters down the road. They also tried to stop me. In the Amharic language, they said, "Why did you not stop back there?" I just answered them in English, which they did not understand. I said, "I must get to my college!" and I just drove on past them.

Then I saw a burning police motorcycle beside the road and stones all over the place. I kept going until I surprised a third set of soldiers who tried to stop me. I just motioned to them that I wanted to turn at the next junction, which was just a few hundred meters further down the road. They let me go, and I got to the college safely enough. I saw an ambulance coming up the hill towards me.

At the college, I was surprised to find a lot of students and other people milling around and talking about the horrible events that had just taken place. Classes were suspended, and most of the teachers, who had children in schools, had been called to collect their children and take them home. The worst shooting had taken place at the Wonderad High School, a quarter mile from our college. Students had fled in all directions, some up the mountain with soldiers in hot pursuit, shooting as they went.

This morning, we learned that Etagegne, one of our cook's nineteen-year-old son was among those killed. So, we went to the wake before the burial. She is a member of our church. This boy had come home from school, but the neighbor lady's son had not come. So, she begged him to go back and find her son. When he reached the highway, the soldiers just shot him. Friends found a taxi and rushed him to the hospital, but he had lost too much blood and was dead when they arrived.

The news media would not report any injuries or deaths, only the crimes of the hooligans. It is a horrible thing when a government of a nation kills its own children, simply for the crime of being on the street at the wrong moment. No accusation, no warning, no arrest, no trial, no sentencing, just summary execution. And no executioners were held accountable. The funeral was quiet. There were similar sad scenes all over the city today as the grieving citizens buried their children. The hatred of this government is growing hour by hour.

Today, the soldiers were going around, rounding up any young boys they could find, and taking them off to detention camps. Only God knows what they will do with them there. Those who know from experience tell us that they will punish and torture them, until they tell all they know, and are totally terrorized so that they will never challenge the government police again. This is a dark day for Ethiopia. There is a God of justice somewhere, waiting. But why is he waiting? That remains our unanswered question.

A month after the riots, the elementary and high schools were back to functioning, but the university was still closed. The students refused to attend classes until their fellow students and leaders were released. Thousands had been arrested. Their leaders who had not been arrested disappeared, presumably in hiding or gone into exile. The government used this unrest to crack down on all opposition political leaders, blaming them, fairly or unfairly, for the disturbance. It was an easy excuse to dispose of all government opposition. Civil or human rights organizations were accused, and their leaders imprisoned. The people were extremely angry.

Fall Semester, 2001

In early August 2001, the MK College Board of Trustees formally requested Vera and I to travel to North America for six weeks to do fundraising for the building of the campus from November 1st through December 15th. The board would pay the expenses. They wanted Vera to go along, not to fundraise, but "as an appreciation for the good work she has done, let her visit her children and grandchildren over Christmas."

I did not really want to do this; I would rather have stayed to teach. Yet, I realized it needed to be done, and I was the most logical person to do it, so I was willing and ready to go.

However, without explanation, presumably due to the conflict, the executive committee vetoed the board's August decision that Vera and I go to North America on the fall fundraising trip. It seemed to me that the committee had no concern about funding the development of its college.

CHAPTER 10

Disruption by Conflict: July 2001 – September 2003

MK College worked under the authority and supervision of its board of trustees, which was appointed by, and answerable to, the MKC Executive Committee. It was a capable board, made up of competent people. All had bachelor's degrees, nine masters, and one doctorate, all qualified and competent in higher education. In their professional lives, they were church administrators, preachers, teachers, university and college professors, businesspeople, engineers, and researchers.

At that time, 2001, half of the trustees were also members of the executive committee. Through this appointed board, it was obvious that the church exercised total control of the college. Therefore, the conflict came as a shock. I would never have imagined that a serious breakdown of relationships could ever have happened between us, at the college, and the executive branch of the church.

Throughout the early years of my involvement as principal, I often sat in MKC Executive Committee meetings. Apart from two minor disagreements over the name of the college and over the logo, issues in which I deferred to the wishes of the committee, I always felt that we were working together in unity and harmony. At some point I was no longer informed or invited to their meetings. I was busy and did not notice.

Sometime in the spring of 2001, there was disagreement over the appointment of new members to the board of trustees. The board sent a list of its nominees to the MKC Executive Committee for confirmation. The board's list was rejected, and others were appointed by the executive committee whom we felt were chosen by their closeness to the chairperson. They were chosen for control, rather than for effective leadership in developing the college. Our protests were not heard.

I first became aware of rising hostility of the executive committee, and especially of its chairperson, towards our administration in early August 2001. It was after the embarrassing incident over the MK College Link issue in the USA. After his return home, the chairperson put the blame on the college administration and on the board of trustees for being secretive and doing things behind his back and embarrassing him in that international setting.

Later that month, we received a rather rude and insulting letter from the new general secretary of the church, accusing us of trying "to separate the college from the church" and of ignoring their directive to include a course on the faith and polity of the church. We had, in fact, implemented that directive. We felt falsely accused, insulted, and diminished. I wrote a lengthy and emotional response, appealing for understanding.

Partly in response to that letter, Hailu, Bedru, and I were called to a Sunday morning meeting with members of the executive committee. Here I became aware of how difficult communication can be between a direct culture and an indirect culture. Some Ethiopians still value the indirect culture of "sem' ina work" or "wax and gold." Clever people take pride in speaking indirectly, hiding the "gold," the real meaning under a surface or apparent meaning, the "wax." To speak bluntly or frankly or simply say the obvious meaning is an indication of a less cultured, or simple individual, and can be despised.

This committee had spent four hours trying to decipher what "gold" my "wax" was hiding in that letter. What did Carl really mean by this, and this, and this? I tried to explain to them that I was hiding nothing. I simply said, in the plainest English, clearly exactly what I meant. Nothing hidden. That was too "foreign" for them to accept. Carl is too intelligent for that. There must be something more?

They were still suspicious. I did not know it at that time, but apparently someone from the college, an insider, had divulged to them that Carl and some leaders in the college wanted to separate the college from the church and make it liberal. The example cited was that, once upon a time, Harvard University was founded under the control of the church, but later, its leadership took it away from the control of the church. Today it is secular and liberal. Therefore, MKC must control the college, protecting its ownership.

I tried to explain that what they perceived to be our trying "to separate the college from the church" was simply that we wanted the church to help explore a way for the college to register with the Ministry of Education as a legal entity, for purposes of: (1) seeking accreditation, (2) seeking tax exempt status for the importing of building supplies, equipment, textbooks, thus saving significant scarce money, (3) seeking a status that would enable foreign students to be granted a student visa, so they could study in Ethiopia, and (4) to legally secure property that was donated for college purposes. We believed this could be done under the direction and control of the church.

We knew something terrible had gone wrong in our relationship with those that count most among the members of the executive committee. However, we had no way of knowing what that something was.

It seemed to us that the church leaders did not trust us and were unwilling to even discuss the issues with us. All we needed was for them to treat us like colleagues, respect us enough to consult with us, and explain their fears or reasons why they were opposing us. We did not appreciate being insulted.

Conflict Continued

By the beginning of 2002, the MK College Link issue had not yet been resolved. I was still out of their good graces and must lay low for a time. We had been quietly and patiently waiting for Dr. Paul T. Yoder, of MK College Link, and the church leadership to put together an agreeable revision that would satisfy the concerns of the church, meet the needs of the college, and still meet the requirements of USA law. I had come to doubt whether that was possible.

In early January, Paul wrote a letter, giving suggestions for changes to the unacceptable paragraphs in the Link document. The executive secretary delayed response. In early February, he replied to Paul, saying, he did "not have time to read your suggestions at this time." It seemed to me they did not want to settle it, and at the same time, they did not want to be responsible for rejecting it outright.

I felt really discouraged. With our one-year home leave coming up, I doubted we would return if things were not resolved before we left. The whole vision for the development of the college looked very dark. This sapped my energy and dampened my enthusiasm for the work. However, we still felt called to this task and took comfort in the thought that it is God's problem, not just ours.

MKC's Golden Jubilee

June 16, 1951, was the day that the Mennonite missionaries conducted their first baptisms in Ethiopia. To mark the fiftieth anniversary of the birth of the Meserete Kristos Church, the leaders put on a major jubilee celebration on January 18–20, 2002. They made elaborate plans and sent out invitations to leaders in many organizations of the Mennonite world. They also invited many other international organizations, friends, and especially former missionaries who had a part in the founding of MKC.

Many foreign guests came to Ethiopia to experience and participate in this celebration. It was held in the new 3,500-seat Misrak Addis Ababa MKC worship center. Conceived in difficult conditions, birthed in suffering and hardship, nurtured in opposition, matured in persecution, and now exploding with exuberance in the power and vitality of young adulthood, this booming Meserete Kristos Church was in a truly optimistic and celebratory mood.

Among the early arrivals, Dr. Calvin Shenk and Pastor Harold Miller came to teach two three-week block courses while the *One Year for Christ* program was running. They stayed on to participate in the church's Golden Jubilee celebration. Chester Wenger, accompanied by three of his eight children, two sons-in-law, and three grandchildren, were also there. They brought with them six boxes of textbooks. Other international guests, former missionaries, members of the diaspora, official representatives, and friends of Ethiopia began to arrive to do some sightseeing or visiting before the gala event.

Other friends and supporters did not come but sent their gifts in support. For example, Dr. Joe and Helen Burkholder, veteran missionaries back in the fifties and sixties, forfeited their trip to attend the Jubilee, thinking it better to contribute the money their trip would have cost. Instead of attending, they sent Cdn $10,000 to the college building fund.

All aspects of the church's far-flung ministry were celebrated, except there was a deafening silence regarding the existence and work of the college. We of the college administration, our existence, our work, our contribution to the whole of the church, were completely ignored. The report I had prepared in response to the leadership's request was not given. Our names were not mentioned. Obviously, the conflict was not forgotten. We felt the pain in silence.

Update on the Conflict:

After the Jubilee, our EMM overseer, Susan Godshall, and Paul and Ann Gingrich, older pioneer missionaries, attempted to broker a reconciliation between the church leaders and the college leaders. They took on a mediatorial role, doing a kind of "shuttle diplomacy," first interviewing me, then reporting to and discussing with the leaders, then returning to me. Tilahun Beyene and his wife, Heywet, also came to mediate. Then Mamo and Mary Ellen Dulla and Peg Engle and Peter Dula also gave us a hearing.

Out of this exchange, it became clear that there were two non-negotiable executive committee decisions regarding MK College that they felt I was challenging. First, the church leaders were intransigent about the possibility of our college registering as a separate institution. MKC as a denomination was registered with the government. All its institutions fall under the legal umbrella of that registration. The leaders felt it would be potentially dangerous for the college to incorporate separately. They held that one registration is enough to cover all our needs legally.

Our questions remained: How do we get accreditation from the Ministry of Education if we do not register with them? How do we get student visas from the Ministry of Immigration if we do not have a registration number from the Ministry of Education? And how do we get a tax exemption from the Ministry of Finance for building supplies and equipment for the new campus if we are not a registered college? The executive committee did not offer any answers to these questions, and they would not even discuss them with us.

Secondly, they assured us that the vision of the MKC leadership for a college with multiple majors had not changed. The land at Bishoftu was granted for this purpose. The first, urgent priority was to continue to train pastors in biblical, theological, and related subjects. Other majors would be added later. The vision is long term but must be implemented by priority.

This was exactly our priority also, and it was exactly what we were doing. I could not understand this to be an issue of disagreement. In retrospect, we may have come across as being too ambitious to get on with implementing the full vision. It seemed they wanted us to slow down and take more time before implementing the liberal arts vision. If they could have just sat down and discussed these issues with us face to face, we would have resolved the misunderstanding, and the conflict could have been settled right there. However, they would not speak with us.

They did tell the mediators that they were thankful to God for the Bible college and the ministry of all personnel working there. They also expressed a desire for good, cooperative, working relationships, including candid discussion. How we longed for evidence of that statement's veracity!

In discussing our situation with Susan, we all agreed it would be best if we take a full year's sabbatical, beginning in early June 2002. It was not clear just what we would be doing during that year. If relationships healed a bit more, I felt I could do some public relations and fundraising for the college.

My opportunity for direct talks finally came when I was invited to share my complaints and requests with the MKC Executive Committee which met on March 22—23, 2002.

I shared my disappointment in the way they were keeping our friends in North America in suspense over the Link issue those past eight months. I explained that Link is bound by USA law that requires USA control of any tax-exempt charitable organization. Just like they cannot control MCC, EMM, or TEAR FUND, they cannot control MK College Link. They either must accept its aid or reject it. If they accept, they can write a memorandum of understanding, like they do with EMM. They responded that they would decide at a different meeting.

I asked them to tell us whether the vision for which they assigned us to work six years ago had changed. If not, why were they opposing us? What were we doing wrong? What did they want from us?

I then asked whether Vera's and my work was finished in Ethiopia? When we accepted the call to help develop a Christian college, we knew it would take a long time. We were willing to commit ten years of our lives towards that goal. Six years had expired, and we were still willing to work at it until our retirement. I told them that our first five years of working with the church were a highlight of my life, but the last eight months had been exceedingly painful for us, and we still did not know why. We did not know what we had done wrong.

I reminded them that I had served as coordinator and then as principal of MK College since September 1996. The time was coming when we were entitled to one year of home leave to re-connect with our children and grandchildren and report to our supporters.

Finally, I asked them, since we were going home for a year, if we should plan to return, or should we be looking for a different job? We did not want to push ourselves on a reluctant church. I told them we needed a clear frank answer.

They gave me fair hearing. I think my speech shocked them. They were silent for a while and then asked me to leave the room so they could discuss what I said. After a half hour, they called me in and the vice chairperson (the chairperson was absent) said, "You are right. We want to work on the issues you raised." I noted that they did not attempt to be forthright in answering my questions about what we were doing wrong. However, they assured me they still had the same vision, and they wanted us to be a part of bringing it to fruition. They would write a formal letter to EMM requesting us to be sent back after our rest period.

That should have satisfied my feelings, but the chairperson of MKC, visiting in Germany, was absent from that meeting. After his return, we saw no change. The longer the shunning went on, the more I felt we should terminate. Both Vera and I were past sixty years of age. We did not come to Ethiopia to fight with the church. If developing a college meant we had to fight with church leaders to get it done, then we were losing interest. It was their college, and we should let them do it their way.

However, it filled us with deep concern that, after a good beginning, it could fail. For my colleagues, for the church, and for a great many Christians in the future, this would be a great tragedy. The thought filled us with deep sadness. I felt responsible to the hundreds of friends whom we persuaded to share their gifts to support this great vision. If it failed, I would not know how to face these friends again. What would I say? How could I explain what I did not understand myself?

Although I felt a little better, I mourned the extensive damage that had happened to our staff's morale, especially the loss of Kebede Sima. I mourned the fact that, after eight months, they still could not take any action on the MK College Link issue. I mourned the fact that they seemed completely insensitive to the college's financial difficulties and offered no alternatives to the ways they blocked our fund raising. In a conflict, no one wins.

Since that executive committee meeting in March, there was mostly silence, and since time was passing and our furlough was quickly coming up, I arranged an appointment to talk with the chairperson in private. We had a frank talk for over an hour. I came away feeling that we made some progress. I suspected the real problem was that he had been misled by someone whom he should have been able to trust, but who led him to deeply believe that we did want the college to separate from the church. Whatever information I shared with him or MKC leadership was not given as much weight as the information he obtained from his trusted source.

The chairperson had his own definition of the phrase "register with the Ministry of Education." For him, that meant we wanted to sign the college over to the government and remove it from the hands of the church completely. So, I asked him what he would recommend, when the time came to offer degrees for paying students in the fields of business or whatever, and the potential students would ask about our accreditation. He outlined what he would expect us to do, and it was exactly what we meant by our word, "register." Sometimes we need to clearly define the terms we use, especially when engaging in cross-cultural communication. I came away from our exchange feeling more hopeful.

CHAPTER 11

Growth Under a Cloud in 2002

Financial Woes:

As the year 2002 unfolded, distrust and tension were still in the air and colored much that we did. While the mediating exercise involving Paul Gingrich and Susan Godshall brought us more understanding, it failed to improve the relationship between the college leadership and the church's executive committee.

In the meantime, donations to the college had gone down significantly. The college had to borrow from the building fund to keep going. Out of our total operating budget that fiscal year of $170,000, at the end of February 2002, we were running about $31,000 or 18% behind. The executive committee showed no signs of concern that we were having financial stress.

Considering the financial downturn, it turned out to be a blessing that enrollment failed to grow. Although it had not been a year of growth in numbers of students, it was a stable year. In the face of many challenges, remaining stable can also be considered a success.

In programming, we made some changes. To encourage and equip many good church leaders who, due to their mature age, were unable to learn the English language, but who had potential to improve their ministries, we added a new two-year diploma program taught in the Amharic language.

International Flavor

The Seattle Mennonite Church Leadership Council, with assistance from the Mennonite Board of Missions, agreed to sponsor Sisay Desalegn, their Director of Urban Ministries, to come to teach in our college for one semester per year for four years. He would be their "missionary" to Ethiopia. Sisay began his annual trips to teach in the spring semester of 2002 and continued each year until the spring semester of 2005. It was a big sacrifice for Sisay, and especially for his wife and children, as he left them at home and came to Ethiopia to teach for four months each year.

During the spring semester, Peter Dula, a doctoral student from Duke University, taught one course while doing his doctoral research in Ethiopia. Myron and Esther Augsburger from Harrisonburg, Virginia, Paul and Mary Zehr from Lancaster, Pennsylvania, and Duane and Lois Beck from Elkhart, Indiana, all came to teach block courses in the summer. Myron Augsburger was the graduation speaker for our first four-year degree students who graduated on July 6, 2002.

Also, a group of six young people were sent from the German Mennonite Church to work with the church for about six months as volunteers. They lived in a rented house near our college. During the day, they would go out to the different churches to do ministry. They usually ate their food at the college and interacted with the students.

One of our students, Fanosie Legesse, agreed to assist them in learning the Amharic language. As a result, he and the group leader, Dianne Dobbie, started up a courtship that resulted in his migration to Canada and marriage. Another student, Zewdu Habte, also initiated a romance. After marriage, Zewdu and his wife Martina returned to Ethiopia as a missionary couple, teaching deacons and priests in an underground Orthodox renewal movement.

New Anabaptists

In April, two of our students, leaders from one of the many Orthodox renewal groups who were given scholarships, asked me to baptize them.

They were taking my class on Anabaptist History and Thought and were re-evaluating their stance on baptism. For years they had discussed in their group whether they should be baptized as adults or remain with their Orthodox infant baptism. They had decided that infant baptism was enough. However, 300 of their members had left their association to be baptized. After taking this course, the leaders decided they must do what became increasingly evident that they ought to do.

With our encouragement, they brought six of their fellow leaders, and with Hailu Cherenet and Sisay Desalegn assisting, they were baptized in the bathtub in our house. They would now go back and baptize the remainder of their followers. Anabaptist theology and practice was spreading its influence far beyond the boundaries of the Meserete Kristos Church in Ethiopia.

Laying the Foundation Stone

On April 28, 2002, an impressive "stone laying" ceremony was held at the empty, fenced, Bishoftu site. Some tents and chairs were brought and set up to welcome visiting dignitaries and prominent church leaders. A sound system was connected to the generator. Four rented buses brought all the students and many guests from Addis. A crowd of about 300 came for the program that began about 10:00 a.m. Women from the Bishoftu congregation prepared and served a nice meal at noon. Their church choir and the college choir provided special singing. As an international guest, Sisay Desalegn preached a sermon. MKC Chairperson, Solomon Kebede, laid the stone and led a dedicatory prayer. I gave a short report on the college's present activities and future vision. This was a watershed experience for all concerned, a kind of rekindling of hope and excitement about working together. We had positive feedback from many.

My report included the following encouragement:

> The Meserete Kristos Church was founded some fifty years ago because of a wholistic ministry. The

missionaries fed the hungry and founded clinics, hospitals, and schools before the people listened to their preaching of the glorious gospel of God's love. Education was a core value from the beginning. Mission elementary schools were founded in the remote parts of Harar Province like Deder and Bedeno. Dresser Bible schools were opened in Adama and Deder. A school for the blind was opened in Addis Ababa. Then the Nazareth Bible Academy was opened as a full secondary school. The growing church opened primary schools at Wonji, Shoa, Metahara, and Addis Ababa. Then the Dergue government closed the church and nationalized all her educational and medical institutions in 1982.

Indeed, education remains a high priority in our nation. Education is essential for the reduction of poverty. There is a direct correlation between the dismal quality and restricted availability of education and the pervasive poverty in our land. In 1998 only 45% of primary school aged Ethiopian children were in school. Of secondary school aged youths, only 9.7% were enrolled in schools. When it comes to the tertiary level of education, enrollment is miniscule. Only ONE out of every 7,000 Ethiopians graduated from some form of post-secondary institution of learning in 1998.

In 1994, the Meserete Kristos Church re-affirmed her continuing commitment to this core value of education by opening the Meserete Kristos Church Bible Institute....

But we at the college are still "nomads" without a home. Like the children of Israel, we are wandering in the wilderness of Kotebe. But our eyes have seen the "promised land," this 60,000 m² plot of land that was given to us as a permanent home for our future campus....

We are still on the border, like Moses at Pisgah, with eyes of faith, we look over into "Caanan." We see large buildings standing in green spaces and lovely flower gardens, connected with sidewalks duly shaded with flowering trees. We see 2,000 students moving about in the campus and halls utilizing the classrooms and library. We see 100 teachers intermingling with them in lecture halls, laboratories, and cafeteria.

We are going to cross over to possess the land. However, we must go gradually, step by careful step. Phase I of the development plan calls for buildings enough to accommodate 500 students....

We will start with what we have, then continue with what we get. With God's help, we will build the academic building then the first dormitory, then the dining hall and kitchen, and the administration building, and finally, an auditorium that can seat 600 will complete Phase I by the year 2005.

This is an ambitious, costly undertaking. It is also a necessary and worthwhile undertaking. It is possible, if we all work together, each doing what he or she can. Students can all help by praying and promoting the project in their home areas. Church leaders can help by promoting the college in their congregations and supporting their young people who desire to attend. Church members can help by generous and sacrificial giving.

Let us be strong and courageous! Go in boldly to "take possession of this land"! Let us build a campus for the glory of God and to bless this nation!

This stone was laid, but little did we imagine that construction, delayed due to the conflict and the consequential shortage of funds, would not start until July 2004, two years and two months later.

*Chairperson Solomon Kebede laying the
foundation stone on April 28, 2002*

Departing Gracefully

In line with my conviction that expats like us should not stay long in leadership positions, but turn the work over to nationals as soon as possible, I informed the board of trustees, in early March, that we were planning on a one-year home leave, and that I hoped to be relieved of the duties of principalship, that it was time to appoint another person, preferably an Ethiopian, to assume that role.

At their next meeting, the board agreed to appoint Bedru Hussein as principal in my place. When the executive committee reviewed the minutes, they appointed Bedru as "acting principal."

The CDC and the architects met at the beginning of May. The architects reported it would take another two months for them to finish their design work. It would be two full years since we were granted the land. I was disappointed. Vera and I were to leave on the first of June. We would not even see the final blueprints, let alone the beginning of construction before we left. I had been looking forward to that day for the past six years, and now I would be absent when it occurred.

Preparing for an upcoming furlough is usually very hectic, and this was no exception. First, there was teaching the last class, administering the final exams, correcting the results, and calculating, then handing in the final grades. There was tidying up the office and handing over important documents to my successor. In between these duties, our spare moments were given to sorting and packing our belongings, storing the furniture and important things, and giving away the "trash." The last act would be packing our four suitcases, moving out of the house, and saying goodbye to all our friends. We were leaving this fair land behind, with all its challenges, trials, disappointments, and victories.

However, before we could leave, there was one more final test of our patience. That involved the production of a promotional video, which we had contracted with Shalom Advertising, a company that specialized in TV commercials and production of documentary videos. The contract called for a 15-20-minute documentary plus a five-minute executive summary both in video film and digital formats. It was to be completed at least two weeks before our departure.

The contractor did not take seriously the "two-week before" stipulation in the contract. The narration was not finalized until Friday. We were scheduled to fly out on Saturday evening. Then they worked frantically all Friday night mixing the narration with the pictures and the music. At 11:00 am, Saturday morning, Bedru and I went to their studio to review and approve the final product. Finding a lot of need for improvement in their draft, we worked with them on corrections all afternoon. They were so exhausted; they could not seem to understand our concerns or suggestions.

It was about 5:00 pm. when we walked out of the office with copies of the video, but without the digital copies. They would finish them on Monday, and Bedru would send them to us in Alberta by courier service. The check-in time at the airport was 7:00 p.m. I was less than impressed with their sensitivity to customer satisfaction.

While I was devoting my last precious hours to finalizing the video, Vera and Jerry had to complete the moving of everything out of our house and all the other business without my assistance. I did not even have a chance to say "good-bye" to our faithful guards. I found Vera at Jerry Grosh's house. She was quite exhausted.

We finished packing the last suitcase, quickly devoured Ann's delicious apple dumplings, and then rushed to the airport. Muluwork, our loyal house help, with her husband and son, Temesgen and Paulos, were waiting at the airport to say their tearful farewells. Then we moved into the queue, putting the six and one-half years of living, that included the guards, the house help, and the Mekonnen Feleke house, behind us. We turned our attention to checking in our luggage.

For us, it was the end of an era. If, and when we returned to Ethiopia, it would be with a different role, a different house, and probably different workers.

CHAPTER 12

Testing in a Dark Valley

The High Costs of Conflict

For missionaries, furlough meant retreating from one's place of service, taking time to rest, to recuperate from one's stresses, to re-connect with family and supporting community. It meant to re-enter one's own culture, to refresh one's energy, and re-focus one's vision in preparation to return with fresh enthusiasm.

For us, it meant making our home in Harrisonburg, Virginia, where we could re-connect with our children and get acquainted with our grandchildren who resided there. We also expected to travel a lot during the year.

We went home to rest, but the conflict went with us. It sapped our energy and dampened our enthusiasm. The temptation to quit kept recurring. I did not want to push myself onto a reluctant church. Maybe our children and grandchildren needed us more than the church did?

Yet, we felt called to this task and took comfort in the thought that it was God's problem, not just ours. From time to time, I sensed the presence and peace of our Lord amid the storm.

Fundraising Travels – 2002

We left Ethiopia without a clear understanding of what the church expected of us on our furlough year. We did not know what our job description would be after our return. We did not know if we were expected to be fundraising, or not, since we were blocked from doing so the previous fall. There was no "Thank you!" or "Goodbye!" from the leaders. There was no "Best wishes!" no "God bless you!" no "See you again!" and no directions. Only painful silence.

One of the qualities of good leadership is, when in times of crisis, to keep a long-range view, seeing beyond the immediate circumstances. It would have been helpful to know how to plan our year if we knew what was expected of us. It was left to us to look inward to discover what God was leading us to do. And that, albeit imperfectly, is what we did.

Events of the past year had confirmed to me that I was not working "to please men." The denominational leadership was not my "lord." If it were, I would have resigned. I had felt a call to a higher purpose that was not yet complete. The images of hundreds of eager excited young people, men and women, longing for basic educational opportunities, was driving me to do all in my power to be faithful to that call. I would utilize the furlough to raise the funds that were needed to build the college to train leaders for the churches of Ethiopia. I would do it without the encouragement of those currently in leadership.

For us, furlough included a lot of travelling, first to connect with widely scattered family members and friends, to connect with and encourage supporters, to tell the story of what God was doing in Ethiopia, and to challenge new people to become supporters of the MK College.

We arrived in Washington DC on June 2nd, stayed with our children in Harrisonburg for two nights, then flew to Calgary on June 4th. We visited folks in Alberta for eleven days, attending a family reunion and speaking in churches. On June 15th, we flew to Seattle on the west coast to speak in Sisay Desalegn's Seattle Mennonite Church and visit the area for a few days. Then Sisay drove us to Oregon to attend the Pacific Northwest Conference meeting at Salem the following weekend. There, we were given time to inform their leaders about the growth of the church and the needs of MK College. We flew back to Washington DC and Virginia on June 25th.

We attended the third biannual Friends of MKC Conference, held

119

on the EMU campus near our home over the weekend of June 27th to the 29th. We reported to about eighty people, mostly former missionaries and Ethiopians of the diaspora.

There, Arlene Leatherman and Clara Landis were honored for their major contribution to developing the MK College library since 1995. During the following seven years, they had contributed the equivalent of one and one-half years of work time (a salary dollar value of about $40,000 – $60,000) in preparing more than 10,000 labels and cards for our library books. We gave them each an Ethiopian souvenir book as an expression of appreciation.

We traveled to Belleville, Pennsylvania, to visit Vera's family for one week. From there we drove to the EMM headquarters at Salunga for debriefing and to attend a missionary retreat and other activities for ten days. After resting in Harrisonburg for two days, we moved on to attend the annual Virginia Mennonite Conference in Newport News. After the conference, we stayed with our daughter, Karen and granddaughter, Jasmine, in their home in Virginia Beach for a few days. After returning to Harrisonburg, we enjoyed staying with our daughter, Sheryl, and her family for two weeks.

On August 10, we departed for another sixteen-day trip, driving to Goshen, Indiana, to arrange for a fundraising meeting later in the fall. There, we visited Peter and Jan Shetler, who had served with MCC in Ethiopia during the late seventies where Jan taught at the Bible Academy and Peter worked in MCC projects. Peter helped our college establish a website and served as webmaster. He paid for the website for many years.

From there, we drove to Ontario, Canada, and stayed with Darrell and Florence Jantzi for nine days. With them, we made plans to co-lead a Tour Imagination tour that would visit Ethiopia on the way to Zimbabwe to attend the Mennonite World Conference in August 2003.

On our way back, we stopped in Pennsylvania for three days promoting the college building fund. On Sunday, we spoke at Weaverland Mennonite Church. Their offering for the college yielded $11,300. We arrived home on August 26th and moved into a rented apartment. Finally, we settled into our own rented home after living out of suitcases for three months. Does "furlough" mean "rest"?

That first eleven-day trip to Alberta in June was mostly for family reasons. In the fall, we made another seven-week fundraising trip back to Alberta. That first trip was fast, by airplane. On September 26th, we set out by car, enabling us to meet a lot of people in a lot of places along the way, both going and returning.

In Winnipeg, Manitoba, we had meaningful discussions with representatives of MC Canada. I challenged them to explore the possibility of establishing fraternal relations with MKC in Ethiopia. Twelve years later, it became a reality.

After spending a month visiting family, friends, and supporting churches scattered in various parts of Alberta, we set out for home. On our way back, we spent three days with Paul and Ann Gingrich in Goshen. They, with Zenebe Abebe, Mel, and Elfrieda Loewen, organized a fundraising gathering. Attendance was good, and $10,075 was raised for the college. We arrived home on November 15th, a completed.

Two days after completing our seven-week, 7,000-mile journey, on the evening of November 17th, the MK College Link Board held a fundraising banquet at our church. About sixty people contributed around $5,970 that night. One piece of good news was the reception of Cdn $50,000 from the DeFehr Family Foundation in Winnipeg.

On a Sunday evening in December, we made a presentation at Landis Homes, a large retirement community near Lititz, Pennsylvania. The many elderly missionaries and other supporters welcomed us. They had a prayer group which met monthly to pray specifically for the MKC and its college in Ethiopia.

Developments in Ethiopia

Shortly after our arrival in the USA, Dr. Paul T. Yoder informed us that MKC had agreed to accept the Link organization, provided the Link Board agreed to their revised *Memo of Understanding*. Finally, after almost two years, that contentious issue was settled! MK College Link was free to do its work on behalf of the college.

Back in Ethiopia, the architects completed the designs. The Municipality approved them, after the College paid $75,000 for a building permit. It was the mandatory fee of 2% of the estimated cost of the construction. It was a tax the government put on all business construction.

The General Secretary of MKC sent me a copy of my future job description in October. I would be given the title, "Resource Development Director." It was okay, as I had been doing that anyway. However, it was not okay with our sponsoring agency, EMM.

Restructuring the College

In November 2002, the MKC Executive Committee decided to restructure the college. They felt they could make it come even more under the direct control of the church. I felt sad. There were so many more important things that should be occupying their attention. It would be wonderful if we could just feel that they were working to support and promote their college rather than keep digging loose the foundations. The executive committee had complete control of the college already. They appointed all the trustees. By definition, "trustees" are people they "trust." Most of the trustees were either employees of the MKC head office or were serving on the executive committee. How could restructuring bring the college any closer to the control of the church?

Of course, after five years of their college's functioning, it would be entirely appropriate for the church to carefully review and evaluate its operations and make appropriate adjustments.

However, I was disturbed by this news, not that I thought the structure was perfect. This was being done without any systematic evaluation of the college's achievements in relationship to its goals, the appropriateness and outcomes of its programs, or its administrative and organizational relationships. It was done without consultation with any of the administrators who had an inside knowledge of the college's functioning. The committee members had taken it upon themselves to unilaterally restructure the college. There was no explanation as to why it needed to be restructured, nor of how restructuring would make it more efficient, or help it to achieve its goals.

Their restructuring called for a new body which they named "The Education Commission." It was to oversee all educational activities of the church. One of its responsibilities was to nominate people to serve as trustees on the board of the college. The executive committee was to give final approval. Leadership in the college was changed. Since it was to be a multidiscipline institution, the college was to have a president and two deans. One dean would oversee the seminary, and the other would give oversight over the science or secular wing of the college.

In the spring of 2003, the MKC Executive Committee appointed Mulugeta Zewdie to serve as president of the college. He was notified while still preparing to graduate with a master's degree in peace studies from AMBS. Upon his return in the summer, he would give overall leadership and facilitate the working relationship between the church and the college. Mulugeta had served effectively as general secretary for the church before he went to study at AMBS. He was known as a person of integrity and peace-loving. The acting principal, Bedru Hussein, was appointed to be vice president for the seminary.

The Valley Darkens

A "cold" new year, 2003, blew in with a shocking letter from the General Secretary of MKC, which cast a frosty pall over my soul. It called into question our future involvement with MKC and MK College.

It was a reaction to EMM's letter of response to the job description prepared by the church for our future involvement. The church had decided to invite Vera and I back to serve for two more years as "Resource Development Director" and included a lengthy list of duties that would "develop and expand the financial resources of the college."

EMM leadership had objected that "it outlines a new role for an EMM missionary. In the past EMM has not sent missionaries to serve as resource development directors. We understand developing financial resources for MK College to be a task that would be done by a member of MKC rather than an EMM missionary."

They then suggested the title might be changed to "Resource Development Trainer and Interim Director," and that "The purpose is to establish good procedures for resource development and train a person chosen by the college to do this work long-term."

The general secretary's January 5th letter of response to EMM was terse and final: He wrote:

> From your response, our appointment of Carl Hansen as MK College Resource Development Director does not fit the way EMM has been operating so far and may not be acceptable. Consequently, the executive committee has discussed your suggestions and the issues surrounding the case to a great extent, weighing the pros and cons, and has come to a unanimous resolution. The Executive Committee feels that suspending the appointment and the invitation for the Hansen's to come back to Ethiopia is a better decision.

When Vera and I received a copy of this correspondence from EMM, we were shocked and numbed by its tone and intent. For some weeks we internalized it. We kept quiet and did not share it with anyone, not even our adult children.

However, we began receiving letters and phone calls of support and sympathy from many people as the news spread. We did not want to talk about it or put the church in a bad light. Yet, it was difficult to keep on promoting the college with enthusiasm when there was the nagging doubt that the church would allow the vision to succeed.

Over the next five months I went through a period of mourning, soul searching, and uncertainty. I took comfort in the words of Paul in Romans 8:28: "*We know that in all things, God works for the good of those who love him, who have been called according to his purpose.*" (NIV)

It is sad when the enemies from outside interfere or destroy the work of God's people. How much more tragic when it is the brothers from within who destroy what God is doing through his people. The only one to gain is the enemy of God's Kingdom. On January 14, 2003, I attempted to make the best of it as I wrote in my diary:

> We get some consolation in the thought that already many church leaders have graduated from our college. Even if the college should collapse, a permanent impact has been made upon these courageous "soldiers of Christ" who are and will pass on to others what they have learned. That gives me great satisfaction. It has been a great privilege for Vera and me to have played a small part in shaping their lives. Institutions and buildings can come and go, but humans live on forever.

But the questions still haunted my soul:

> What about the future and our involvement in shaping it? At our advancing age, we will not be hasty to draw conclusions. It is MKC's problem, I mean the whole membership of MKC, not just three leaders. It is EMM's problem as well. And above all, it is God's problem. We will keep on doing what we feel we can from this end. We are leaving it to the Lord of the church to settle the leadership issues involved there.
>
> In a way, it will be easier to just settle down here with family, forget about the vision and the pain, and start a new life in this beautiful valley. But, at our age, what kind of employment can we get? And, most troubling of all, what do we tell the supporters of the college?

On January 28, like the ancient biblical Job, I poured out the bitterness of my soul in lament:

> It seems incredible that in a church of over 100,000 members, three people have so much power that they

can destroy a church's institution and the loyal servants who run them, and the members quietly accept their actions. There must be some constitutional way that the members can challenge the actions of their leaders. The church of Jesus is not a dictatorship of the one or few over the many. Christian leadership is to be servant leadership, not crushing tyranny.

It is ironic that, while we have succeeded in building warm working relationships around the world, which have resulted in keeping the college going and growing, we have failed miserably in maintaining working relationships with those who wield power over us in our church and workplace. Over the last eighteen months, we have seen this relationship turn sour and break down. All the steps we took to find the root cause, make peace, and restore harmony have failed. We still do not know what our "sin" was. We do not know what we were doing wrong. We do not know what their alternate vision for the college was and is. They would simply not communicate, only oppose. When we tried, they turned a deaf ear. Now it has come to this drastic conclusion. What is next?

However, we have not totally despaired. The church belongs to Jesus Christ, and he is the only head. He can overrule his stewards. Many people are praying for us. We are waiting to see what the rest of the Ethiopians do about it....

Yes, we felt called by the Lord to do this work, and all that we did was in response to that call. I never felt I was doing it for certain leaders, but for the Lord. However, when the stewards of the church, the designated leaders, withdraw their confirmation of that call, there develops a contradiction between my sense of call and the church's cancellation of their call. Is the same Holy Spirit leading both parties? Does God contradict himself?

So, I decided I must back off and let God and his church sort it out before we can return. It might take some years. It might never be. I cannot work with such a contradiction. Eighteen months of disharmony is enough. I must be open to the possibility that my mission is accomplished in Ethiopia and that the Lord has other plans. "He must increase, I must decrease!"

I think I have poured out enough of the "bitterness" of my soul. God is on his throne. Let us keep close to him!

The Human Resources Department of EMM, recognizing that Vera and I were under a lot of stress, arranged for us to take a two-week retreat at a workshop for cross-cultural workers provided by Heartstream Resources of Liverpool, PA., February 3 – 12, 2003.

The Retreat was like medicine for Vera and me. It was especially designed for missionaries who are going through struggles relating to their calling or who are dealing with burnout. We found it helpful to share with counselors who understand. We decided we need to simply forgive. Perhaps they do not know what they are doing. As foreigners, perhaps we do not know what we are doing. We must be open to the possibility that in working across little understood cultural barriers, we most likely have offended more than we realize. We must hang loose, be repentant, work where and when we are wanted, and move on when the work is done, or when we are no longer wanted.

Fundraising Travels - 2003

Towards the end of February 2003, I wanted to make some more major fundraising contacts but felt discouraged. How could I approach people again, people who gave for the building program three or four years ago, when we still did not have any building to show for their generous responses. They would not think that we were serious. I could not ask them again until there are some foundations to show that we are serious.

At the same time, the attitude of the MKC leaders alarmed me. If they are not interested in the development of the college, why should I be? Even if we raise the money, will the campus ever get built? Might the money, already raised and in the college bank account, be diverted?

Although the "wind was not blowing in our sails," we did make some appointments to keep promoting the college. In March, we shared in a missions' conference in Pennsylvania and spoke in the Huntingdon Mennonite Church in Newport News. Then we drove to Florida, partly as a tourist/vacation trip, to see unfamiliar territory and old friends and partly to promote the college. We showed our display at the annual MCC sale in Sarasota.

At the beginning of May, I flew to Alberta to be guest speaker at a missions' conference at the Coaldale Mennonite Church, a new contact for us. On May 8 – 12, I flew on to British Columbia to do a four-day fundraising trip that was organized and hosted by Bill Armerding, the Director of Overseas Council Canada. I was hoping to make our cause known among the many wealthy Mennonites there. It was my first visit, so, in four days, not much could result.

Bedru Hussein visited the USA in April. He tried hard to encourage us to keep on planning to return. He reminded us that we were in a spiritual battle. People cannot be treated like machines, used, and then thrown away. He was very optimistic that God was in control, the decision would be reversed, and the misunderstanding corrected. I agreed, but was still mystified: How can it be that the key antagonists are men supposedly "filled with the Holy Spirit"? It seemed terribly sad to me.

As time went on, our assurance grew that we would eventually be re-invited to return to work at the unfinished task. We felt strongly that this was not the Lord's time for us to withdraw from the work we were doing at the college. This was just a "test." We felt we should give at least four more years. However, if the Lord showed us something different, we wished to be obedient. We placed our future in his capable hands.

By faith, we were planning to return, but we could not see any green light ahead.

Further Developments in 2003

Bedru Hussein, Acting Principal of the college, suffered a stroke on April 17, 2003. Thankfully, it was a minor stroke. He was able to walk and talk and recovered his many abilities quickly. People were suspecting this might have been a direct result of carrying too much stress as the principal of a college in conflict with the church leadership.

Woudineh and Shewaye both graduated from MBBS in Fresno on April 27th. Woudineh earned a master's degree from the seminary. Shewaye earned two master's degrees, one from the seminary and one from Fresno Pacific University, plus she gave birth to their firstborn, Eden, a daughter. They had proven to be dedicated, diligent, hardworking, and competent as students. A job well done. They returned to pursue their calling as teachers in the college. In addition to teaching, Woudineh worked closely with Hailu, relieving some of the burden of the dean's work.

In May, the MKC Executive Committee decided against inviting the long-term missionary couple, Jerry and Ann King-Grosh, to return for another term of teaching at the college. They said, the college "has enough teachers," while in fact there was a shortage. Again, they never consulted the college administration nor with Jerry and Ann, nor did they consider their superb qualifications, previous contribution, and relationships.

The college was gifted once again with the presence of Dr. John Miller who came to teach two summer courses. This time he came with his wife, Doris, who assisted in the library, relieving the librarian to take the summer courses.

Sisay Desalegn came from Seattle and taught in the fall semester after attending the Mennonite World Conference in Zimbabwe. Also, Tefera Bekere joined the faculty in the fall of 2003. He had just graduated with an MA degree in Missions from EMS. He taught in the field of missions and anthropology.

An Unexpected Diversion

The MKC Executive Committee sent a revised job description to EMM in June, inviting Vera and I to return to work. I was to work in a new position they created: *"Interim Educational Resource Development Director"* for the education department of the church. I was to work directly under the control of the executive secretary at the head office. I was to find financial resources for the whole of the educational enterprise of the church. The college was not mentioned in the job description. They were to remove us from the college altogether.

Our inclination was to reject this offer. First, there was no hint of reconciliation of the damaged relationships. Secondly, it had never been the policy of EMM to send a missionary to work solely as fundraiser for any church. Also, it was not the policy of the Ethiopian government to give work permits to foreigners to work in Ethiopian churches as "missionaries." My legal permission to work had been as a "teacher" in a college. Further, fundraising for MKC would be much more difficult since public trust had been seriously eroded among the potential donors. I could not, in good conscience, promote an organization that I, and many others, could no longer trust.

Furthermore, the job of fundraising did not fit with my areas of interest, gifting, nor calling. I viewed myself as a teacher and only did the other jobs, like fundraising, out of necessity because it needed to be done.

After much prayer and discussion with EMM personnel, we unanimously agreed that they would not be sending us back to work with MKC at this time. We must give the Ethiopian brothers time to settle their problems without the added dynamic that our presence seemed to generate.

Our decision was prompted by the MKC Executive Committee's procedure. They did not consult Vera and me at all about the restructuring or about the job description they prepared for us. They did not explain why their invitation was suspended for five months. They did not explain why we were to be moved out of college work altogether. They did not tell us what our faults were. They did not take into consideration our gifts and calling. They did not explain the practical implications of the new assignment. In fact, they did not contact us directly, even once, during all those months. EMM does not assign missionaries that way.

We are a spiritual family of God's children, and we discern God is leading through prayer, discussion, and sensing together what seems good to the Holy Spirit and to us. We were not used to arbitrary, bureaucratic, authoritarian, or impersonal assignments. We were not machines to be used, abused, or discarded at will. Seen in that light, we and the EMM Human Resources personnel decided together that it would be better to decline the invitation. We would not be going back to work at this time. Our employment with EMM, after twenty-eight years, would be terminated.

EMM would give us three more months of support while we searched for a job. They would send us back to Ethiopia to dispose of our stored furniture and possessions. After that, we would co-lead the Tour Imagination group in Ethiopia, August 1 – 6, as we had promised two years before. We would then go on with the tour group to Zimbabwe and the Mennonite World Conference. Then, we would return to Ethiopia on August 20, pack up our things, settle our affairs, say our goodbye's, and leave that country for the last time. Our employment with the mission board would end on August 31st. We would arrive home in the USA on September 2nd and start a new chapter in our lives. Of this story, this would be: THE END!

This was the most painful breakdown in relationships I had experienced in my entire life. It felt like a premature death in the family. It just did not seem right. We tried to relinquish all desires, wishes, and expectations, and defer judgment to our Lord. It was his church and his work. We were his. We were deeply sorry we were not able to see the vision to its completion. Even Moses did not get to enter the promised land. I never dreamed that our involvement with MKC would end in this inglorious fashion, but it had come to that.

Our Dilemma

I was deeply troubled by one haunting question. As principal, over the previous five years, I solicited funds from my family, friends, former missionaries, the Ethiopian diaspora, organizations such as MCC and various foundations, and from the congregations of Christian brothers and sisters in the USA, Canada, Germany, and the Netherlands. In the process, I boasted of the wisdom, strength, integrity, and spiritual commitment of MKC's top leadership, and of their vision for a large multi-disciplined Christian college to train leaders for their growing churches.

Many hearts were touched, and many responded with their gifts and their prayers. The college was able to grow, and almost 400 students had already graduated. We had been granted land for a permanent campus, and we had close to $800,000 in our building fund bank account.

These hundreds of brothers and sisters, who trusted us and trusted the church through us, deserved accountability from us. Since we were dismissed, these people, upon hearing rumors that we were not returning, one by one, wrote to or called me, seeking the truth about the rumors and the reason for this decision to exclude us from our work in MK College. I did not like to talk about it. I did not want to besmirch the church's or anyone's reputation, but I could not lie about it either. I believed that, in God's work, there must be transparency and openness. It gave me fresh pain to damage the relationship of trust that had been built up through the years between these supporters and MKC. This was my dilemma.

CHAPTER 13

Into the Light

According to plan, Vera and I arrived in Addis Ababa on July 23rd, 2003. Upon our arrival at the college, the students came pouring out of their classrooms and library in mass, welcoming us with clapping and shouting. They presented us with a bouquet of roses! We felt quite overwhelmed. The college faculty and staff also warmly welcomed us. However, the key leaders of the church chose not to meet us.

We spent the next several days sorting out a few possessions, which had been stored in some rooms behind the house Jerry and Ann King-Grosh had occupied. The furniture belonged to the mission and would stay. We selected a few memorable things to fill the four suitcases and sold or gave away the rest of our possessions. Then we spent the next few days preparing to receive the Tour Imagination guests, arranging hotels and transportation.

In the meantime, the church held its annual General Assembly of Delegates. We heard that there were elections, and that Pastor Siyum Gebretsadik was elected as the new chairperson.

On August 1st, the group of sixteen tourists from Canada and the USA arrived. As guides, we spent six days escorting them, introducing them to some of the highlights of Addis Ababa, the culture, and the history, showing them where the first Mennonite missionaries founded the Meserete Kristos Church in Nazareth.

As we led the tourists around, visiting the different churches, in each place, one of the elders would draw me aside and quietly express his deep displeasure at what the leaders had done and expressed that their prayers and support were with us. We were deeply touched.

According to plan, Vera and I accompanied the tour group to Zimbabwe to experience the Mennonite World Conference at Bulawayo. Along the way, in South Africa, we visited in Johannesburg, saw Soweto, and toured a gold mine. In Zimbabwe, we visited the Victoria Falls and the Hwange National Game Preserve nearby.

Resolving the Conflict

On August 20, upon returning from Zimbabwe to Ethiopia to collect our things and say "Goodbye," we found Pastor Siyum, the new chairperson, looking for us. He invited us for lunch at the classy Gihon Hotel. There, he ordered the best in Ethiopian cuisine. He wanted to make things right that were wrong. He begged us to forgive and reverse our decision and return to the work that we had begun. He did not, and perhaps could not, reverse any of the executive committee's decisions, but he tried to explain them and minimize the impact of those decisions.

We did not resolve anything, so he made another appointment to meet with us on Monday afternoon. The leaders were facing a lot of pressure from a growing number of members who sharply disagreed with the actions that were taken.

We had four separate interviews with Siyum over the last week we were there. We assured him that it was not a lack of commitment or the fading of the vision that moved us to terminate. It was the continuous hostility and resistance we felt from the executive committee and the resultant anger and hurt felt by so many disappointed members of the church, especially our colleagues.

We laid down four conditions that must be met before we would consider returning: There must be, (1) complete reconciliation and healing of broken relationships among those with whom we must work; (2) a retracting of the decision to restructure; (3) a more open and consultative style of leadership, rather than the secretive dictatorial style of the recent past on the part of the executive committee; and (4) a convincing appeal to Eastern Mennonite Mission that our services are wanted and needed.

As a positive sign before we left, the leaders formed a peace and reconciliation committee of five respected elders, not current office bearers and not employed by the church, to do an independent investigation and begin a reconciliation process. Vera and I were the first to be interviewed before our departure.

During our last ten days in Ethiopia, we witnessed the return of 120 students and the beginning of a new semester. We felt encouraged. While this conflict had delayed the building of the new campus, the teaching was going on and would be making a significant impact on the leadership of the church in the days ahead.

We had lunch with one of our earliest graduates, Pastor Zerihun Tesema, who was now a pastor of a congregation in Addis. It was less than ten years old and had a membership of over 1,000. About 300 members were added in the past year alone. His church had also spawned three daughter congregations.

We left with a hopeful feeling. If the church met these conditions and the mission agreed, then we would be open to return. We departed Ethiopia on August 31.

On Recognizing the Role of Partnership

During those troubled times, I pondered on what had gone wrong in the relationship between the church leaders and those of us responsible for the college. I finally concluded that there was a failure to recognize that organizations can only thrive when there is a deep recognition of the essential role of partnership.

Partnership is not about one giving and another receiving. It is sharing resources to accomplish something all partners want to see happen. In the case of Meserete Kristos College, all parties believed it would be a desirable thing to train leaders for the benefit of the church population, as well as for the nation.

While the church is the originator and owner of the vision and provides the on-ground human implementing energies, other partners provide enabling spiritual, financial, material, ideal, and human expertise resources. If each partner contributes his/her fair share, with mutual respect, achieving the vision or goal is possible. The goal is for the expansion of the Kingdom of God and the exalting of the name of Jesus Christ in Ethiopia and beyond. For this goal we all work together in love, unity, and mutual respect.

It seemed to me that the executive committee members failed to understand that the college was built upon and functioned as a complex partnership between the church members, the church leadership, local administrative and teaching staff, and local expatriates who shared many years of their lives. They also had a partnership with supporting agencies abroad (MCC and EMM), congregations, foundations, and a host of sympathetic individuals who shared their wealth and prayers to support the college. These believed in the goals their Ethiopian brothers and sisters were striving to accomplish. Without a collaborative partnership, the college, as the leaders envisioned it, could never have become a reality.

The executive committee failed to realize that if they would like the support of the international community, they must open themselves to the full meaning of partnership. Partnership implies accountability both ways. There are obligations and responsibilities on both sides. When outside donors contribute to any MKC program or project, they become partners in that ministry. Partnership, even informal partnership or silent partnership includes accountability. Accountability means reporting back, and sharing information, including progress and problems. It means being open to hearing criticism and valuing advice.

How then could the church leaders assume that we outsiders should have no say in how the college is structured and managed? How could they think that we foreigners have no business asking questions, giving suggestions, or being consulted? My first job description was to be "a teacher and consultant" when the church invited us to return to Ethiopia back in 1996. Without notification and without explanation, my consultant role had been de facto terminated, and my welcome to sit on the executive committee meetings as a non-voting contributing member had been withdrawn.

Further Challenges

Another obstacle of a different kind rose up to complicate Vera's and my return. We were informed that because EMM changed its policy, we missionaries would be required to raise our own support. Before, EMM did the fundraising to support those it sent. Now, those being sent had to carry the additional burden of finding their own support. This would take some time.

At the end of September, the church sent us a formal invitation to return, along with a revised job description. They assured us that peacemaking was in process but was not yet completed. In the following days, we heard some very encouraging reports of repentance and reconciliation among the leadership members.

We felt that God would turn this conflict into something positive for the growth and development of his church and his people. Conflict is not always a bad thing. It may be a necessary growing pain, an indicator that something is out of date, something needs to be changed. In this case, it seemed there was a leadership style that was increasingly out of date, and perhaps certain individuals accumulated too much power for too long. This does not mean they were bad, but simply were making wrong assumptions, were not listening, were not understanding, or were not communicating clearly. Changes were needed before we could go on. The whole culture of leadership needed to be evaluated and restructured.

With such amazing church growth and human nature being what it is, an occasional conflict should not be surprising. What matters most is how conflict is managed. It can be turned into something good, a "growing pain," or something destructive, a "death pain."

Due to recent tensions, growth at the college had stagnated. Enrollment in the fall of 2003 remained at 120. The need to train leaders was still there, the campus was there, the teachers were there, the administration and staff were there. However, contributions to the operation of the college had fallen critically below what they were the previous year. It took a daring leap of faith to accept the 120 students and adopt a budget of $142,000.

Up to that time, a total of around $800,000 had been received in the fund for the building of the new campus. Some of it had been spent on fencing, well drilling, architect's fees, and building permits. About $679,000 remained safely in savings accounts. Actual construction was delayed by the uncertainties surrounding the conflict. It was already more than three years since the land was acquired and a year and a half since the historic ground-breaking ceremony took place.

The MKC Executive Committee appointed Mulugeta Zewdie as the new principal, changing the title to "President." My assigned role, besides teaching, was to be "Director of Resource Development" for the college.

In mid-October, I decided to resume fundraising activities which I had suspended in June. I wrote a letter of appeal and sent it to over 850 friends and supporters on our mailing list. In the letter, I explained our situation clearly and honestly. Support improved.

In mid-November, EMM agreed that we could prepare ourselves to return to Ethiopia to work. That meant we needed to begin the lengthy process of raising personal support and meeting the requirements for reappointment. We began that by organizing a "Missionary Support Team" (MST) which relieved us of that burden.

While waiting for the outcome of this peace-making process, we made our home for a full year in Harrisonburg, Virginia. Being jobless, we moved in with our son-in-law, Eric Payne, and our two grandsons. Later, Vera got a part time job in a school cafeteria. Being an alien who could not legally work in the USA, I applied for permanent resident status, a process that, thanks to the USA immigration services, took twenty months to complete.

Meanwhile, in Ethiopia, the reconciliation process faced difficulties. There was resistance from a few of the key leaders, who were under the influence of those who were opposing the college in the first place. Consequently, there was a delay in getting the results we wanted before we could give ourselves whole-heartedly to returning. Our friends there encouraged us to be patient, saying, "It usually takes at least as long to resolve a conflict as it does to start one."

In mid-January 2004, a disturbing letter came from Bedru, informing us that the college land at Bishoftu was in danger of being taken back by the Oromia government because we failed to build on it and that the church seemed to not care overly much. I responded in my diary:

> If the church lets the land go back to the Oromia government, that would be a major disaster and defeat. I was reading Joshua chapter one this morning. I know the struggle we went through to find a suitable site for our campus, and the acquiring of this plot was a clear answer to much prayer and the details of how we got it was nothing short of a miraculous and unusual provision of God.
>
> How then can the church leaders just dismiss it and let it go back without a struggle? What has happened to our faith? Are we responding like the ten spies who saw only the obstacles to the conquest of Canaan, or the two spies who held onto the promises of God and said, "We are well able to take the land!"? Let us believe that the God who gave us the land will also give us the money to build. But we must move ahead, put our feet in the "water," start building with what we have in hand. The rest will come.

Unplanned Visit - Breakthrough

Suddenly, outside of our expectations, EMM, with the financial backing of MCC, sent me back to Ethiopia on March 14, 2004, for five weeks to teach a block course on Anabaptist History and Thought and to have in-depth face-to-face conversations with the current church leadership to clear up some issues. Then, if things were cleared, we would be sent back for another term in July or August.

Siyum, Bedru, Woudineh, and a driver were all waiting at the airport when I came out late that night. After a brief welcome, they took me to the college where the students were still up awaiting my arrival. They had decorated the place with a banner and flowers. After we talked a bit, since it was late, they escorted me to my room and bade me rest well. What a welcome!

Bedru informed me of the bad news that the government had reclaimed our land and updated me on changes in the church leadership. Of the three leaders who had given us such a challenging time over these past two and one-half years, one completed his term of service and was replaced. One was facing discipline for moral infractions and apparently resigned from the church. The third one had just been transferred from his office to a department where his gifts were much more suitable and useful.

Hedwig Unrah, our "Paraguayan daughter," was staying at the college guest rooms also. The next day, she and I drove out to the still empty college land and walked over to the stone that marked the dedication. We stood there and prayed, reminding God that we had dedicated this land for his service as a Christian college site and complained that now the government has reclaimed it. Will the government or God have the final say in this matter? We left it to God to decide. We got home after dark.

Bedru Hussein and Mitiku Zena, our accountant, frantically put together a large dossier of evidence, showing that we had prepared the blueprints, paid for construction permits, dug the well, had raised funds, and were ready to start construction. With this, they filed an appeal and presented it to Ali Abdo, the head of the Oromiya land office. After due consideration, Ali Abdo gave the church one month to get started with the building program. Ours is a God who hears!

Consequently, an urgent board of trustees meeting was called to activate the building committee. A lot of decisions had to be made immediately. The re-constituted Campus Building Committee called for an urgent meeting with the architects. They decided it was best to put out for bids a contract to build half of the academic building. My month was up, and I returned to the USA.

The CBC faced a major unexpected problem; the bids submitted by the contractors for the half-building were double what they expected, due to inflation and the high demand of the building boom over the past four years. This meant the half-building would cost close to one million dollars. We had less than $800,000 in the building fund. This was a disturbing development. They were waiting for my advice. I was not sure I was the right one to give advice in this situation. It would have to be decided by Ethiopians.

However, back in the USA, I discussed this matter with a few of the Link Board members. Their opinion was that we have come this far over the past seven years against great obstacles. The need for the envisioned Christian college had never been greater and would only grow as the church grows. If we give up now and stop, history will judge us badly. Therefore, if we really believe this vision is from God, and if we really trust God, let us move on, sign the contract, and start the construction. We will all work hard at fundraising and find the money by December. However, we did not want to advise the Ethiopian brothers on what to do.

Personally, I approached this from a spiritual perspective. Our questions should not be, "What do we have on hand today?" but rather "What does the Lord want?" If this vision is really of him, and he bears witness in our spirits, then he can also be trusted to provide what is needed. The "over-flowing Jordan river" should not deter us! Let us put our feet in the water!

If Yahweh does not build the house,
in vain the mason's toil.
If Yahweh does not guard the city,
in vain the sentries watch. (Ps. 127:1 The Jerusalem Bible)

This created a dilemma for the church leaders. They could not sign a contract committing themselves to pay a contractor without adequate funds on hand. However, if they did not sign a contract very soon, they would like to lose the land. If they lost the land, they would lose all that had been invested in the fence, well, architect's fees, building permit, soil tests—everything. They would also lose credibility with the broader church membership, fellow Ethiopians, as well as the international donor community, not to mention the government.

While this decision was under discussion, someone advanced an alternate plan. Why not forget the liberal arts college idea, let the Bishoftu land go back to the government, and concentrate on making a good little Bible college on the Misrak MKC compound or use the funds we had in hand to purchase the present rented compound in Kotebe from Wezero Senait?

After much deliberation, the leaders decided to stay their course and move ahead in faith. The church needed a college now, and the need would only increase as the church grew. How would future generations view these leaders if they made that easier decision?

I was told by someone who was present in the meeting that the decision to proceed with the larger plan was won by one vote. Sometimes one vote does count!

The academic building in question was to be a five-story structure of ninety-one rooms with a total usable floor space of 54,600 ft^2. It would be enough to house all the classrooms, library, offices, and dorm rooms to keep 300—400 students. The cost of the whole building would be about two million dollars. This would provide government regulation quality construction using reinforced concrete skeleton and cement blocks with finished interior and low-maintenance exterior.

While we were raising funds in North America, the board of trustees in Ethiopia signed a contract with Pyramid Construction to build the first half of this building. The contracted price was $832,000. Construction started in July 2004. The contract stipulated it would be completed by October 2005.

CHAPTER 14

Re-Gaining Momentum

Launching Construction – The Academic building

Bulldozers began scrapping off the topsoil in July. Then, laborers began digging the trenches for the foundation by hand. By October, the contractor was laying the foundation and the ground floor.

The contract was to have the building completed in sixteen months. However, from time to time, there were shortages of cement, reinforcing steel, and bricks due to a building boom throughout the country. Besides shortages, mismanagement, and other pressing priorities on the part of the contractor, the time schedule had to be extended several times. It was not until February 2007, two and one-half years later, that the facility was ready for use.

Although progress on the building was slow, the heavily reinforced concrete foundations and pillars were impressive. The building standards took into consideration that Bishoftu is in an earthquake susceptible zone. Mersha Sahale's Engineering and Consultancy firm (AEC), which did the architectural work, was also doing the supervising. They kept an engineer on site to see that all things conformed to the specifications of the plans.

Fundraising Travels – Summer 2004

While our missionary support group was gathering support for us, Vera and I continued with fundraising for the school through the summer of 2004. We mailed out a letter of appeal to 850 addresses, then combined fundraising with a family visit. We traveled by car to Winnipeg and Alberta in June. We made a ten-day fundraising trip to Ontario in mid-July, and then spent a weekend in Newport News and the Virginia Beach area in August. We made some promising contacts. Some turned out to be only that, "promising." Others delivered what was promised. We raised about $60,000.

People responded in different ways. For example, Sisay Desalegn tactfully and consistently put the need before his congregation. Through his effort, Seattle Mennonite Church held a special fundraiser which yielded $5,500.

Rhoda Nolt, a faithful supporter, organized a fundraising event at the Mellinger Mennonite Church in Lancaster which netted over $10,000. Karen Yoder planned and conducted a similar event in Belleville in November. Assefa and Grace Haile used the occasion of their 30th wedding anniversary to appeal to their friends to contribute to the college. Besides having a party, they raised $4,800. These are just a few examples. Many others were also doing special things to raise awareness and support for the cause.

Re-Entry

Our Missionary Support Team did an excellent job of soliciting our support, but by the time all the details were worked out, the fall semester of college had already started. We flew back to Ethiopia on October 5th, 2004.

This journey marked the closing of our two years and four months extended home leave, or, as we experienced it, our "exile." It had been a traumatic chapter in the story of our lives. It had been costly in terms of emotional stress, extensive introspection, and testing of faith. It was also costly in financial terms, living without support or a job for over a year. Yet, it was reassuring to us that throughout this trial, we continually experienced the providence of God. We never felt material need, and never really wavered in our conviction that the vision and calling were on target.

Upon our return to Ethiopia, we were hosted in a guest room on the Kotebe campus for a few weeks while we searched for and found a house to rent within walking distance. It so happened that Jim and Peg Engle and Sisay Desalegn were also staying in some other guest rooms. We enjoyed their fellowship and shared some meals together.

The college was functioning smoothly. Instead of continuing to rent the second house outside the compound, the administration had rented the whole 2,000 m² adjacent compound from Wezero Senait. That added a large warehouse, which provided a spacious library room and three additional dorm rooms. Behind it were another three dorm rooms and three guest rooms. Facing the warehouse across an open courtyard, which served as a volleyball court, was an additional building, which provided four rooms, including an office for me.

On staff, there were a lot of positional changes. After serving as president for one year, Mulugeta Zewdie had been transferred back to the church where he served another term as general secretary. Hailu Cherenet moved into Mulugata's office and had been appointed "acting president." He still also served as an academic dean. Woudineh Endaylalu was appointed "assistant dean" and moved into Hailu's office. Shewaye was appointed "dean of students." Girma Teklu returned to the college to resume his teaching role.

Bedru's role as "vice president" was ambiguous. Following his stroke, he took an eight-month leave of absence while doing a contract for Global Discipleship Ministries. He still gave leadership with regards to the building project. In January 2005, he returned to serve as "associate director of resource development" with a particular focus on local fundraising and taught some courses. Vera resumed her role as head librarian. Tigist Alamirew, her assistant, had been managing the library while taking classes part time.

Overwhelming Feelings of Inadequacy

In the year 2004, over 14,000 new believers were added to the church membership. This report reinforced the overwhelming sense of urgency that was driving me. God was building his "flock." Our small role was to provide a resource to equip the servant-leaders to "shepherd" them. Sensing that we were called for such a time as this, I journalled my overwhelming feelings of inadequacy:

> Who are we, ordinary people with limited gifts and skills, so short of energy and wisdom, struggling with early signals of our approaching mortality, surrounded with such material poverty, equipped with limited resources, to tackle such a huge task as developing a "university"? We look at the huge need, and the "few loaves and fishes" in our hands, and turn our eyes to our Lord, and cry, "but what are these few among so many?" Unless the Lord blesses and multiplies ... Unless the Lord builds ... all the little time we have left, all the limited talents and declining abilities, all the few pathetic resources we can contribute will never be enough. We need, as never before, his intervention, his strengthening, his blessing of our inadequate efforts, his multiplying of our resources, his wisdom to override our foolishness, his life to override our dying!

Funding the Construction

In the last six months of 2004, the college received donations amounting to $219,000. Of this, $9,000 was a tithe from my 84-year-old mother who sold her house and moved into the senior citizens' lodge in Brooks, Alberta. Another wealthier couple had given $50,000 for operations. That alone was enough to alleviate the disaster that was looming. That which had been borrowed for operations from the building fund was now being returned. We were encouraged.

An October local fund drive and fundraising banquet raised $9,540 in cash and pledges. In addition, the faculty and staff gave or pledged to give $1,834 to the building fund within the year. Several of the lower-paid staff members pledged to give one month's salary.

At the close of December 2004, we had already paid $393,000 in preliminary expenses including topographical survey, fence, drilled well, architect's fees, building permit fees, soil tests, and electricity installed on site. Further, we contracted the construction of the 1st half of the academic building for $832,000. We also budgeted $140,000 for equipment for the new building. In summary, we were committed to spending $972,000 to complete and equip the present construction. Of this amount, we had already collected $875,000. We still needed to raise $97,000.

We planned to continue building the second half of the academic building as soon as this first half was completed. That would require another estimated $1,200,000, allowing for inflation and contingencies. However, more urgent was the need for a kitchen, dining hall, and toilet block, not to mention the ongoing need for operations and scholarships.

Leadership Transitions in 2005

Early on February 8th, 2005, all the workers came on time and got busy cleaning and polishing the campus. They slaughtered two unfortunate sheep and prepared a large feast. The occasion for all these preparations was the long-anticipated ceremony for the official installation of Hailu Cherenet as the new president of Meserete Kristos College.

The program began around noon, after the guests, students, and staff assembled in the small chapel room. The college choir sang, the church chairperson, Siyum Gebretsadik, gave a short message, and the executive secretary, Mulugeta Zewdie, gave the charges and led in a dedicatory prayer.

Also included in the ceremony, Woudineh Endayelalu was

commissioned as the new academic dean, Shewaye Yalew as dean of students, Mitiku Zena as administration and finance head, and Bedru Hussein as associate resource development director. The ceremony was followed with a *beg wat* (sheep stew) feast.

Everyone was sorry to learn that Kebede Bekere, after teaching for four years, resigned to accept a position with World Vision International. Although missed as a full-time committed faculty member, Kebede continued to teach on a part-time basis. He has become known for his solid teaching and his published books in the areas of psychology and counseling.

Three visiting professors and three local teachers taught seven block courses during the summer of 2005. Dr. Allen Black, a known professor of New Testament at SW Baptist Theological Seminary, taught a three-week course called NT Greek Exegesis. He authored several Greek textbooks including the popular, *It is still Greek to me*!

Dr. Tesfatsion Dalellew, co-director of the Africa Desk, MCC, Akron, Pennsylvania, taught a course called "The Church and Development." Brent Segrist, from Nairobi, Kenya, taught a course on "Old Testament Historical Books." Sisay Desalegn returned for the fourth consecutive year to teach for three months.

Another development was the sudden departure of Tilahun Bekele, a part-time English teacher, to a full-time assignment in Awassa. Just as suddenly, God provided a suitable substitute in Nancy Charles, an MCC volunteer from Winnipeg, who accepted the challenge of teaching English for the full academic year, 2005-2006.

After teaching for four years, Selamawit Stephanos was awarded a well-deserved scholarship to study at Eastern Mennonite Seminary in Harrisonburg, Virginia. She departed in late August 2005, leaving a void in our faculty and a much bigger void in the lives of her husband, Pastor Abebe Siyoum, and two children who remained behind.

Gemechu Gebre, after teaching for three years, left his post to pursue other interests.

Solomon Telahun joined the faculty as lecturer in Christian education. He was not new to the college, having served as an adjunct faculty member periodically since its beginning. Solomon came with a master's degree from the Ethiopian Graduate School of Theology (EGST). He had served MKC in many capacities, but especially as a teacher, preacher, writer, translator, editor, board member, and elder. He also had worked for six years in the Pentecostal Theological College as academic dean and lecturer.

German Mennonite Involvement

In October 2005, a delegation of eight people from the Mennonite churches in Germany and The Netherlands made a one-day visit to our college and the new campus building site. The workers were busy putting in the brick partitions and plastering them. The fraternal guests were committed to helping the Ethiopian Church. They had sent 20,000 Euros ahead of their arrival: 10,000 for the college, 5,000 for the HIV AIDS program, and 5,000 for the Wollega Bible Institute. They brought us a new video projector and two used laptop computers.

Missionary Training

Tefera Bekere Kumsa, head of the MKC Department of Missions and Evangelism, brought forty-three young men from almost every region of Ethiopia to the campus for an intensive one-month Missionary Training Program. He described the purpose of this program as "recruiting, training, equipping, transforming, and sending young adults to Gospel-needy areas, to preach and plant indigenous churches."

After completing the training, these young graduates were to be sent out as missionaries. After six months, they would be evaluated. If they passed the evaluation, they would be given an additional one-month intensive training before returning to continue their work.

Translation of Anabaptist Materials

"The teachers are Anabaptist, but the books are not." This was a common complaint heard from Amharic diploma students. Indeed, the biggest challenge in offering a diploma program in the Amharic language was the paucity in good Christian-oriented textbooks and reference works. And finding Anabaptist-oriented books in Amharic was wellnigh impossible.

The college took steps to face this problem. With a grant from MCC, it undertook to translate Anabaptist and peace textbooks. A 2004 graduate, Kassu Kebede, was employed to translate pertinent books, articles, and chapters to form a *Reader in Anabaptism* in the Amharic language. This Reader was published and made available to the public and used in the college as a textbook in the Amharic diploma program. Also, Kassu translated the little book, *Anabaptist Seed,* by Arnold Snyder, and 10,000 copies were printed.

CHAPTER 15

Renewal of the Public Relations Office

Renewal of Public Relations Activities

Upon returning to Ethiopia, besides teaching a full load, I assumed my responsibility as Interim Resource Development Director and Trainer. It was understood, by myself and my sponsors (EMM), that I was to carry this responsibility for a two-year term and that the person whom the board selected to be trained would be prepared to replace me when that time expired in August 2006.

The person assigned to work with me as "trainee" was Bedru Hussein. The weakness of this assignment was that my brother Bedru and I were almost of the same age and experience. We made a good team. I learned from him as he learned from me. However, when it became my turn to depart it would almost be his time to retire as well. My contribution as a trainer would have had a lot more meaning, for the long-range benefit of the college, if I were assigned a much younger, energetic, committed, and capable person to continue this important work in the decades to come. However, my overseers in the church did not seem to be thinking ahead that far. As it turned out, Bedru retired before I did.

I was doing many of the international aspects of this work informally since 1997, even during my "exile" in 2002 – 2004. Bedru and I officially began to work together to foster local ownership at home and to promote the Meserete Kristos College abroad.

An Unforgettable International Public Relations Trip

To meet the huge challenge of campus development, the board of trustees decided to undertake a major public relations/fundraising campaign. They requested Bedru Hussein, along with President Hailu Cherenet and me to undertake a two-and-one-half month public relations journey to the USA, Canada, Germany, and The Netherlands.

At the beginning of 2005, we began to make plans for this trip. Hundreds of pages of email correspondence resulted in an exciting itinerary. With Shalom Productions, we produced a revised edition of our promotional video and printed 6,000 copies of a new brochure. We also produced another newsletter in English and in Amharic.

The aim of this trip was four-fold: (1) to increase awareness in North America of the existence of the church in Ethiopia and what is happening there; (2) to encourage fraternal relationships between Christians in North America and their brothers and sisters in Ethiopia; (3) to visit and encourage partners who were supporting the work of the college, (4) and to reach out to others who would be willing to become partners in raising the rest of the money needed to complete the second half of this large building. This last goal was Bedru's and my main concern. We wanted to have the funds available so that when the first half of the academic building was completed, we would be ready to get started building the second half.

We were inexperienced amateurs in raising funds, and we had the serious handicap of a lack of credibility. Coming from a largely unknown, third-world country, representing a barely known church, and asking for a lot of money to build a big campus, who would believe us? Had we not been canvassing for seven years for funds to build a campus? Had we not received generous support? However, we still had no building to show for our efforts, nor for the gifts already given. Previous donors saw no results. What could convince them to give any large amount this time?

Hailu and Bedru were excellent communicators and preachers. Both were seminary graduates and had years of North American exposure.

Both could represent the Ethiopian church and college very well. I felt privileged to be their escort.

Unfortunately, Vera would not be traveling with us. In sympathy, the board encouraged her to take a vacation by going to the USA for one month to visit our children and grandchildren while I was traveling.

So, on March 30, Hailu, Bedru, and I left Ethiopia. Upon landing at Dulles International Airport, we immediately ran into a big problem that overshadowed our whole trip. The Ethiopian brothers passed through immigration and customs without any problem ahead of me. When they got to the other side, I was nowhere to be seen.

While waiting for my "green card" application to be approved, I had been traveling on a special travel abroad permit, which had expired. Therefore, when I presented my documents to USA Immigration, I was immediately charged with attempting to enter the country on an expired document—a crime! They hustled me into a private room and put me under arrest, took away my passport, and appointed a trial date set for two-and-one-half months later, July 13, 2005. Then they released me to travel as I wish within the country. I was under "house arrest," not allowed to leave the USA!

Two hours later, I emerged from Immigration to find two very worried Ethiopian brothers waiting for me. In those days, we did not yet carry mobile phones. Fortunately, they had connected with my daughter, Karen, and son-in-law, Eric Payne, who had come to pick us up, in the waiting area.

We rejoiced in our reunion. However, this complication became a dark shadow that hung over us throughout the rest of our journey. I would not be able to accompany the brothers into Canada, my home country, nor on to Germany and The Netherlands.

We made a lot of important contacts. Some of the contacts included meeting with the Link Board, and sharing with former missionaries, who fathered and mothered the Meserete Kristos Church. We preached and shared our presentations in many different congregations, ate meals and shared updates with interested donors, visited nine different denominational headquarters, and introduced ourselves to six different mission agencies. We visited eight different Christian colleges, universities, or seminaries. We also shared with small Ethiopian diaspora groups in most of the regions where we visited.

In Harrisonburg, we participated in a fundraising banquet sponsored by MK College Link Board featuring Ethiopian food. About $16,000 was raised. In Goshen we met more of the pioneer missionaries. Paul Gingrich drove us to Archbold, Ohio, to meet with the Sauder family who encouraged us with gifts amounting to $100,000.

We flew to California, and, renting a car, visited old friends and made new friends among the Ethiopian diasporas. We also visited our students at Fresno Pacific University and shared with faculty there. Then, Hailu flew to Seattle where he spoke in some churches while Bedru and I drove to Phoenix, where we spoke in three congregations. From there, we flew back to Indiana.

Retrieving our car, we continued our journey westward, visiting supporters at Reba Place in Evanston, and Lombard, Illinois. In Minneapolis, Minnesota, we talked with individuals, small groups, and spoke in three different churches. There, we parted ways. Due to the restrictions placed upon me by US Immigration, I could not accompany Hailu and Bedru to Winnipeg. They went on to Canada by Greyhound bus, and I drove the car back to Virginia.

Bedru and Hailu spent the next seven days visiting the offices of Canadian Mennonite institutions and sharing with friends and supporters in Winnipeg and Steinbach. They learned a lot, and the institutions and people contacted also learned a lot from them about Ethiopia and its Meserete Kristos Church. They then went on to Europe, spending twelve days in Germany and The Netherlands. They returned home to Ethiopia on June 15th.

While I grieved that I could not accompany my Ethiopian brothers to Canada and Europe, it felt good that the long grueling trip was over for me. We met a lot of old friends, made acquaintances with a lot of new people, spoke in many churches, showed our video many times, gave the same information about as often, and handed out our 6,000 brochures. We had covered many thousands of miles without any mishap and had only one breakdown in Ohio, remedied by a new alternator. As Bedru kept reminding us, we "planted many seeds," and it would be exciting to see how they grew!

While our aim was to raise $1.2 million for the building and equipment, we did collect $260,000. Some potentially significant pledges were made of unspecified amounts. Although we were not successful in reaching our goal, we expected more to trickle in during the weeks and months ahead.

As planned, Vera had come home to Harrisonburg for vacation in the month of June. It was good to be with her during my "imprisonment."

In the meantime, while we were waiting for my house-arrest status to get cleared, we tried to make the most of the situation by doing what we could. We collected several hundred more books for the library. We contacted Equipping the Saints, an organization that specializes in assisting missionaries and churches around the world by supplying good used equipment and furniture. Together, we collected enough used equipment to fill a 40-foot shipping container, which was sent to Ethiopia in September. The equipment included used computers, office desks and chairs, computer tables, classroom desks, hundreds of chairs, bunk beds, filing cabinets, tables, kitchen equipment, white boards, maps, projection screens, overhead projectors, library shelves, and used books.

Then, suddenly, I was informed that I should come to Washington to pick up my passport. The court case was cancelled, thanks to diligent efforts of my $4,000 lawyer!

So, early Tuesday morning, June 29th, our friend, Joe Mast, took Vera and I to Homeland Security and Immigration in Fairfax for the all-important interview for which we had waited eighteen months. After waiting inside for three-and-one-half hours (while Joe waited as long in the hot humid outside), we were surprised when the officer gave me back my passport with the permanent resident permit stamped in it! The process was complete. Imagine my joy! Even the lawyer was surprised. They would send the final "green card" in the mail in due course. Finally, I was legally a resident of the USA with all the rights and privileges, except voting.

The timing could not have been better. I received the permanent resident permit at noon. Joe and Vera took me straight to the airport at 2:00 pm, and I boarded the plane before 6:00 pm. My ticket was to expire the following day! Vera's return ticket was for the day following mine. "All is well that ends well!" We praised God that ordeal was over.

Follow-up

Upon our return, we did the necessary follow-up on the contacts we made, updated our database, prepared the July issue of our MK College Newsletter, wrote letters of thanks to those who contributed, and made a few visits to potential donors in Addis Ababa.

Fundraising is all about relationships. That year we strengthened and renewed old relationships and started a lot of new relationships. We added about 500 names of new supporters and potential supporters to our database, which grew to over 1,300 addresses in all.

We wrote a total of 487 letters of thanks to people who had made one or more gifts during that fiscal year. God had truly blessed us with many sympathetic and willing partners in this great work. Without these partners, our college would not exist.

Evaluation, a Public Relations Failure

From the beginning, those former missionaries, family members, and friends which we had approached were people who knew us and trusted us. They supported us because they knew who we were, not because of some credible track record.

Up to this time, in our external relationships, while we "sowed seed" that would grow and yield something in the months and years ahead, we were disappointed in the immediate results of our efforts. While we were thankful for each of the many hundreds of supporters, we failed to persuade the potential large donors to become partners. People capable of making large donations are wealthy because they are careful. They do not easily support causes that do not have a proven track record. And we still lacked that convincing credibility.

We tried approaching potential big donors and some foundations, but they rejected us outright because we had no track record. Now, after ten years of persistent struggle, our college was still in existence and was sending out quality graduates, and we were constructing the first building on our new campus. We had proved our staying power. We were beginning to have a track record. Was it time to approach the foundations and other donor organizations once again?

Internally, in Ethiopia, we had failed to get much meaningful financial support from our own people. We had projected it would be reasonable to expect to collect at least $65,000 from Ethiopian sources, but we only received $3,754 from local sources that year.

Another weakness was that the church executive committee members, as well as the college trustees, did not take any responsibility to raise support for their college. In the same way, those trustees neglected to keep the CDC on its toes. There was no one coordinating, doing the many things that needed to be done in time to utilize the campus when the present contract was completed. For example, nothing was being done about constructing a sewer system, a temporary kitchen, a campus gate, driveway, landscaping, planting trees, applying for additional land for a sports field, or a staff housing plot.

We invited about 150 people, mostly businesspersons, to Misrak MKC for a fundraising banquet and program on October 15, 2005. Only forty attended, mostly church leaders who were not well-to-do, and some of our underpaid staff. The businesspeople did not show up. The amount raised was only about $4,000, about enough to cover the cost of the wasted food at the event. However, in addition, the faculty, staff, and students pledged about $2,000.

However, Bedru and Mitiku followed up, contacting all the invitees who failed to come. They got more pledges and donations. It was not so bad, but we learned that having banquets is not always the best way to raise money.

Strategic Planning

On February 22 and 23, 2005, a group of seven administrators and teachers spent two days in Adama in the Adama Ras Hotel engaged in an intensive strategic planning exercise for the college. This exercise was continued for three days in August. This time it was at the Ararat Hotel for uninterrupted, twelve-hour sessions each day. It was a helpful exercise, clarifying direction and purpose.

However, to be fully effective, progress in implementing strategic plans needs to be measured and evaluated several times per year. Shortfalls must be accounted for, and plans amended. Under new leadership, this did not happen.

CHAPTER 16

Another Chaotic Leadership Transition - 2006

It had been more than a full year since we returned to work in Ethiopia. Vera had picked up her former work in the college library. She enjoyed her work and the relationships she had formed. But it was different for me. I used to be the principal and was at the center of all the action. This time I was an "emeritus." The action went on without me. I was on the sideline just in case I was needed. This was as it should be, but it took some adjustment on my part.

The new college president, Hailu Cherenet, had applied and was accepted into a PhD program at Trinity Theological Seminary in Deerfield, IL. However, his August 2005 application for visas for himself and his family was turned down flat twice by the US Embassy. Twice, they took his $600 application fee and rejected him outright without even looking at his evidence. He consoled his discouraged spirit with the realization that probably it was best for the college that he remains on duty at this moment in time.

Then, without explanation, like a lightning bolt out of the blue, in late December, Hailu received a letter from the US Embassy, notifying him that he had been granted visas to go to the USA with his wife and three of their children. Suddenly, they were preparing to leave on January 9th, 2006.

The college staff put on a farewell dinner for Hailu and his family. Hailu would be gone for PhD studies, looking to take at least four or five years. That left us unsettled one more time—three presidents in three years. Who would take his place? The MKC Executive Committee met to decide.

Then on Friday morning, the 6th of January, I was informed that the committee, in their meeting the previous night, had decided to appoint me to serve as interim president "until a search committee could find a longer-term person to be the president."

Yes, notification, appointment, and taking charge the same day. Like Saul, son of Kish, I was found, informed, and installed the same day! This came as quite a shock since I had a full-time job and since I relinquished the CEO post some three years and seven months before.

Hailu made an amazingly quick settling of his affairs, handed over the presidential office that afternoon, and departed with his family on Monday evening. He with his family were received and hosted by Reba Place Fellowship in Evanston, Illinois. I had worked closely with Hailu as a dear brother for seven years. We had been through a lot together. Suddenly, he was gone. We, especially I, would miss him terribly.

A Historic Visit with My Hansen Siblings

My interim presidency fell upon me like a bombshell and was followed by an explosion of activities. I was appointed on January 6th, moved into the president's office on the eighth, and received all my Hansen siblings, who came for a twelve-day visit to Ethiopia on the 11th.

History was made when we welcomed my four brothers, their wives, and my youngest sister in the dark of night to Addis Ababa. Yes, except for George, who visited us on his way home from India thirty-seven years earlier, this was the first time in all our years of service in Africa, that my siblings, Peter and Margaret Hansen, Paul and Irene Hansen, George and Marilyn Hansen, Charles and Wynona Hansen, and Freda King finally came to visit us. It was exciting having them all come at once. This deserved every minute of our attention as they wanted to see as much of Ethiopia as possible.

So, I left my three-day old presidential office to show them the great historic monuments at Axum, Lalibela, and Gondar; the Timket celebration on Entoto; and some of the places in which we had lived and worked including Nazareth, Sodere, and Addis Ababa. We introduced them to some of our many friends and Ethiopian "families." Of course, we had to introduce them to the college in Kotebe and the construction going on at Bishoftu. At the end of twelve days, they regretted they had not allowed themselves more time to see more of this intriguing country. They were fascinated by all they saw. They went home and became loyal supporters of our college.

After my siblings departed on the night of January 23rd, I had one day to adjust back to the presidential office before taking off for a three-day Faculty Advance in the town of Adama. It was an encouraging team-building experience.

For the next seventeen days, I faced a lot of challenges like drafting an application for more land for a sports field and staff housing at Bishoftu, doing fundraising correspondence, while preparing and teaching the first week of a new course on Peace and Justice Issues. At the same time, I was overseeing the making of heavy decisions about the building program, sorting out some staff and procedural issues, taking in forty-eight new students, and launching an extension program with thirty-two students enrolled in three courses (part-time) at Adama. It would be administered locally by church elders there but supervised by our office. Our graduates there were to do most of the teaching. At the same time, we were making the logistical preparations to welcome our first *Experience Ethiopia Tour.*

CHAPTER 17

External Resources

From the beginning, external support enabled MK College to become what it was and accomplish what it has.

Experience Ethiopia Tours

By the year 2006, our friends, Darrell and Florence Jantzi, had retired from their previous employment and volunteered to assist in promoting our college in their home province of Ontario. Darrell began soliciting friends and acquaintances, collecting money, and forwarding it to the college. Over the next fourteen years, he was the college's best fundraiser.

Together with Darrell and Florence, we had gained experience with the Tour Imagination group back in 2003, escorting them around Ethiopia for six days and then accompanying them to Bulawayo, Zimbabwe. Since that time, we planned how we could use the medium of a tour to give North Americans exposure to the country, its history and culture, and especially to the vibrant life of MKC and the challenge of training leaders through its college.

We hoped that such a tour would generate profit, which would be added to the resources needed to run the college. More than that, we hoped such tours would gain long-term friends who would support the college with their prayers, their enthusiastic promotion in their home areas, and through their generous financial support. Out of this vision emerged the *Experience Ethiopia Tours*.

The tours were advertised in our *Newsletters* and in denominational periodicals. In North America, Darrell and Florence received and processed the applications and organized the flights. We, in Ethiopia, organized the itinerary, transport, hotels, and guides. Darrell and Florence both came along with the participants and assisted with the coordination. Because of my many years and experience in the country, I was the main guide and interpreter. We always tried to include one Ethiopian staff member from the college to accompany the group within the country.

With some variations, these tours followed a basic eighteen-day itinerary that helped the participants to experience various aspects of Ethiopia. We visited some of the spectacular, UNESCO protected, historical and cultural sites such as the ruins of what is claimed to be the 3000-year-old Queen of Sheba palace, the still standing 2000-year-old seventy-nine-foot-tall monolithic Axumite stellae, the resting place of the Ark of the Covenant at Axum, the 12th century rock-hewn churches at Lalibela, and the 16th century castles at Gondar. We showed them where the pioneer missionaries lived and worked in Nazareth. We met with some of the church leaders and learned of the amazing vitality and growth of the Meserete Kristos Church, including some of its work in evangelism, development, and education. We visited a development project being implemented by the church, in partnership with MCC or the Canadian Food Grains Bank. The group also enjoyed cultural events and experienced Ethiopian hospitality and cuisine.

The tours ended with a five-day visit to Kenya, where we visited church/mission involvements in Nairobi such as Roslyn Academy, a school for missionary children; Eastleigh Fellowship Center where the Kenya Mennonite Church focuses on the needs of the poor and refugees, especially Somalis; Methare North Primary School with its 360 children living in the middle of a slum; and visited the Mennonite Guesthouse, recently re-named *Amani Gardens Inn*.

The "icing on the cake" of the whole tour was a three-day and two-night safari in the famous Maasai Mara Game Preserve. There was always an abundance of African animals in their natural habitat.

There, unlike the animals, the guests would luxuriate for two nights in the five-star Mara Serena Lodge.

One time, the group witnessed the dedication ceremony for the new men's dormitory building. Among the tour guests were those who contributed heavily to the building of that dorm.

A few times, after a night in the college's guesthouse, the group went for a pre-breakfast walk to see and hear the thousands of birds having their morning "devotions" on Lake Chelekleka across the road from the campus.

Sometimes we arranged so that the guests could eat a meal in an Ethiopian home and get a sense of local family life.

The tour usually visited the first MKC congregation in Bishoftu. That congregation was started in 1989, while the Dergue was still in power. It was given land along the lake after the fall of the Dergue and religious freedom was restored. A small temporary mud and stick chapel was constructed along the water's edge. As the congregation grew, at least four additions of pole and corrugated iron sheet roofs were added. Now it accommodates over 1,000 members and up to 2,000 people who come to their Wednesday night prayer and healing service.

The congregation also planted many "daughter" churches in that growing city. It also administered a Compassion project, which ministered to 200-300 needy children.

In addition to personal luggage, tour participants often carried from fifty to sixty NIV Study Bibles as gifts for new students, laptop computers and additional office supplies, or clothes for college students' use.

At the MKC Head Office, the group learned about the many ambitious and successful programs the church was conducting across the nation. These programs included wholistic ministries in fifty prisons, sending and supporting over 400 missionaries, some of them in Muslim countries. It also included church planting, congregational and ministerial support programs, Christian education programs, literature production and translation work, and a conflict intervention and peace promotion.

In the MKC Relief and Development (MKC-RDA) headquarters, the group learned of the sixty some projects serving needy people, including food or cash for work in famine areas, afforestation and soil conservation in famine prone areas, adult literacy, medical clinics, an HIV-AIDS program, and child sponsorship programs giving hope and a future to over 16,000 destitute children. All these activities were undertaken with the assistance of Canadian Food Grains Bank, MCC, Tear Fund, and other NGOs which supplied an annual budget of over four million dollars.

In the years between 2006 and 2019, ten tours were conducted. They all took place during the months of February and March, following the same basic itinerary. In total, 146 people participated in these tours.

These ten tours netted an overall profit of $142,093, all of which has gone to support the work of the college. More importantly, the tours have motivated many long-term partners who pray for and support the work through the years.

Miscellaneous Provisions

In January 2006, Jim and Anna Ralph from Bally, PA, arrived at the college with their seven-year-old son, Zach, and a nineteen-year-old niece, Angela. They came for three- months to train groups in prayer counselling. They lodged in the guest rooms of the college. Although their ministry was focused on the churches in different regions, their presence and interchanges with the students and staff were deeply appreciated.

While the regular students enjoyed their January break, about forty evangelists occupied the campus for a six-week refresher and learning program sponsored by the MKC Evangelism/Missions Department.

Some saints in the USA had arranged to cover the costs for Tigist Alamirew, the assistant librarian, to travel there to undergo plastic surgery to remove the scars on her face. Her two-year absence from the library left Vera in a tight situation.

Levi Weaver, retired pastor and dairy farmer from Bath, NY, a long-time supporter of the college, visited in Ethiopia for three weeks in March. Levi helped with maintenance issues around campus. He took time to teach the young Assefa Adugna basics in maintenance. Assefa has since developed to become the main maintenance person on campus. This was an excellent example of how an older retired person can mentor a younger person, passing on his/her skills in a situation where those skills are in short supply.

Anonymous Foundation Gift

On November 8, 2005, we sent a project proposal to a foundation which wished to remain anonymous. We asked for assistance in completing the academic building now under construction, bearing in mind the second half of the building.

On February 2, 2006, we received a positive reply stating they were accepting our application and decided to give us a grant of $75,000. Then, a week later, we received another letter stating they had agreed to increase the grant to $100,000 instead of the $75,000 promised. That grant was received in the month of May 2006.

From Trash to Treasure

It is an oft repeated truism that "The first world's trash is often the third world's treasure." The container, filled with trash—used items—packed by volunteers, and sent by Equipping the Saints in mid-September, reached Djibouti in mid-October. It took another six weeks to transit to Addis Customs. It sat in Customs for another seven weeks until all the import duties and taxes could be worked out and paid. It was released to the College on January 24, 2006.

Like children at Christmas, staff and students gathered in eager anticipation as a big truck backed the huge forty-foot high-cube container into the Kotebe campus's narrow gate. When the door finally opened, the crowd of volunteers surged forward with eager hands lifting down the chairs, tables, desks, bookshelves, dishes, filing cabinets, and computers. It was 4:30 p.m. that day in February when they began to unpack. Dusk settled in and sunk into night as they continued to unpack.

At 10 p.m., the last computer was removed. The container was empty, but the yard and library and staff room were full of its treasures. The rented container needed to be returned immediately. Everyone was exceedingly excited and grateful for all the good and useful treasures that it contained. The unloaders were amazed at how much a container can hold. Everything arrived in good condition.

The bad news was that Customs charged us about forty-one dollars per day for storage for the seven weeks it took to negotiate the tax. It ended up costing us about $2,000 to have the container sit in their large open empty yard. There was also the extra charge we had to pay for extending the container rental. You win some, you lose some!

That same October 2005, we had submitted a wish list to Crossroads International in Hong Kong of items we needed for the new academic building under construction. On April 3rd, 2006, the brothers and sisters in Hong Kong sent their container. This charitable organization was paying for everything, including the shipping. We would only have to pay the taxes.

That container made its way from Hong Kong through the complicated shipping and customs systems and arrived in Addis in July. This was a huge bonus and encouragement for us. It raised our inventory of chairs, tables, student desks, office desks, a few TVs, whiteboards, overhead projectors, stoves, refrigerators, cupboards, dishes, cookware, curtains, and drapes. Together, these two shipments would furnish and meet most of the needs of the new building for the first few years. Our people were grateful.

The ninety used computers were highly valued. With these, the students could learn how to type their papers and use a computer for the first time. With a new server computer and the other computers, it was now possible to computerize the library. However, later, we discovered that the true meaning of the word "used" sometimes also means "unusable." Half of the computers did not work but served as spare parts to make the other half usable.

In January 2006, with advice, encouragement, and by raising several thousand dollars, Clara Landis and Arlene Leatherman enabled the college to obtain the necessary program software and equipment to computerize the library. From 1996 up to 2006, they had written the catalogue cards and labels for over 15,000 volumes and sent them to us. To expedite this change of technology, these elderly saints ordered software from Book Systems with barcode labels and a barcode scanner. This meant the old card system was obsolete. The company printed labels for all the books that had been registered, based on the information sent to them from the beginning.

Staff Provisions

Although not new to the college as a teacher, Pastor Getaneh Ayele joined the faculty fresh from graduating with an MDiv degree from AMBS. He taught biblical and pastoral subjects. As Sheweye Yalew was away on maternity leave, her duties as Dean of Students were shared with Getaneh, who gave pastoral oversight to students as well.

Ruth Girma Ayele was hired to manage the photocopy room. Due to the excessive cost of books, most textbooks and class handouts were copied in that room.

In April 2006, the board of trustees asked our teacher, Solomon Telahun, to pick up the mantle of "College Advancement Officer," and Solomon agreed. This meant he would be working more with us in the public relations and resource development areas and less as a teacher in the classroom.

After five years of faithful service as Finance and Administrative Head, our gifted and beloved Mitiku shocked us, announcing that he would be leaving the college on the first of June. The opportunity for much better pay and career advancement proved irresistible. What a disappointment! How could we develop a bigger college without staff who are committed to working with us? And how could we keep them without more attractive pay packages?

Two months later, Amere Eshetu was hired to assume the responsibilities of Finance and Administrative Head. He came with the maturity born of many years of experience, including some years with the MKC Head Office and its Relief and Development Agency.

Appreciation for Provisions

Building the campus and desiring to increase student enrollment weighed heavily upon my mind. We had to give more attention to fundraising. The people in the First World that we were looking to and inviting to become partners needed to understand that we were a desperately poor church in a desperately poor society. We were educating 125 full-time students, including providing tuition, room, and board on a budget of less than $150,000 per year. Would this cover the costs of six students at a college in the USA? We were all making sacrifices, the teachers, the students, and especially the support staff. Yet, all these groups mentioned were extremely grateful for the privilege of teaching, of learning, and of working. Although there was nothing left for luxuries, there were only a few who complained.

One time we held a convocation with the whole student body and staff where we shared vision and information, then opened for questions and comments. I was emotionally overwhelmed by the many expressions of deep gratitude and praise to our gracious God for the very existence and growth of our college. Each felt it was a great blessing and privilege to study there. In their own sight, they were nobodies, from nowhere, the poorest of the poor, coming with nothing but their deep love for the Lord Jesus Christ and his Church. They had a deep desire to learn, so that they could return to rescue their people from the darkness of ignorance, superstition, demonic oppression, and sin. They studied, hoping to equip themselves with abilities to help their people find release from the prison of poverty with its perpetual hunger, debilitating disease, and premature death.

As such, they had no adequate words to express their deepest appreciation for every dollar of support granted by the invisible network of supporters and partners, a continent, and an ocean away. These were brothers and sisters whom they had never met and whom they would never meet—the mystery of Christian fraternity!

It is that need, that hunger, and that spirit in our students that captivated me and energized me to stay and struggle with them for the realization of the church's goals for its college.

CHAPTER 18

Challenges in the Pivotal Year 2006

Contracting a Consultancy Service

As I assumed the responsibilities of my interim presidency, I entertained a naive hope to open the new multi-disciplined programs as early as January 2007. In April 2006, cooperating with the board of trustees, we began laying the groundwork. Upon the recommendation of the General Secretary of MKC, we hired Melaku Bekele to assist us.

To speed up the process, we contracted Ethio-Education Consultants (ETEC) to work with Melaku and our team. The contract called for them to do the research and prepare all the documents needed in our application to the Ministry of Education for pre-accreditation. They began their research at the end of June.

By the end of October, the consultants presented their interim report of 370 pages in six separate documents. We distributed copies of them to thirty-four selected experts to read and make written remarks. These were professionals with experience and expertise in the areas we were considering.

These experts came together for a one-day workshop to share their comments. Their suggestions were then fed back to the consultants, who incorporated the best suggestions into their final draft report.

This draft was then presented to a validation workshop held on December 8th. On that Saturday, twenty-eight professionals participated. It was the first meeting to be held in the not-quite-finished building.

Specialty committees examined the curricula. Incorporating their suggestions, we believed we had a superior structure with administrative and financial manuals, a manpower plan, and a superior curriculum.

Almost all these twenty-eight experts were evangelical Christians, many of them members of MKC, and most of them directly involved in higher education. Their comments added immensely to the quality of the foundational documents upon which the proposed "Meserete Kristos University College" would be built. Together, these people represented some of the best thinking about education in Ethiopia. They represented a pool from which we hoped to attract some of our administrators and teachers in the years ahead.

After sorting out the suggestions gleaned from the validation workshop and incorporating the best insights into their documents, the consultants submitted their final report in February 2007. It consisted of six documents including a *Financial Manual*, an *Education Policy Manual*, an *Administrative Manual*, a *Pre-accreditation Application*, a 100-page *Curriculum* document, and a seventy-seven-page document describing what they renamed as the *Meserete Kristos University College*. These documents represented serious work and a good foundation upon which to launch a quality program.

Beams of Optimism

The African saying, "A guest is a blessing," was proved true again in the summer of 2006 when six visiting professors from the USA and Canada—John Peters, Peter Frick, Fanosie Legesse, John Miller, Doris Miller, and Dalton Reimer—brought fresh insights and excitement to the summer school. Dalton Reimer team-taught a course on peacemaking with Girma Kelecha of Ethiopia. All, except Fanosie, were older people representing a great treasure trove of experience and wisdom. The students were very pleased.

Vera and I set out on our scheduled home leave for the two-month period, May 24 to August 2. Like we often did, Vera and I put work ahead of family. We began our home leave by fundraising for a week in Ontario. There, we had a reunion supper with members of the first Experience Ethiopia Tour. We were mightily encouraged when that small group collectively pledged to give $100,000 for the building fund by December.

Flying to Alberta, we spent three weeks with our siblings and friends. We spoke in three different supporting churches on Sundays. It was only afterward that we went to Virginia, to spend the month of July with our children and grandchildren before returning to Ethiopia.

Later, in October, the Northwest Mennonite Conference formalized a relationship with the Meserete Kristos College. They signed an agency agreement, opening a direct legal way for funds to travel from Canada to Ethiopia.

The prospect of Pyramid Construction completing the academic building and the moving of our campus from Kotebe to the new campus in Bishoftu in January 2007, was becoming an exciting possibility.

After the summer classes ended and the guest lecturers departed, about 100 student leaders representing Christian organizations on the campuses of various state universities came for a fellowship and training time for two weeks.

A Praying College

The MK College was born in prayer and sustained by the prayers of many people, both at home in Ethiopia and abroad. The provision of scholarships were the answers to the prayers of many evangelists, pastors, and lay leaders who earnestly cried out to God for an opportunity to study to develop their gifts and ministry skills.

Prayer continued to be an integral part of campus life. Students had their private prayers as they wished when they rose in the morning. Some of the teachers began their lectures with a brief time of prayer. There was chapel time each morning and prayer time every evening. On Fridays, they began the day with fasting, devoting the morning to a communal time of prayer and intersession in lieu of classes.

The question was not to pray or not to pray, but rather, how much prayer is the right amount in a busy and demanding academic setting, where students complain they could not get their assignments done? And should participation be compulsory? Some dared to raise this question. Opinions differed. However, most complied with the expectations, perhaps not wanting to risk appearing less pious. In visiting the campus in recent years, I noticed that many students found it convenient to skip some of the chapel services and prayer meetings. God knows their hearts and intentions.

For a seminary to not degenerate into a cemetery, it needs to encourage students to keep up and deepen their personal relationships with God through meaningful spiritual exercises.

Fall Semester 2006

At the end of August 2006, the fall semester began with a certain amount of confusion mixed with hope. First, the academic dean had taken a leave of absence without my approval yet tried to control things from his place of residence in Fresno, California. His wife was also with him, having taken maternity leave to give birth in Fresno. The absence of these vital people left a gap in the teaching faculty. We had to resort to more part-time teachers.

A young man, Zegaye Tadessa, was hired to work with Vera as assistant librarian. With his help, Vera downloaded the library software and started the process of entering the 15,000 library books into the computer. Zegaye spent a lot of his time assisting staff members with their computer problems.

Bekele Bedada from Bahar Dar, one of our outstanding graduates, was hired and taught for two years. He was then awarded a scholarship to do graduate studies at the Mennonite Brethren Biblical Seminary in Fresno in January 2007.

We were blessed with three volunteer teachers. Sonya Stauffer Kurtz of Colgate Divinity School, Rochester, New York, USA, taught a course on Anabaptist History and Thought. She came to Addis Ababa with her husband, Roger Kurtz, a Fulbright scholar who was doing research on African literature, and their two sons. Sonya taught for the full semester.

On October 13, 2006, our first teacher from Asia arrived. Hironori Minamino was a pastor of a Mennonite Brethren Congregation in Osaka, Japan. He taught a two-week course on *The Prophetic Books*. His two biggest challenges were learning to eat injera b'wat and rice without chopsticks or forks and teaching in the English language.

Ron Klaus, of Goshen, Indiana, USA, also taught a block course on *Pastoral Theology* for two weeks. Ron was traveling around the world promoting and teaching new concepts of the church as a community of disciples. Other senior courses were suspended while the students concentrated on taking those two block courses.

Attempt to Acquire Additional Land

The land grant given for the college was much too small for the kind of campus we envisioned. Our appeal, six months earlier, to the mayor of Bishoftu to add more land was rejected. Melaku encouraged me to go together, bypassing the mayor, and make our appeal directly to the president of Oromiya. He knew some of the people at the president's office in Addis.

At the end of August, Melaku and I were finally granted an audience with the president. We presented our case to *Abadula*, (meaning "Father of the big stick" as he was affectionately called.) He was a former Minister of Defense and a well-known retired general. He promised to come out personally with the mayor of Bishoftu "on Tuesday next week" to see the site and to give us additional land if what he saw us doing gained merit in his sight. He even said, "If what I see is favorable, I can even give you the whole mountain." That would give us access to the crater lake up the hill behind the campus. This would be a great incentive to develop the retreat center idea right there on the mountain as we first envisioned. We returned excited.

But our hope was short lived. On Monday, we received an apology by phone, saying the president could not come on the appointed day as his superiors in the Federal Government had called him to appear at an EPRDF (the ruling party) meeting in Tigray. However, he promised he would give us a call "as soon as possible." Melaku and I waited, but the call never came. After making many futile trips to the president's office, we finally gave up the plan. We never saw Abadula again.

The dream of developing a retreat center on additional land was finally squelched in 2009. The municipality decided to develop the entire hillside, surveying and selling plots to individual developers to cover it with hotels and residential houses.

The discredited former socialist government had terraced the steeply sloping hillside and planted a forest, turning it into a protected community park. Now, with it being sold to private hands, the citizenry went up and cut off the entire forest in a few days. Then bulldozers cut through the terraces, developing rough access "streets." A few entrepreneurs started laying foundations but were not able to complete anything before the government halted all development. Under the direction of UNESCO, the hill surrounding Hora Lake was declared to be a protected cultural heritage site.

Since then, in response to Prime Minister Abye Ahmed's initiative to plant 4.7 billion trees, the municipality rallied the people to turn the whole hillside back into forest.

Knowing how governments come and go, and how policies change with them, is the vision of having a retreat center built on the hill totally dead? Out of the picture?

CHAPTER 19

Migrating to the Permanent Campus

Progress, or the lack thereof, in constructing the academic building was a major cause of frustration. Having started construction two-and-one-half years earlier, the building was supposed to have been completed in sixteen months, which was October 2005. Due to shortages of materials and other excuses, the contract was amended, pushing the completion date ahead to April 2006, and then to August.

In August, they assured us that the building would be done by October. In good faith, we set our goal to start the spring semester in the new campus on February 4, 2007. That meant we must move the whole college from Kotebe to the new permanent campus at Bishoftu in January.

Such was the plan. However, the reality was that Pyramid Construction kept falling behind, extending completion dates passed October to November. Then it was Christmas, then January, and the finishing touches were still not done.

The college needed to make separate arrangements to have the septic tank and sewer system constructed. We felt we should not start this construction while Pyramid Construction was still occupying the construction site. There would be confusion and maybe hostility with two or more companies occupying the same construction site. Earlier, we assumed their finishing date of October gave us a three-month window of time to build the sewer system, temporary kitchen, dining hall, and toilet/wash house block.

However, as our moving deadline approached, we could not wait any longer. We had to take the undesirable action of placing three separate construction crews to work in the same yard in which Pyramid was still working. Therefore, while the contractor went about adding those final changes to the building, we contracted Tibebu Endeshaw to construct a septic tank and drainage system. He worked on that during November and December 2006.

Also, there were other campus functions for which the academic building was poorly suited. First, there was no place for a kitchen nor a dining facility. While we could sleep a hundred men in rooms designed for classrooms and office space on the fourth floor, the toilet facilities were inadequate. Also, the basement of the library could be used as a temporary assembly hall and chapel, but where could we put the stacks for the library books?

Therefore, we hired Araya Selassie Zemichael, a 65-year-old retired builder, to design and construct a kitchen, dining hall, and washrooms behind the large permanent building. These were to be simple, one level structures, large enough to accommodate the immediate need of 250-350 students.

Complications and Disappointments Along the Way

I felt overwhelmed by chaos in the fall semester of 2006. The dean had manipulated the board, in my absence, to grant him the three-month leave. With the dean being absent and his stand-in being ineffective, there was a certain amount of anarchy in managing the academic performances.

Solomon Telahun, who began working with me in public relations along with teaching responsibilities, assumed his role with enthusiasm and lots of creative ideas. However, he soon clashed with the dean on many issues. This made it difficult for him to work with integrity. The board and its chairperson failed to support him or to help him work out the differences and bring reconciliation with the dean.

Sadly, one year after his appointment, as we were struggling to meet our moving deadline, Solomon handed in a letter of resignation which was accepted without comment or protest by the board chair. His letter of resignation was really a cry for a hearing, a symptom of a conflict, a cry for a change within our administration, which the board failed to address properly. In those days, the board was only listening to the academic dean. Solomon was bitterly disappointed. In Solomon, the college lost another good man.

Consequently, in the years following, the college's leadership continued to neglect promoting awareness among the congregations, raising funds in the country, and improving its relations with sister denominations and with the public in general. While I continued carrying the responsibility of relating the college to the world outside, there was no one assigned to strengthen its relationships within Ethiopia. Obviously, our team had a leadership problem.

A few days later, more unwelcome news came in the form of another letter of resignation, effective by the end of January. This one was from Amere Eshetu, the finance and administrative head. This was the second person to resign from that position since April. Behind it, there were some of the same reasons. Sadly, no one in leadership seemed to notice that there was a big problem brewing in the college.

Then there was the long delay of the consultancy service in producing its final report. When it was finally submitted at the end of December, we were facing all the challenges of moving to our new campus. This was not the time to implement the decisions it called us to make. All those decisions had to be delayed accordingly.

For an experienced administrator working in a similar setting, some of these delays would have been anticipated as a part of the reality. As an inexperienced administrator, I felt like a novice traveler looking at a mountain range in the distance. It looks quite straightforward, and one might estimate that it would not take long to reach the top. But as one gets closer, many previously hidden foothills and ridges pop up that one must climb over, and many curves and switchbacks one must negotiate before reaching the top. From a distance, they were not even visible, but they are a part of the larger reality. So, it is with a novice founding a liberal arts college in a setting where it has never been done before.

In the face of the consultancy lagging a few months behind and the building contractor continuing to fall further behind in each of his promises, the New Year moving date steadily, persistently, unstoppably, kept inching closer each day. I felt further disappointment on seeing that the board also took the side of the dean in his hostility towards me, as he tried to undermine my interim presidency.

My impatience and frustrations were sorely tried. There seemed to be such slow progress, so little to show for our investment of time and energy. It was one of those times which I experienced too often, of "living in the almost, but not yet." Everything was almost done, but nothing was really done. I felt it was time to turn the responsibilities over to a younger person, yet the presidential search was also in a state of limbo, never concluding.

I had been appointed to serve as interim president for a period of "from six months to one year." However, three months passed before the trustees even met to activate a search committee. And seven months passed before the vacancy announcement got posted in the regions of MKC. As the anniversary of my appointment approached, a replacement candidate had not yet been selected, though there were several names on the list.

Rejoicing in Achievements

As the old year 2006 passed, while we could not avoid the reality of serious disappointments, there were important achievements, blessings to give us courage, if we remembered to count them.

On the positive side, all were happy to see the first half of the academic building take its final shape. This sturdy concrete structure exuded beauty and quality in all its aspects. Its five floors offered forty-five spacious rooms with a total of 27,000 ft^2 of floor space, three times that of the former rented Kotebe campus. Although this large structure was only half of the total academic building design, it was large enough to accommodate the whole college including library, dormitory, classrooms, chapel, and offices, except for the kitchen and dining facility under construction outside. Visitors were surprised and made many complimentary remarks.

The academic building nears completion, November 2006

The academic building ready for occupancy, January 2007

Preparing to Move

The big challenge for December 2006 and January 2007 was the preparation and relocation of the entire college from its congested, rented, Kotebe campus to its new home forty-five kms away on the northern edge of Bishoftu. To facilitate this move, we loaded Araya Selassie Zemichael with the additional responsibility of moving coordinator.

As soon as Tibebu's' crew finished constructing the septic tank, they began to construct the much-needed transformer/generator house, so the electricity and water could be connected.

To open an extension campus in Addis, the dean facilitated the renting of a small office and space for a classroom and a computer room, large enough to continue with our Addis extension classes plus opening a computer class as well.

Moving was further complicated by the fact that we had agreed to host a six-week training of fifty new missionaries on the old campus. This would be completed on January 17th.

Transferring the library, setting up the computer labs, and arranging offices and furniture were done while the training was going on. The kitchen, beds, and classroom furniture were moved following that date. That meant that, after the students left, we had two weeks to vacate the premises, repaint, and restore the campus to its original condition, so it could be returned to the owner by the end of January.

At the same time, we needed assistance in setting up the college's computers. The ninety used computers were of assorted brands and ages, either Pentium II's or III's. We needed someone to make sure they all worked and to organize them into two computer labs, one at Bishoftu, and the other in the rented building in Addis where we envisioned a city extension campus.

"Partners in Mission" Volunteers

Ken Horst and Philip Rhodes of the Partners in Mission Program of Virginia Mennonite Missions organized and sent a work team of five men and two women to help facilitate the move. The seven great young people were eager to work and willing to try new things and learn as they went. Their leader, Rick Gullman, was a pastor who grew up in

Ethiopia as a missionary kid. The rest, Dale Brubaker, Josh Helmuth, Eric Showalter, Amanda Showalter, Philip Rhodes, and Gloria Good were all members of the Dayton Mennonite Church.

These seven arrived on Friday night, January 12, 2007, and were housed in the guest rooms on the Kotebe campus. As a part of their welcome and orientation the next morning, they were given a tour of the city. Then they were introduced to the exotic pleasure of Ethiopian cuisine at the Yod Abyssinia Hotel. The next day, being Sunday, they visited the Misrak Addis Ababa Meserete Kristos Church in the morning and the Mennonite Central Committee headquarters in the evening.

Kelly McDonald, a Virginia businessperson, had invested time and money, preparing five suitcases full of computer-related items, and sent them ahead with the work team. He would follow later. Unfortunately, these five suitcases of electronic equipment were held back at the airport for customs payment and clearance. This was an unexpected inconvenience as the group started their work on Monday morning. Bedru and Rick spent the next three days going back and forth to customs at the airport to get the suitcases cleared. This made a significant dent in Rick's contribution, given the two-week limit on their stay.

Customs inconvenience aside, the work team did an impressive job in those two weeks. They dismantled the temporary tin and plastic structures at Kotebe that we had made when we transformed the residence into a campus. They cleaned and painted most of the former campus buildings inside and out. They tied up around 16,000 library books into manageable bundles for easy transport. They loaded and unloaded trucks that took books, furniture, and equipment to the new campus and assembled the steel bookshelves we received from Equipping the Saints. They assembled thirty-five new computer desks, which we had purchased for the lab at Bishoftu. They served with diligence and love for two weeks, then departed on January 26th. We wished they could have stayed for one more week.

Kelly McDonald came as a volunteer to set up the computer labs. At the same time Peace Works, a non-profit organization in Ontario,

Canada, also sent their man, Soon Lem, to assist with this computer challenge. Soon and Kelly worked together very well.

Kelly and Soon arrived two days before the work team departed for home. They lodged with us. They assembled the computer networks for the two labs. They also worked at networking the library.

To ensure ongoing maintenance and success after their departure, we assigned Zegaye, the new librarian who showed a keen interest in computers, to work alongside Kelly and learn as much as he could. He later would also teach the first computer class.

Kelly chose to use Linux as the base operating system rather than Microsoft. Linux was less susceptible to viruses, used free software, and had no licensing issues. This was good until some years later, when MCC sent us another computer expert who did not like Linux. He changed the operating systems back to Microsoft. The virus problems returned.

The lure of freeware was overcome by the fact that we could buy almost any kind of pirated software from the local shops for a ridiculously cheap price. In any poor nation, pirated software becomes the norm. We succumbed to temptation as well at times. Right or wrong, the general feeling was that Bill Gates made his money and could afford to subsidize our efforts in educating the poor of this world. Is there a place for situational ethics? In Ethiopia, the rules bend a little now and then, and sometimes quite a bit!

As a non-literate computer person, I had no idea how big the task was to get the used computers up and running with operating systems and software installed in two different computer labs in two locations, plus networking our library and offices, and all in two weeks. When it was finally done, about fifty-five of the computers were found to be usable. The others supplied spare parts. We were grateful that both Kelly and Soon were available at the same time. They worked harmoniously to do this great service for our people.

Kelly and Soon came at the most challenging time possible, considering that we were busy moving the college and also our home where they were lodged. They adapted to the confusing conditions and worked hard at their tasks. They even helped load our personal furniture into a truck when the time came. They networked thirty-two computers for one computer classroom and seventeen for another, even though they found the power source unacceptably low and some of the electrical wiring in the new building not connected. They also helped set up a computer network in the library, so that we could use computers rather than the old card file system to keep track of books.

They kept up their sense of humor despite trying conditions. They experienced long hours driving to and from Bishoftu each day, both the joys of empty roads and the more frequent terrors of congested roads, invisible potholes on dark nights, and "barbaric" drivers. They enjoyed the native food and tolerated our own offerings.

The construction of the kitchen and dining shelter was moving forward but was not finished within the allotted time for school to begin on February 4th. We were frantically trying to move things ahead, but there was no cooperation from the contractor at the main building. There were still no locks on the doors of the offices or classrooms. We started to move things, despite that fact. Our local team was loading, sending, and unloading about four smaller Isuzu truckloads of materials per day, thirty-two truckloads in all.

By February 3rd, when the students arrived on the new campus, most of the moving was complete. The new semester opened with registration on time the next day. We did not have a grand opening or dedication ceremony. There was no time. We had been too stressed to plan anything.

We moved in, not because we were ready, but because of the semester's starting date. We were determined to start on time at the new premises, and we did. The telephone service was not ready to be connected. We just got the water hooked up the week before. When it was turned on, some major leaks appeared. The most disturbing were the leaks that seeped through the upstairs bathroom floor, dropping water down on the books stored in the library below. The contractor was to have tested the plumbing in advance—incomplete work. There were problems with inadequate electricity. Some sockets did not seem to be connected—again, shoddy work.

The kitchen and dining hall were still waiting for their roofs.

The cooks were happy to be pealing carrots and onions out in "God's kitchen." They cooked food for 110 students over an open wood fire in a tin shelter. The students filled their plates and found a shady spot out in "God's dining hall" to eat their meals with gratitude, special gratitude for the fact it was not the rainy season.

February 5 was orientation day for the students at their new campus. I was unable to attend, due to hosting Kelly and Soon in Addis, on their last day in Ethiopia. When they completed work on the Addis computers, we helped them do some last-minute shopping, took them out for dinner, then took them to the airport that night. Motivated by the love of God, these volunteers came and served a people they had never met, at their own expense.

Classes started on time, but construction workers mingled in the halls with the students, adding the finishing touches and fixing the systems. Having no locks on office doors meant we had to hire more guards to keep an eye on things.

This move was traumatic for the whole college, especially for the faculty and staff, who either had to uproot their spouses and children and move to Bishoftu, or commute ninety minutes each way, every day. The general attitude of students and staff, despite inconveniences, was one of gratitude and praise to God for enabling us to finally reach our long-awaited goal.

Some of the support staff moved, along with the college from Addis Ababa, renting rooms in the local community in Bishoftu. Vera and I also rented a house there and moved our things before the semester began. For those who found it inconvenient to move, we rented a service bus to collect them in the morning. and return them to Addis each evening.

To complicate things, that same opening day, our building supervisor, Araya Selassie, was involved in an accident with the college pickup truck. It was heavily loaded with too many corrugated iron sheets. Araya, driving faster than he should, lost control, and the truck overturned. He and Mamo, the purchasing agent, not wearing seatbelts, were thrown out and badly bruised, but conscious. They were rushed to a hospital in Addis and checked for broken bones and internal injuries.

We were all thankful that they were both discharged at the end of the examination. The truck was not so blessed. It had to spend many weeks in the recovery ward of the auto hospital.

The medical examination was superficial, for later Araya was diagnosed with three broken ribs and a punctured lung that took painful years to heal. He was unable to continue his contract with the college.

CHAPTER 20

Development Under New Leadership

A New President

It took more than a year for the board of trustees and their appointed Presidential Search Committee to reach a decision. The advertisement to receive nominations yielded seventeen applications or suggestions. Of these, the committee produced a short list inviting them to apply. Seven applied. As the committee members studied these applications, some of the members expressed dissatisfaction with all of them. Then, someone suggested, "Why not Negash Kebede?" Negash was not among those who applied, and his age was greater than the committee's parameters. However, somehow, this idea appealed to the committee. So, they approached Negash inquiring of his interest and availability. Negash responded positively.

Therefore, at its next meeting, the board decided to offer Negash Kebede the position of president of Meserete Kristos College. This action was approved by the Executive Committee of MKC. Negash was appointed to a four-year term, beginning March 1, 2007. That was only two weeks away from notification. Negash was able to terminate his services as principal of the Dandi Bora School with immediate effect. (I am ashamed to say that no one ever officially informed the other seven applicants of the board's decision.)

Negash Kebede, president of MK College, 2007-2012

An inaugural ceremony was held in the library basement of the new campus in Bishoftu, on Sunday afternoon, March 11ᵗʰ. Among the important guests who came to participate were fifteen from the 2ⁿᵈ Experience Ethiopia Tour.

Negash brought with him a lifetime of experience in education and leadership. Born in Bedeno, Ethiopia, he received his elementary education there at the Mennonite Mission School. He graduated from secondary at the Nazareth Bible Academy in 1963. He earned a Bachelor of Science (BSc) degree from Haile Selassie I University in 1969. Negash joined the staff of the Bible Academy in 1970, and served as math and physics teacher, academic dean, and for five years as director. There, he met and wed Janet Shertzer, a missionary teacher colleague formerly of Lancaster, Pennsylvania.

During a four-year break in the USA, Negash earned a Master of Science (MSc) in education physics and was a candidate for a Doctor of Education (DEd) degree at Temple University. Without completing the thesis, he and Janet returned to Ethiopia in 1979 where he resumed his post for another four years as director of the Bible Academy. This was just after the "Red Terror" was subsiding and intellectuals were fleeing in the opposite direction. People thought he was mad to return at that time.

In January 1982, Negash was arrested and imprisoned because of his position as chairperson of the Meserete Kristos Church, which was being closed by the Marxist Military Government. During his four-and-one-half year incarceration, he served as health officer to 350 inmates and as a high school teacher and unit leader in an education program for the prisoners. He was released in 1986.

From 1987 to 2004, Negash taught physics and math at the International Community School in Addis. At the time of this invitation, he was serving as principal of Dandi Boru School. He was my age, yet still jogging the annual twenty-km marathon to raise money for Cheshire Home.

People wondered what I would do after March 1st. I had been down this road before. This was my second time relinquishing the CEO position in this college. I felt relief. I was tired and happy to turn over the heavy responsibilities to a national whom I respected and trusted.

The board asked me to continue in the role of Director of College Advancement. First, I would lead the Experience Ethiopia Tour '07 for eighteen days, take a two-week vacation in Kenya, then return to help plan for the upcoming liberal arts program. We expected it to begin in late August. I was also planning for a fundraising trip in May and June to USA and Canada. Then, in the fall I would resume teaching. That was my plan.

The Kenya vacation never happened. Vera's mother passed away while we were in Kenya completing our tour in Maasai Mara. As soon as we returned to Ethiopia, Vera flew to America for the funeral instead.

Building the Campus

As indicated earlier, our plan to immediately start construction of the second half of the academic building had been suspended, as we constructed the urgently needed kitchen, dining hall, latrine, transformer house, and a workshop. With these in place, we turned our attention to constructing a guesthouse and a dormitory for men.

Construction of the kitchen, dining hall, and toilet block began in December 2006, and progressed through the hectic business of moving.

It was not nearly complete when Araya Selassie had his tragic accident which took him out of the picture.

Amere Eshetu, who had officially resigned, extended his service as Finance and Administrative Head to fill the gap left by Araya as best he could until Negash took over the role of building supervisor. Negash was keen to get the campus developed before launching new programs.

By the end of March, those buildings were nearing completion. The kitchen workers moved out of the sunshine and into the kitchen, although it was not yet complete. Water pipes needed to be connected, and the wiring finished. Some plastering remained to be done before painting could be completed.

In mid-May, construction was started on a ten by twenty-meter workshop. The architect's plans were modified, using hydro form blocks instead of the traditional cement block and plaster materials. A local private contractor built it for $40,000 rather than the earlier estimated figure of $65,000.

Tibebu Endeshaw completed his contract for building the transformer/generator house for the equivalent of $60,000.

A Guesthouse

At the same time, my brother, Charles Hansen, and some of his friends, mostly from Duchess Mennonite Church in Alberta, Canada, undertook a special project. They contributed around Cdn $136,000 toward the construction of a $210,000 guesthouse.

Accordingly, on December 3, 2007, another contract was signed. Again, hydra form blocks were used for the walls instead of cement. The blocks were clear sealed on the outside and plastered and painted on the inside. Construction started immediately and was completed the following September 2008.

The guesthouse was a two-story building with six bachelor suites and two two-bedroom family apartments. Three bachelor suites shared a common kitchen and living space on each level. Each bedroom had its own bathroom. Very adequate. It had a full-length front veranda on each level.

The family apartments were designed to accommodate volunteer or missionary families who would come to teach or support the college. The suites were to be used by visiting teachers, single volunteers, and single missionaries. It was fully occupied in the years immediately following. It has blessed expatriate missionaries and volunteers with the security of a home. This guesthouse is sometimes available for rent to local people or groups, as opportunity arises, and serves as an additional source of revenue for the college. Much thanks is given to the generous folks in Canada who provided this facility.

Negash, as a new CEO, needed to process the building decisions himself. His character was such that he did not automatically accept past decisions that could still be changed until he had studied, evaluated, and considered alternatives. We modified the original plan for the guesthouse, making it smaller, more practical, and $50,000 cheaper. With the dorm, we made a complete circle regarding the shape and quality of materials to be used. Basically, we returned to what the architects designed in the first place, although there were modifications in the design that saved money.

The MK College guesthouse, opened in September 2008

Chapel, kitchen, guesthouse, and workshop,
all built in 2007 and 2008

The Case for Building Dormitories

By the fall of 2007, thirteen years since its founding, we felt it was high time to start the long-promised liberal arts programs. The ETEC consultants had done their work and submitted their report and suggestions in January. We hoped to launch the first of the programs immediately. However, there remained one major obstacle. Accommodating a large intake of students would require dormitory space, which we did not have.

We were too far from the centers of population to attract enough day students. Since there were almost no boarding facilities on private college campuses, parents would be willing to pay to place their child in a secure Christian environment. Dormitories would pay for themselves in time.

After housing the 110 students on the upper floor of the academic building for one semester, we realized that crowding too many students into the large classrooms was not ideal. Its sanitary facilities, designed for office use, were not suitable for a large resident student population. It became clear that the next priority should be to build two dormitories before launching the liberal arts programs.

It was a simple business principle. To become self-sustaining, we needed paying students. To attract paying students, we needed decent accommodation. We had classrooms, offices, a library, dining room, and kitchen facilities. Dormitories must be our next priority.

We had little money in the building fund, and, with all our commitments, we did not have the organization to raise the funds needed. The Link Board in the USA disappointed me in clearly rejecting our expectation that it would be an active partner in raising funds through volunteer or employed full-time fundraisers. The Daystar model had six full-time fundraisers in the USA. We did not have even one.

Borrowing money from a bank or any lending source was not considered by a poverty-stricken church that operated on a policy of pay as you go. Leaders would not even think of taking the risks associated with debt.

Negash and I decided to adapt the original architectural design and immediately start construction of one complete dormitory for men. This one would be four floors tall and would have ninety-six rooms. We would start the second one a few months later, if we saw the money coming in. If we could get the men into a new dorm, we could keep up to one hundred women upstairs in our academic building while the second dorm was being built. We began construction in December 2007.

Negash tried using the new shop as a temporary dorm while the men's dorm was being built. However, amid bitter complaining by some of the men about how cold it was, he relented, and the beds were moved back to the fifth floor of the Academic building.

Since he took office as president, Negash bypassed the defunct Campus Development Committee. To build the men's dorm, he decided the college would be its own contractor. He, being the president and having experience in building, would be in charge. He contracted out the labor to Israel Abate, an ambitious young man who proved to be very competent and helpful. Negash and the college's purchasing committee bought the materials. By purchasing the materials and supervising the labor, Negash was able to save considerable construction costs.

The method of construction, being labor intensive, went terribly slow. By the end of May 2008, the foundation was laid, and a year later the walls reached the roof stage. Due to the ongoing building boom, there was a constant shortage of materials, skilled labor, and escalating prices. At one point, after a two-month delay in construction, due to the unavailability of cement, a shipment of 300 quintals arrived at the steep price of twenty-nine dollars per quintal. By comparison, when the first building was started a few years earlier the price was six dollars per quintal.

Being our own contractor saved money but took much of President Negash's time and energy. There were problems with supplies, problems with keeping workers, problems with purchasing, problems with coordination, and problems with decision- making. Looking on from the sidelines, one could find plenty of faults; however, we realized this was a new venture for all of us. It would be, at the end, a great achievement to be able to say, "We did it ourselves!"

According to Ethiopian tradition, when construction of a new building reaches a certain stage, a cow or sheep is slaughtered, and a feast is prepared as a reward for all those who worked so hard to get it to that point. One Tuesday, to celebrate the completion of block laying, an ox was compelled to lay down its life. The workers and staff gathered in the new building where they were treated to a heaping plate of roasted meat and/or big chunks of raw meat, consumed with bread and a soft drink. All were happy as the employers' demonstrated appreciation for their sacrifice and hard work. Such gestures enhanced the laborers' morale.

A contribution of 10,000 Euros sent by the Dutch Mennonites in 2008, enabled us to buy and ship 440 used dorm beds from the USA. Responding to our application, they sent another gift of 20,000 Euros, which enabled the college to purchase locally- manufactured, high-quality foam mattresses for the beds.

A historic moment occurred on October 7th, 2010, when about 180 delegates and guests converged on the college campus to participate in the church's 81st General Assembly. The venue itself was a highlight for the delegates. The occasion marked the first time the church held its meeting on its own new college campus. The completion of forty-eight rooms, the first half of the new dorm, provided ample accommodation for all the delegates.

Following the General Assembly, the male students moved into the dormitory for the fall semester. Compared with the accommodation they had endured in the past, the students felt this was a step up into the lap of luxury. Construction of the second half continued until late 2011.

Four years and two months after the first turning of the soil, the long-anticipated ceremony of dedication of the fully completed dormitory was held on February 11, 2012. The timing was such that international guests, taking the Experience Ethiopia Tour, could also attend. Among the guests were those who had contributed financially to the building of this dorm. It was a time of rejoicing and thanksgiving.

High honors were due to President Negash Kebede, who saved at least $300,000 by personally undertaking the contractor role at great cost to himself. He labored day and night, contracting out the labor and supervising the quality of their work. He shopped diligently for the building materials, comparing prices and quality of materials, then making purchases and arranging transportation.

His perseverance paid off in bequeathing to future generations a very impressive white building, standing four stories tall and sixty meters long. It was of superb quality and elegant beauty, providing ninety-six rooms with a capacity for up to 384 men. In a period of intense inflation and economic stress, the building of this dormitory at an overall cost of $775,000 was truly remarkable.

A special tribute is also due to Israel Abate, who contracted the labor. As a contractor, this young man did not hesitate to don work clothes and engage himself, with his own sweat and soiled hands, in every aspect of the construction. He worked alongside and encouraged his crew. Together they performed a service of the highest caliber.

This building would never have been possible without the generous partnership of hundreds of well-wishers and unseen partners in Canada, the USA, the Netherlands, and Germany. Special thanks to Mr. Harry Voortman of Voortman Cookies of Burlington, Canada, who contributed the final $200,000, enabling the completion of this project.

Among the dozens of laborers sweating in the hot equatorial sun, who can forget the eighteen-year-old volunteer, Alex Freeman from Ontario, Canada? He spent three months without pay, sweating bare chested, alongside hardened Ethiopian workers with hammer and chisel. Together they dug forty-three holes, two meters deep by two meters square, in the volcanic rock for the sturdy foundation upon which this edifice stands.

Men's and women's dormitories

A Terraced Garden Turned into a Student Lounge

The original Campus Master Plan called for a graceful garden terrace in front of the U-shaped academic building. It would be a pleasant outside space with clusters of tables and chairs, where students could relax, visit, or study.

In disregard for the master plan, President Negash decided to construct a roof over the terrace. As the roof took shape, he decided to install hydro form walls, then a cement floor. At first his plan was that the structure would serve as a temporary dining hall, then it was to be a meeting hall and study area, and by the time it reached completion, it had evolved into a student lounge and coffee shop with a TV and an extra meeting room.

The overall cost of this structure came to about $29,000. It served, and still serves, as a practical addition to the campus, but it did not blend into the architect's sense of an esthetically attractive front of the major academic building.

The Poultry Project.

Four friendly German volunteers arrived on November 5, 2009. Their arrival followed a German Mennonite Church contribution of 20,000 Euros to launch a poultry project on campus. Rüdiger Fellman, a seventy-nine-year-young farmer, led the group. He had been to Ethiopia two years earlier and spoke a little English. He came along with his slightly younger wife, Lieselotte, Kurt Beutler, a sixty-six-year-old carpenter, and Robert Beutler, his kid brother who was a mere fifty-nine. Together, they hoped to build an eight-by-ten-meter poultry house with a 500-hen capacity in two weeks.

It did not turn out to be that simple. President Negash's vision of what a poultry house ought to be was quite different than the Germans envisioned. The Germans expected to construct a simple stone and mortar foundation, a cement floor, simple block half walls with screened-in top walls and roofed with eucalyptus rafters and corrugated iron sheets.

Negash's vision was more like building a regular house on an elevated foundation with cement block walls plastered on the inside and out, with small windows, and steel door. Since he was president, it went his way, but the Germans were frustrated. Forty students assisted with getting a proper stone foundation in place, three feet above ground. The foundation then had to be filled with rock material, upon which to pour a concrete slab floor. The whole project took months to complete. The German volunteers went home, having only photos of the foundation to remember their accomplishments.

The vision of having a chicken project on our college campus was good. We anticipated four benefits. Chickens would convert the waste from the kitchen and dining hall into eggs and meat. Eggs would supplement students' diets, and any surplus could be sold on the market.

Chicken manure would fertilize the campus vegetable plots, helping to produce more food for the dining hall. Caring for the chickens would earn pocket money for the neediest of students. Finally, the project would provide a practical demonstration and direct learning experience that students could emulate in their areas of service in the future.

Again, the vision and reality did not mesh. The 500 pullets were purchased and installed in cages where they grew and produced a lot of eggs. The administration did not use kitchen scraps nor green alfalfa to supplement their feeding. They purchased all the chicken food from a feed mill. Also, students were not given any responsibility for caring for them. They assigned two women to care for the chickens. Hence the profit margin decreased, and kitchen scraps ended up in the garbage pit.

CHAPTER 21

Other Developments in 2007

Graduation

After days of frantically cleaning up the debris of construction, workers had the front campus prepared to receive the 500 plus guests, who came to celebrate the first graduation in the new facility. The ceremony took place on May 26, 2007, in the large basement space below the library reserved for the book stacks but was temporarily used as a chapel.

Altogether thirty-seven students graduated. In addition, we conferred honorary degrees upon two elderly church leaders, Evangelist Ertiro Erancho and Pastor Tadesse Negawo, in recognition of their outstanding service as evangelists, educators, and pioneer church developers.

One of the unpopular, but economically pragmatic decisions undertaken by Negash was to discontinue giving students free textbooks. Instead, the college continued to photocopy most textbooks but insisted upon their return at the end of the semester. They would no longer be available for the students to take home. Obtaining private copies would now be up to the student.

Another Public Relations Fundraising Tour

The board decided that Negash and I should make a public relations and fundraising trip to North America after spring graduation. This would be an opportune time for supporters to meet the new president, to get a firsthand update on the college, and to be challenged to assist with urgent needs.

At the same time, we received an invitation to attend the International Committee of Mennonite Brethren (ICOMB) Global Higher Education Consultation at Fresno Pacific University on June 4-10, 2007. This would also be a unique opportunity for us to meet many of the world educational leaders associated with the Mennonite Brethren International Fellowship.

In response, we undertook a six-week trip from June 4 to July 14. The US Embassy denied Negash's application for a visa. While he was re-applying, I flew ahead and took care of business in Virginia, then flew as scheduled to Fresno. At the last minute, Negash was granted a visa and flew directly to California, arriving on the evening of the fourth, just as the consultation was having their banquet opening.

The objectives of this trip were to deepen and enhance relationships between the college and its supporters and sister institutions in North America. We also hoped to find new partners to assist with new building projects. We traveled to California, Ontario, Manitoba, Indiana, Virginia, and Pennsylvania.

The highlights of the trip were visiting old friends. In California, we also visited Dr. Zenebe Abebe, a vice president at FPU, and with Bekele Bedada and Emebet Mekonnen, our faculty members on study leave in Fresno. In Ontario, hosted by Darrell and Florence Jantzi, we met with the MK College Link Canada group, and with old timers like Shemsudin Abdo and Dr. Joe and Helen Burkholder. We met with Mennonite Church Canada leaders in Winnipeg. There, Negash signed an agency agreement with MC Canada Witness for sending and supporting Fanosie and Dianne Legese as teaching missionaries.

I spent an additional four days, July 10-13, hosted by and introduced to the Dutch Mennonites (Doopsgezinde) in the Netherlands. They were deeply disappointed and embarrassed that Negash was denied a visa to join me in visiting their country.

A highlight of the trip was the generous hospitality and welcome we received along the way. We did not spend a single night in a hotel, and most meals were eaten in the context of fellowship with our hosts.

With regards to success in fundraising, we did not feel that we were successful, but we made many contacts.

Losing the Dean

The academic dean had been installed a year before I was drafted as interim president. I gradually became aware that there was much discontent with his performance. It came in the form of negative reports from both students and staff, on one-by-one quiet reporting. The nature of the complaints was mostly around dysfunctional relationships.

When I tried to discuss these concerns with him, I found him hostile and extremely defensive. All the complaints were unfounded. He was right, and they were wrong. In fact, he too had many criticisms of them.

His relationships with his workmates became increasingly problematic. After Negash Kebede took my place, the dean came into conflict with the board and the executive committee of the church. He had circulated accusations levelled against certain church leaders that had no basis in fact. He refused to retract those accusations or bring evidence to substantiate them. After an attempted, lengthy, two-month reconciliation process failed, the church took the strong measure of dismissing him from his employment with the college.

This sad turn of events was a great disappointment to all of us at the college and to the leadership of the church. It was a sad story of disappointing relationships that could not seem to be corrected. What happened to our "ministry of reconciliation" (2 Co. 5:18)? In church, is it necessary to perform surgery to restore health? Sometimes.

The college lost another faculty member when FPU awarded Fekadu Negussie a full scholarship to enter its Masters in Peace Studies program. He departed in late July, leaving his wife and two children behind. Five college faculty members were studying abroad. Fikadu's wife and children joined him later when arrangements were worked out.

Signs of Progress

The fall semester of 2007 began with 124 full-time students enrolled on the Bishoftu campus, plus seventy-four part-time students in branch campuses in Adama and Addis Ababa.

The loss of these teachers was mitigated by the arrival of Fanosie and Dianne Legesse and their children, Zachariah and Lydia, in early August 2007. Fanosie had been our student, fresh from the countryside near Sire, Arsi, where he had been an evangelist near the beginning of this millennium. After he met Dianne Dobbie from Fergus, Ontario, he migrated to Canada where they were married.

After Fanosie completed his BA degree and earned an MDiv degree, they came as a missionary couple assigned to MK College for a three-year term. Fanosie was a very dynamic and beloved teacher. They lived in a rented house in Bishoftu for the first year, then moved into the brand-new guesthouse when it was completed in September 2008.

The college also welcomed Marege Habtu, a recent graduate of EGST, to teach on a full-time basis.

Dr. John Peters visited Ethiopia at the end of September 2007 to teach a two-week block course on Community and Culture. This was the second time this retired sociology professor came to teach a block course. He was fascinated by the college and the growing Ethiopian church and had become an ardent advocate in Canada.

He had joined with Dr. Peter Frick, Darrell and Florence Jantzi, Beatrice Wideman, Fanosie and Dianne Legesse, and others to form an informally organized support group called "MK College Link Canada." He was instrumental in getting Soon Lem, of Peaceworks, to come to Ethiopia to assist with setting up the computer labs the previous January. He was also largely instrumental in collecting 316 boxes of used books in Ontario for the successful library and textbook drive. To us, John was much more than a "guest lecturer."

Other guests in 2007 included Dr. Calvin and Marie Shenk, representing Eastern Mennonite Seminary, who came to teach for a few weeks and to explore the possibility of closer cooperation between the two institutions at the graduate level.

In July 2007, David Eagle, Pastor of Saanich Community Church, Victoria, British Columbia, and Dr. William Webb of Heritage College, Cambridge, Ontario, taught block courses. The students appreciated their quality teaching and friendly interaction. The administration appreciated their contribution to the enrichment of the college experience.

Having been without an academic dean since August, the board approved the appointment of theology lecturer, Belihu Delelegn, as "Acting Academic Dean" effective the beginning of December 2007. Belihu accepted that role on top of his teaching load.

For eight years, MK College had benefited from Belihu's knowledge and gift of teaching. Becoming the academic dean was a way for him to continue serving in an area where he had a strong vision and passion. He was excited about contextualizing the curriculum in an appropriate way, that was sensitive to the Ethiopian context.

Having grown up in the Ethiopian Orthodox Church, Belihu put his faith for salvation in Jesus Christ alone many years earlier. Faced with persecution, he left the Orthodox church and helped found a new evangelical Baptist church called *Addis Kidan* (New Covenant) with the Southern Baptist Conference. He discovered that his vision and calling was to educate others. He began teaching and offering Bible courses through this new church to pastors and church workers in the area. After twelve years of pastoral and academic experience, Belihu joined the Meserete Kristos Church and took up teaching in Meserete Kristos College in the year 2000.

In my new role, I enjoyed the peace and quiet of my spacious office on the fourth floor above the president's office. I could be a simple teacher without the weight of responsibility. I was happy to leave the presidency in the capable hands of brother Negash.

The year 2006 had been a hard year for me, emotionally and spiritually. I was disappointed that I could not build a team. We lost Kebede, Mitiku, and Solomon. I helplessly and sadly watched the academic dean withdraw from the team, and the board was of little support.

It was time for me to fade out and relinquish the dream Vera and

I had given twelve years of our lives to achieve. It was time for other capable, committed people to assume the challenges. The details of the dream would change, but I trusted the vision would live on and become a reality for the next generation.

Importing a Service Bus

Along with the move to the new campus in February 2007, we needed a bus to shuttle faculty and staff between Addis and Bishoftu. We thought we could buy a new one in Ethiopia, but there was not a single new bus at any of the dealers. It would take six months to have a new one delivered from Japan. We started looking for a used bus, but they were not available either. People counseled us to buy a used one from Dubai.

Therefore, we contacted a local dealer in October 2006 and ordered a used Toyota Coaster bus from Dubai with the promise that it would be delivered "in a few weeks."

The "few weeks" stretched to eight months. Finally, after renting a contract bus for the full spring semester, our thirty-two-passenger, used, Toyota Coaster bus from Dubai finally arrived at our compound in June.

Ordering this bus was a big mistake and was managed poorly by the Christian brother who imported it on our behalf. After the hassle of processing through customs, it needed to be refurbished, serviced, inspected, licensed, and insured. This took months while we continued to pay rent on the temporary contracted bus. We wondered if they drove it around the world via China, instead of across Arabia.

We learned a few things to never do again. It would have been cheaper and faster to have ordered a brand-new bus from Japan, even though there was a six-month waiting time there too. Anyway, it was a nice bus. Apart from occasional breakdowns, it shuttled the staff and a few students who lived in Addis to and from the Bishoftu campus for five years.

Developments in the Fall of 2008

Paul and Sandra Joireman, professors at Wheaton College, came to teach for a month in July 2008. Ernie and Lois Hess, a retired teacher and nurse from Lancaster, Pennsylvania, arrived in September to teach for ten months, sponsored by MCC. Later this contract was extended for a second year. They made their home in one of the newly completed bachelor suites. When they returned in the fall, Fanosie and Dianne Legesse, with their two children, moved into one of the family apartments. Jim and Peg Engle also arrived to teach for the fall semester. They lived in another family apartment.

Jim & Peg Engle, Carl & Vera Hansen, and Tigist Alamirew enjoy "heavenly food" together.

During the first two years on the new campus, several important projects were completed. Construction of the large men's dormitory was well underway. The library, with 25,000 volumes, was computerized. Several hundred trees were planted. Some landscaping was done. Telephone lines were connected. A campus-wide water system was installed that enabled the irrigation of trees and two acres of vegetables. A big transformer was installed and connected to the grid.

Due to the general pervading level of poverty in the nation, the successful building of this campus (even partially) stirred a feeling of pride and self-respect among the owners (members and community). Morale was high among the staff.

Another Fundraising Trip in 2008

Vera and I took a seven-month extended leave in North America from June through December 2008. We began our activities with a fifty-day, 8,900-mile road trip starting from Virginia and heading west. We combined visiting family and friends with informing, encouraging, and challenging our college supporters along the way.

In Elkhart, we marveled jealously at the new library and renovations on the campus of the Anabaptist Mennonite Biblical Seminary (AMBS). What a wonderful adequate campus, but so empty, so few students!

In Evanston, Illinois, we spent the night with Hailu Cherenet and Yeshi and their family. Hailu was living in Evanston but commuting to the Trinity Evangelical Seminary in Deerfield for his PhD work.

A highlight in Canada was a short visit with Dr. Paul and Laila Balisky in their retirement home in Grand Prairie. This remarkable retired couple spent forty-five productive years as missionaries in Ethiopia with SIM. As church planters, pastors, teachers, theologians, professors, writers, founders of Evangelical Theological College, and SIM Country Directors and much more, this couple had made an enormous impact in the Kale Heywot Church and on the evangelical churches of Ethiopia.

Our journey took us on to Coaldale and Lethbridge, then on west across the Rocky Mountains to the Fraser Valley, Abbotsford, Vancouver, and on to Victoria, meeting people on the way.

In Victoria, we had a very warm welcome from Dr. and Mrs. Carl and Lorraine Garry to their spacious beachfront home. On Sunday morning, we shared a ten-minute update in the Saanich Community Church. The next morning, they took us to see the famous Butchart Gardens.

In the fall, we took another major personal trip to Cusco, Peru, where we visited our daughter Cindy and her husband, John Kreider, and four of our grandchildren for three weeks. On our way back, we stopped in Texas to visit Vera's sister, Vernane Stutzman and her husband, Dick.

In November, we undertook another ten-day fundraising trip through Pennsylvania and on to Ontario.

Besides traveling, we helped Equipping the Saints to pack another forty-foot container with used university dorm bunk beds, seventy used doors salvaged from an EMU dorm, boxes of library books and textbooks, library shelving, and assorted used furnishings.

CHAPTER 22

Life in Bishoftu

Our Home

Vera and I arrived back in Ethiopia in January 2009, just after Ethiopian Christmas. Having departed the USA in the dead of winter, it felt good to be back home in Bishoftu, to wake up to the familiar sounds welcoming another warm Ethiopian day.

First the clear, crisp, electronically assisted voice of the priest, chanting from his church on the hill, penetrated our sleep with his pre-dawn liturgy, worshiping our God and challenging his people in the Orthodox way. Then, the birds, at first, one or two, then a mighty chorus of the feathered choir joined the priest in worship, in the avian way, until the sun peeked over the horizon of another cloudless day. Finally, we heard voices: the workers, greeting one another as they arrived at the college construction site; night watchmen putting away their night clothes and getting ready, anxious to be relieved of duty, so they could go home to breakfast and possibly sleep; and students excitedly chatting as they emerged from their dorm, heading for breakfast.

We spent the next two days moving our things out of storage into our new apartment. We were welcomed to a dinner with our fellow missionaries, Fanosie and Dianne Legesse and Ernie and Lois Hess, also living in this building.

We were incredibly happy with this new apartment. It had two bedrooms and two bathrooms, a large living/dining room and an open kitchen, and a small den/office. It shared a laundry room with an automatic washer with other residents. It had a full-length balcony with a beautiful view of Chelekleka Lake and Yerer Mountain. The rooms were large, not luxurious, but very adequate, better than any we ever had during our thirty years as missionaries. There were a few things still to be done, like getting phone lines installed with internet access and landscaping outside.

Since it was January, the regular students were on vacation. A small group of twenty-five evangelists were taking missions courses for the month. Vera went back to working in the library, and I prepared to teach in February. I also began sorting out the logistical details for the upcoming Experience Ethiopia Tour.

Construction of the men's dormitory had reached the third floor. The terraced dining hall was also being built. Slowly, slowly, the college campus was taking shape. The trees planted a year ago were growing nicely.

The Climate

Nature endowed Bishoftu with two vastly different states of existence, the long nine-month, dusty, desert-like, dry season, and the shorter, three-month rainy season. By the beginning of September, the whole country is clothed in the greenest garb, like Ireland. The seasonal Chelekleka Lake spreads-out three-and-one-half kms below the college. Long flowing grass, little green trees, and beautiful flowers adorn the campus, a fitting reward for our horticultural efforts the previous spring. One can hardly imagine it to be the same dry, dusty, hot country it was three months earlier.

As Chelekleka Lake slowly recedes during the dry season, the community of birds increases. As other sources of water and food dry up, this lake continues to provide nutrients and shelter, a welcome oasis, a living sanctuary for our hungry and thirsty feathered friends.

The farmers surrounding the lake also compete for the scarce, life-sustaining water. They diligently cultivate their small vegetable plots and keep them productive, deep into the dry season by irrigating until the lake recedes beyond the reach of their small, gasoline-powered pumps.

At the college, the irrigation of vegetables continues throughout the dry season, thanks to a good drilled well. The availability of water turns what would be a dry barren wasteland into a paradise of blooming flowers, shrubs, and trees.

The Town

During the last few decades, the sleepy little town of Bishoftu, formerly known as Debre Zeit, came alive with new developments. The building boom that was transforming Ethiopia was also transforming this town. New buildings housing businesses such as hotels, restaurants, shops, factories, schools, and vast new residential areas, were springing up. The municipality cooperated by leveling, draining, and cobble-stoning all the dirty, rutted back streets. They also put in cobblestone sidewalks along the main streets.

Using cobblestones was a wise and beneficial decision. Each of the millions of cobblestones, cut by hand into four-inch cubes and laid in place by hand, one by one, gave employment for thousands of needy people. In doing so, they used abundant, cheap resources instead of importing expensive bitumen. With all the streets and sidewalks along the main road being cobblestone, the cleanliness and orderliness of the town was improved. Mud puddles and traffic dust were diminished. Also, any street repairs were easily implemented by the simple adjustment of stones.

We were surprised and pleased when the municipality transformed the dusty, or sometimes muddy, road that ran past our campus gate. By building it up, putting in bridges, and asphalting it, they connected the campus with the main highway in the west and with the east side of town, about a four or five-kilometers distance. Besides making travel smooth, clean, and quick, it also increased the traffic and encouraged accessibility of taxi service. Solar-powered streetlights were installed in 2016.

Student Life

Life for the students was not just lectures, books, and papers. Especially around 1:30 pm after the noon meal was finished, students would find their way to "Elsa's Cafe." An empty classroom filled with small tables and orange plastic chairs, a TV, and a few checker boards formed the social hub of the college. Steaming *makiatos* or a cup of hot milk with a dash of expresso was served up in quick fashion for about ten cents a cup. Spiced Ethiopia tea was cheaper yet.

When their eyes got tired of reading, or their brains got tired of thinking, the café was where you would find the students. Here, you might find them relaxing, chatting, playing checkers, watching the news, a televised soccer game, the *God Channel,* or some other miracle-working tele-evangelist, offering solutions to all your problems.

You might find a few students in the shade of an acacia tree, surrounding the one ping pong table, watching their friends competing with well worn paddles. Or, if it was late afternoon, when the sun was less hot, you might find teams playing volleyball over a torn net, with fans cheering on both sides.

Celebration and Life in the Guesthouse

Jim and Anna Ralph had returned to Ethiopia for a two-year open assignment with the church. One of the many wonderful things they did was to complete the decoration of the campus guesthouse. They did an excellent job of making the bare rooms feel comfortable and homy. We enjoyed living in this new building very much.

St. Valentine's Day, February 14, 2009, marked the forty-fifth anniversary of the pivotal occasion when Vera accepted my proposal for marriage. If I remember correctly, Vera was quite naively happy over the prospect at that time. Little did she realize what she was getting into, when she impulsively consented with an eager "Yes!" Anyway, from my side, there were no regrets over her decision.

To celebrate, we went out for dinner to the Air Force Officers' club restaurant. It was a delightful, outdoor, terraced restaurant that sloped down to the water's edge, on the far side of Hora Lake. They served tasty food in the darkening twilight. Ducks swam on the lake, dipping their little heads for their supper. Other birds called from the treetops where they were settling in for the night. The electricity was shut off in that part of town, so it was quiet, dark, and romantic, but, as always, the time came to go back home.

At home, we invited our colleagues, fellow pilgrims in the guesthouse, to our apartment where Vera shared her wonderful valentine cake. Our guests included Ernie and Lois Hess, Dr. John Miller, Dr. John Michael Miller, and Fanosie and Dianne Legese and their two children.

Ernie and Lois were people with whom we went to college forty-four years earlier. They had recently retired from teaching and nursing and were now MCC volunteer English teachers. John Miller was a seventy-eight-year-old retired missionary, Bible professor, and bishop from Leola, Pennsylvania. He was there for two months for his third round of teaching. The other man, Dr. John Michael Miller, a retired chaplain, one-time college professor, and United Methodist minister from Atlanta, Georgia, was close to the same age. He came for a four-month period. These two professors/churchmen were longtime friends who had been colleagues teaching at Oral Roberts University in an earlier era. We differentiated the two John Millers by calling the second one "J. Michael" or simply "Mike."

With a nice group of eleven expats to live with, we celebrated each other's birthdays and any other special occasion of which we could think. We would share cakes, cookies, goodies, and kitchenware or furniture, as we were able. We shared stories from various parts of the earth and different traditions, all human and all interesting. We enjoyed living in this community!

Richard and Karen Thiessen from Columbia Bible College (CBC) in Abbotsford, British Columbia, joined us, arriving in May with their three sons, Abram, Solomon, and Isaac. They were on a three-month sabbatical and stayed in the guesthouse. Richard, as the head librarian of CBC, lent his expertise assisting the librarians. Karen, a pastor on sabbatical, gave time to home-school her sons and to take self-care time to relax and rejuvenate. The teenaged sons volunteered to be useful in any way they could—a nice family. Richard, years later, was instrumental in collecting books for the MK College library.

We heard hyenas whooping to each other about every night. They would pass through the village looking for something to scavenge. The dogs would howl in response. Some came into the college compound.

One Sunday morning, I found a hyena near the dorm construction site, lying dead with an electric wire in its mouth. We know that the life of a hyena is not that attractive. Perhaps he was looking for an escape? Anyway, whether intentional or not, he electrocuted himself. They are reputed to have the dangerous and often deadly habit of chewing on electric cables. Not a recommended habit. Ernie Hess, the naturalist, extracted some teeth to embellish his collection back home.

The Orthodox priests celebrated their mass and other ecclesiastical duties faithfully every Saturday and Sunday at their church on the nearby hill. They also celebrated other special days in honor of their favorite saint or some other religious holiday. To engage the believers (and annoy the unbelievers and Muslim neighbors), they sometimes started their liturgy as early as 2:00 a.m., but usually closer to 4:30 or 5:00 a.m. They would turn up the volume on their loudspeakers. The clear sound carried over the still night air so that it seemed as if they were just outside our window.

It was disturbing at the early hour, but by 7:00 a.m., it became a part of the grand chorus of praise, along with the morning singing of the birds. I guess, we all, alike, were created to give God glory. But some of us decadent types wished it was at a saner hour. It was also one of the trials borne by students who "burned the midnight oil" to prepare for exams the next day.

One Sunday, we decided that we would all walk to the Metropolitan Tabernacle for the Sunday service. It was only about one and one-half kms east of our college. It was a new church introduced to Ethiopia from Ireland. Missionaries from there started an elementary school for the poor that spawned a new church. The pastor, Bezebah, a seminary-trained Ethiopian, also taught a course in our college. We liked him.

With good soil and available water just outside our house, gardening was a relaxing and rewarding hobby. We ate healthily with fresh vegetables and got the bonus health-benefit of a little exercise on the side.

By the summer of 2010, all the other residents of this guesthouse disbanded, each returning to their home or going on to the next challenge in their pilgrimages. In their place, one Mennonite Central Committee volunteer, Thelonius Cook (called "Mr. Tee"), a single African American computer expert from Virginia Beach, came to assist with computer problems. He came for a three-year term to help the college, as well as all East African MCC programs with their computer problems. He only stayed for one semester, terminating his contract early. Perhaps he was too lonely in the guesthouse with just us?

Travails

Life on campus was not to be equated to that of paradise. There were some problems. In 2009, a pump failure left the campus dry. To meet student and campus needs, water was hauled in barrels and cans by pickup truck from a nearby Dutch neighbor's well. It took months to have the pump repaired. An emergency line was installed, connecting the campus to the city water supply. However, city demand allowed only a trickle to reach the campus, filling a few tanks at night. Irrigation of the campus had to be discontinued until the pump was fixed.

Three years later, the well went dry again. The Kale Heywot Church Water Development Department drilled a second well in March 2012. This eighty-meter deep well was situated just inside the campus gate. They found an abundance of water. However, just as we were rejoicing and before they installed the curbing, the walls caved in below forty meters. The contractors failed to rectify this problem, and after some months of unpleasant interchange, they left the college with a big bill and a forty-meter well that yielded water in the rainy season but ran dry in the dry season. It tarnished the good name of that church's water department.

These two wells alleviated the water problem. Limited irrigation allowed the production of vegetables for the students' use and some to sell. They tried to keep a few flowers growing on the compound, but it was not like before.

Again in 2014, during the dry season, when the vegetable fields were growing green and lush, suddenly there was not enough water. The second well was dry, and the first one had limited supply, just enough for human and animal consumption and for the building construction needs. Management stopped all irrigation. The fields quickly withered and turned brown. A sad loss.

One of the big trials we endured was the sporadic service provided by the government's Electric Power Authority. Throughout this period, the campus suffered, and still suffers, with frequent power outages. Sometimes it would just flicker off for a few seconds and then come back on, just long enough to shut down the desktop computers, the washing machine, and other electronic devices.

Other times it would remain off for many hours, shortening the workday for computer users. It would often go off just around evening, leaving the campus in the dark, often until morning. Students had to study by candlelight or by the lights on their cell phones, if they were the lucky few who had such. Or they did not study at all—not a helpful solution when there was an exam or assignment due in the morning.

The government-owned phone service, Ethio-Telecom, was equally aggravating. The guesthouse was wired for telephone service along with the other buildings. However, after a period of several years of repeatedly calling on the service to come and restore the phones to working order, we finally gave up on land lines and resorted to mobile phones. Even those worked only intermittently.

These unsatisfactory public services constantly reminded us that we were in a part of the world that was moving from a feudal age into the 21st century, all within one lifetime. That was a quantum leap, and a hitch here and there should be no surprise. When compared to Europe, Ethiopia was making a 500-year leap in one generation.

International Evangelical Church – Bishoftu

A partnership between Double Harvest America and Double Harvest Netherlands launched the Genesis Farm in November 1996 at Bishoftu. Dutch Christians settled in as missionaries, developing a fifty-two-hectare integrated agricultural enterprise as a ministry. By promoting modern agricultural production, they aimed to ensuring food security and poverty reduction in rural and urban Ethiopia.

Genesis Farm accomplished its mission by employing between 450 and 600 people. They trained them in horticulture and animal husbandry, with many spinoff businesses. While they learned new transferable skills, these employees also learned to appreciate the Christian gospel and world view. Many of them, after learning skills, went on to good jobs or to start their own enterprises. The quality vegetables, poultry, and dairy products of this self-supporting mission farm were highly valued in the city markets.

In the years that followed, other Christian investors from the Netherlands undertook to follow that pattern, establishing about a dozen different "business as mission" industries in the vicinity of Bishoftu. All of them were set up as a combination business and human development enterprise, being a blessing to the community and the country. They did not repatriate profits, but re-invested them in further development for the benefit of society.

These businesses were developed and managed by committed Dutch experts who came with their families. This meant that quite a large Dutch population grew in the area. Most of them did not know the local languages very well, and they felt the need to maintain their own social and spiritual lives. So, they started their own Bible study and prayer times.

There were also other expatriates in the area such as Sudanese and Rwandanese students in the Defense Engineering College or the Veterinary College. There were also a YWAM missionary couple from India, a Nigerian missionary couple, plus Americans in the Peace Corps, and those in charge of Rafiki Village, an orphanage in Mojo.

Finally, there were we expatriate staff at MK College. We all felt more comfortable worshiping in English rather than in the local language.

Seeing the need, the Dutch took leadership in organizing an International Evangelical Church in Bishoftu in 2008. They gathered in a meeting hall at Genesis Farm for their Sunday morning services. They had a schedule of lay leadership and lay preachers. We expats each took our turn, that is, we who were males, as they did not approve of females giving teaching or pastoral leadership over males.

We expats from the college often drove or walked the four kms around the lake to the Genesis Farm for church services on Sundays. Besides the regular people who lived and worked there, it seemed that most Sundays there would be visitors. The Dutch had close contact with "the folks at home." There was a steady stream of visitors and short-term volunteers coming to encourage and work with those who were living in Ethiopia.

In 2010, the Bishoftu International Church weekly service venue was changed from the Genesis farm's hall to the much larger MK College chapel. The attendance fluctuated between fifty and seventy, depending on the number of guests visiting the area.

On some Saturday afternoons, we foreigners from the guesthouse would walk to one of the nearby Dutch compounds to socialize around a volleyball court. Other families would join us. Sometimes we would celebrate birthdays or enjoy other social activities together.

Maintaining Non-Resident Legal Status – An Expat Problem

Entering and working in Ethiopia legally as an expatriate, became an increasingly difficult challenge under the EPRDF government. Back when Vera and I returned to work under EMM in 1996, we were given an entry visa and a work permit as a *missionary* that allowed us to live and work in Ethiopia. That status expired in 2002 when we returned to the USA. When we sought to return in 2004, the government was no longer giving work permits to missionaries.

We found a way around it by applying for, and receiving, a *business visa*, the *business* being a teacher in a church college. This allowed us legal entry, and to our advantage, did not require a work permit, nor a residence permit. However, it required me to leave the country and re-enter every six months. This was expensive and awkward, but manageable for a time.

Sometime later, I found I could come on a three-month tourist visa and have it renewed within the country. I did that for a few years until it created a crisis. On January 25, 2010, I went to Immigration to have my tourist visa renewed. I was told that the regulation had changed. They would only renew my tourist visa for one month, up to February 25th. When that day came, they would not renew it again because it was illegal to work, holding a tourist visa.

I had a job to do. Besides teaching, I was committed to lead another Experience Ethiopia Tour, expected arrival being March 4th. What could I do? The immigration officer told me I would have to get a business visa. To do so, I would have to return to my country of origin and apply at the Ethiopian Embassy there.

With no time to waste and some earnest prayer, I ordered tickets to fly to Washington on Saturday, February 27 and return on March 5. I did not realize that the Ethiopia Embassy would be closed for Muhammed's birthday on Tuesday, and my return flight was set for Wednesday. That left one day, Monday, as the only window of opportunity to obtain the coveted business visa.

Prayers were answered when, on Monday morning, it took only twenty minutes plus $70 for the Embassy officials to grant me a one-year business visa. I was grateful. However, it was very costly that I spent $2,000 on air travel, plus seven days of my time. In my way of thinking, it would have been a much more efficient use of our limited resources to put that small stamp in my passport right there in that immigration office in Addis for the good of all concerned. Such are the efficiencies of some government policies!

I arrived back in Addis around noon on Friday, March 5. The tour group had arrived the evening before. Vera had arranged a welcome for them in my stead.

CHAPTER 23

Transitions and Developments

Personnel Changes

There were major changes in personnel at the college in the year 2010. Pastor Getaneh Ayele ended his employment as teacher. Yohannes Shiferaw was hired to work at the circulation desk in the library. He had good credentials, including a diploma in library science and good recommendations.

As we hinted earlier, there was a major exodus of those from the guesthouse at the end of the spring semester. Among them were Fanosie and Dianne Legesse and Ernie and Lois Hess, who completed their contracts and returned to their homes.

Fekadu Negussie graduated from Fresno Pacific University with an MA in Peace Studies and returned to teach sociology and cultural anthropology in the fall. Hailu Cherenet returned for the summer to teach two courses. He had been gone for four-and-one-half years.

In the fall, we welcomed a new MCC SALT volunteer, Ben Chleboun (pronounced *Clay-bone*) from the USA. He came to teach English for one year.

Also, we welcomed Fantahun Beerara from California. An Ethiopian by birth, Fanta migrated to the USA with his family twenty-six years earlier. Having given up his secular teaching career and graduated from a Lutheran seminary in Minneapolis, he returned as a volunteer at his own expense. He taught courses in wisdom literature, counseling, and comparative world religions.

We were blessed to have Paul Wytenbroeck, a retired shop instructor from British Columbia, Canada, volunteer for seven weeks. He was just the right person to guide the maintenance crew in organizing and setting up the workshop. He also helped them get the used machines in working order and taught them how to use the welder.

Ruth Girma was promoted from working in the duplicating room to serve as cashier. Wondimu Gichumo, a guard, was promoted to take her place in the duplicating room. In addition to her responsibilities as treasurer, Roman Gemeda took on the additional responsibility of guesthouse host.

One tragic Saturday morning in October 2010, Tesfaye Makongo, an alum and part-time teacher, was killed in a tragic accident while traveling from his home in Addis to teach in a leader's seminar in Adama. He was one of eleven people killed when the minibus, trying to pass a tanker truck, was crushed in a head on collision with a container truck on a narrow bridge just south of Mojo.

Tesfaye, a much-loved evangelist and church planter, came to our college in 1999 and graduated with a BA degree in 2002. Since then, he served in Addis Ababa, planting the Fransawi MKC congregation, pastoring in another congregation, and teaching part time at MK College. He was also among those thirty graduate students taking the MA courses offered by EMS each summer. Tesfaye left behind his young widow, Ruth Asfaw, and their two-month-old son.

Team Spirit

Sometimes there was a question of fairness, maybe discrimination, or class distinction. Wolansa Yisahak, our faithful young secretary turned registrar, served cheerfully for eleven years. To better herself, she enrolled in a master's level program with a distance learning arrangement in India, majoring in sociology. She had asked the administration for scholarship assistance, but the board turned down her request, allowing scholarship assistance only for teachers.

She had purchased a laptop computer on loan, and the president asked the board whether the college could assist her with that purchase. However, since the computer was also for her family's use, this suggestion was also denied. I wondered whether more consideration, for the betterment of those who serve faithfully, would not have built a more positive team spirit. It is not surprising that Wolansa no longer works at the college.

When assessing internal organizational strengths and weaknesses, there were complaints from the staff that the leadership did not listen to them. The lower-level staff felt neglected, even though they loyally served the college for many years. Their complaint was a cry for justice.

Another problem in developing team spirit was the composition of the staff. Some key positions were occupied by non-MKC members. The other staff complained that these people lacked commitment to advance the college. They were satisfied to maintain the status quo, as long as they received their salaries.

A proper staff development plan, including competitive salaries, recognition of staff contributions, and an openness to hearing their concerns, would have helped to build a better team spirit. The college lacked those things.

Security

A troubling incident occurred when it was reported to Negash that the head of the guards was carrying a Kalashnikov at night. Local police had issued it to him without the president's knowledge. This being an Anabaptist college that believes in pacifism and nonresistance, the president was not amused. He ordered the gun to be returned to the police authority with a message of "Thanks, but no thanks!" It would be better to suffer loss at the hands of a hungry, or not so hungry, thief than to have the blood of an enemy, or anyone else, on our hands.

One day we were all startled by a mighty explosion that shut down the campus electrical system. Investigators found that the damage was in the transmission line, not the transformer. However, the stiff corpse of an electrocuted cat was found in the campus powerhouse. Its clandestine entry into forbidden space may have triggered the explosion. How did the cat gain entry to that building? Were we doing all we should be doing to keep our campus safe?

Liberal Arts Programs

From its inception, the vision of the founding fathers of MK College was that after establishing its Bible and Christian ministry programs, non-religious or secular programs would follow. Such programs would attract paying students, and the college would move towards self-sustainability.

To do so, the college would need to be accredited by the Ministry of Education. To get accreditation, it would have to be registered as a profit-making educational institution. As such, the government's policy required that it must be open to all Ethiopians, including non-religious people as well as those of the Islamic faith. If we went that way, we would have to respect the law of the land. Could we have biblical/theological programs and secular programs on the same campus? This possibility raised heavy questions in the minds of many in the leadership.

If the door were open for all, how would that impact the moral and spiritual life on campus? Would committed Christian students utilize the opportunities for evangelism that the presence of the secular and non-Christian students presented? Should, and would the church be willing to do that?

However, the church was also aware that in the huge evangelical community, young people were attending secular universities, exposing themselves daily to the thinking and behavior of the secular environment. For that reason, the idea of having liberal arts programs taught from a Christian perspective, in the context of a believing Christian community, was attractive.

Earlier experience with the Nazareth Bible Academy fortified my belief that offering liberal arts programs in a church-owned college would mostly attract students sympathetic to its standards. Also, considering the alternatives offered in government and private non-religious universities,

MK College's programs would only appeal to the kinds of students we would be comfortable having on campus. It could be that the student population would be composed of mostly evangelicals with a small mix from outside, as used to be the case in the Bible Academy. We were already receiving inquiries from parents about the timing of the launch of the liberal arts programs.

In 2009, Negash started to work on getting pre-accreditation from the Ministry of Education for three liberal arts programs. However, the Ministry of Education required the applying school to have qualified teachers on its payroll in advance of getting pre-accreditation. We needed student fees to pay the required teachers. Yet, to attract students, we needed an accredited program. It was a vicious circle. At that time, the lack of finance to hire the required qualified teachers, plus the limitations of dormitory space, held him back.

The following year, the Ministry of Education drastically changed the requirements for private schools to gain accreditation for university level programs. They dropped the pre-accreditation arrangement and required applicants to have fully developed programs up and running. That included that all lecturers be in place for the full four-year program before they could even apply for accreditation. They were demanding all programs to be 70% hard sciences and 30% liberal arts.

This presented a huge challenge to MK College because of its commitment to having a strong theological faculty and wanting to include religious courses in its secular programs. This would entail a huge budget to get all the required things in place.

With the board's approval, Negash decided to take a more gradual approach, introducing non-accredited programs, if students would apply. He would start the liberal arts programs with what we had on hand, without accreditation, then build up our capacity before applying after our program was running.

Accordingly, he introduced a Bible degree with a major in community development. He hired Lloyd Kiros, who came with an MA in Community Development from India, as a lecturer. In time, many students were attracted to this major to get better employment opportunities. This raised some concerns that many would leave theological studies and go to this major in the future. Others chose Bible and peace studies.

Faculty-Staff Retreat

It had been a long time since the faculty and staff had a retreat. This fact became a cause of disagreement between the teaching faculty and the administration. The tension centered around the question of what constituted the desired retreat, and how much expense the college should bear to enable it to take place. The custom had been that the employer paid for the retreats, and it was the worker's right (the entitlement argument). In our situation as a non-profit institution, the administration felt that the faculty was demanding an elaborate retreat and wanted the participants to at least bear a token of the cost. This created resentment on the part of some. Without agreement, there was no retreat.

To break the stalemate, mid-level staff appointed a planning committee. It suggested a participatory scheme in which workers would pay in proportion to their income, and the college would pay a larger share. In the end, twenty staff members opted to participate, while most of the unhappy teachers decided to boycott the retreat.

Consequently, on a Friday afternoon in late September 2010, we set off on the college service bus and headed south to Awassa. We arrived at the Heywot Birhan Church Retreat Center just before dark. After stowing our luggage into our rooms, we went out for supper at the Lewey Hotel. After supper, we returned and deposited our tired bodies in our modest beds and slept well.

Most of the rooms were created out of shipping containers and were small but satisfactory. Priced at thirty birr ($3) per night, they were much cheaper than those in a hotel. Us respected foreigners were put in a house on the compound. Vera and I had a room, and Ben and T shared another room with a shared bathroom. We heard no complaints from anyone, except that there was only one communal bathroom to serve the other sixteen.

On Saturday, we went to the same hotel for a buffet breakfast, after which we went on a morning excursion to Wondo Genet, a resort center about twenty miles away. There we enjoyed a good swim in the hot pools of the Wabe Shebelle Hotel. The Wondo Genet Valley is a beautiful fertile place. It is densely populated, and subsistence agriculture is the dominant activity.

We returned to Awassa in time for lunch at the hotel and then toured the new Haile Gebre Selassie Resort. It was so attractive that we stayed most of the afternoon. Rooms cost from US $80 to $100. That evening, back at the Retreat Center, a sheep was slaughtered and roasted over an open fire. We enjoyed a time of storytelling, laughter, singing, and feasting around a bonfire in the dark.

Sunday, after a morning devotional, we went back to the Lewey Hotel for breakfast. Following that, we visited the Lewey Resort, also owned by the same man. After admiring that Resort and dreaming of how nice it would be to stay there, we reluctantly got on the bus and set out for home.

We stopped at the Sabana Lodge on Lake Langano for a two-hour break. Those of us, who were so inclined, swam in the cool water for an hour before having a late lunch.

We arrived home in Bishoftu near sundown. It was truly a pleasant and relaxing retreat. It was a significant experience for the poorly paid staff, who labored faithfully, day by day, year around. They worked for a minimum wage, with no frills, barely earning enough to cover their rent, food, clothing, and educating their children. For them, this break was a treasured highlight. We think the non-cooperating teachers missed a lot!

Faculty Transitions

Kassu Kebede resigned his teaching post to accept employment with World Vision. Benjamin Chleboun completed his one-year commitment under the MCC SALT program as English teacher and returned to the USA. Lecturer, Workineh Ayele, class of '04, graduated with an MA from EMS and EGST and became a full-time lecturer in the fall, teaching NT Greek and Study Skills.

CHAPTER 24

Growing a Library

A Library and Textbook Drive

In our preparations to launch a fully accredited liberal arts curriculum, we needed relevant library books and lots of textbooks. To meet this need, in January 2007, we sent out a circular letter, *An Invitation to be a Partner in a Library and Textbook Drive for Meserete Kristos College,* to about one hundred addresses of friends and supporters. We encouraged them to solicit and donate good library and textbooks relevant to the programs we envisioned offering. The drive was to end in mid-May.

The response was very gratifying. Offers came from places scattered across Canada and the USA. The most outstanding response was the selfless and energetic effort put forth by Dr. John Peters of Waterloo, Ontario, Canada. Being a well-known, respected retired academic, he contacted his many friends and persuaded them to share their books. He sorted the books according to quality, relevance, and age. Soon he had his garage full of books ready to send.

In our letter, we invited all parties to send their books to Equipping the Saints at Weyer's Cave, Virginia. This NGO was in the process of gathering used furniture and equipment to fill and send us a second forty-foot shipping container. However, getting the books sent from Canada through US Customs and all the way down to Virginia was a challenge.

Here again, John Peters found a solution. He learned of an organization called "The Theological Books Network" operating out of Grand Rapids, Michigan. This group was sending a container of theological books to the Ethiopian Graduate School of Theology in early May 2007. Their books were to be divided out between six different theological schools in Ethiopia, including the Meserete Kristos College.

John contacted them and arranged, since their container was not full, to include four or five pallets of non-theological books for our college. He invited Willard Swartley to take the books they gathered in the Elkhart/Goshen area to Grand Rapids as well.

The Network sent the container in the summer. It arrived and was cleared through customs in October. That time coincided with Dr. John Peters being in Ethiopia teaching a block course. It was exciting having him help to load those boxes one more time, this time into the college's vehicle in Ethiopia. There were 316 boxes containing over 8,000 volumes in that shipment.

The municipal government in Richmond had built a new library and wanted to repurpose the old one. This meant they wanted the shelves removed. Equipping the Saints had purchased all the shelves and furniture for our college for less than $300. As I was in Virginia at the beginning of June, I, along with five men from the Harrisonburg Mennonite Church, drove to Richmond, along with a truck and crew from Equipping the Saints. There, we dismantled the shelves, loaded them into the truck, and took them back to Weyer's Cave. These quality steel shelves would later be included with the 247 boxes of books, dorm beds, and other useful goods that were shipped in October.

The total cost of purchasing and sending this container was around $6,047 to the seaport of Djibouti. From there, it took another $2-3,000 in costs to transport it inland from Djibouti, through customs, and to our campus in Bishoftu. Although the cost was high, we got a lot of books, plenty of book shelving, and useful furniture and equipment, including dorm beds. The long container became a useful storage facility in subsequent years.

This total of 560 boxes of books was a big challenge for Vera and Tigist to sort, label, and stack. They were incredibly happy for the assistance of Chris Brnjas, a volunteer from Elora, Ontario, Canada, who spent two months entering thousands of books into the computer.

It was a daunting task to open all the boxes and sort out the books. There were those that would be added to our library holdings, those that could be used as textbooks, and the duplicates and others that would be distributed to various colleges, church libraries, or elementary schools.

Again, in 2010, we received another twenty-four boxes of books through Theological Books Network, most of them from donations in the Elkhart-Goshen Indiana area.

The Meserete Kristos Library

A Saga of Dr. Negussie Ayele's Library

Dr. Negussie Ayele, a noted historian and professor of history on the campus of UCLA, had a life-long connection with MKC. One of the earliest evangelists and teachers in the School for the Blind back in the 1950's, he went on and earned his doctorate at a university in Florida, where he became a lecturer. In the late 1960's, he returned to teach history and political science at Haile Selassie I University in Addis. At that time, he re-connected with the MKC and served as chair of the Bible Academy Board of Trustees for a term.

After the revolution, Dr. Negussie was appointed as ambassador to Norway by the Dergue regime. With the fall of the Dergue, he moved to the USA where he served as a professor in UCLA for many years. With retirement and declining health, Dr. Negussie decided he would like to donate his substantial library to MK College. Getting these books from California to Bishoftu was a major challenge.

It took two more years before Dr. Negussie got around to sorting his books. Friends helped to box the books, and Million Belete paid a couple thousand dollars to ship forty-five boxes to Harrisonburg. We stored them in a shed, waiting for news of a container that would take them to Ethiopia.

The books were stored for another two years until I learned of a container leaving for Bishoftu from Florida. So, I rented a van, and with my grandson, Justus Payne, loaded the boxes, along with ten more boxes we had collected, and took them to Florida where we placed them in charge of the Rafiki Village officers. They put our boxes in their container to be shipped. Six months later the books arrived in Bishoftu. Again, the boxes sat in the college library, waiting for someone to record them and enter them into the computer before attaching the labels and putting them on the library shelves. From beginning to end, it took about eight years to get those books into their Ethiopian repository. Many thanks to Dr. Negussie Ayele, Million Belete, Rafiki Village, and the many who helped!

Continuing Flow of Books

Vera had set up a bookstore in the library to dispose of duplicate and unwanted books at cheap prices. It was popular with students and other visitors. It also generated income to offset the high cost of shipping.

However, book collecting was not over. For three more years, John Peters continued to collect books in his Waterloo, Ontario home, while Richard Thiessen was collecting the same in his Columbia Bible College library in Abbotsford, BC. How to get them all to Ethiopia? That was the question. Finally, in October 2013, ninety-six boxes were shipped from Abbotsford to Winnipeg. Erb Transport kindly delivered them free of charge to Baden, Ontario.

In November, John set out with a rented truck loaded with the 264 boxes of books, crossed the border into the USA, and delivered them to the Theological Books Network in Grand Rapids, MI, for shipment with other books to Ethiopia.

Again, Vera, upon her 2014 winter vacation in Bishoftu, accepted the challenge of a neglected library, and worked there to bring it back up to her Swiss Mennonite standards of cleanliness and perfect order. This prompted editor Teku Kebede, in the March 2014 issue of the MK College Newsletter, to comment:

> It is known, and for good reason, that the MK College Library is named "Hansen Library" after Vera Hansen who has tirelessly donated eighteen of her best years to its growth and development. And even now, having come out of retirement for the past five months, she is still found there, organizing, and entering new acquisitions.
>
> It could not be an exaggeration to say, "For Vera, books are like her children." It is an indication of how she loves Meserete Kristos College.
>
> Within the last month, immediately as the students went to their homes for vacation, she began to disassemble then reassemble and extend the library shelves. She searched for several students to assist. When these could not be found, she persisted all alone. Though she was very busy welcoming guests from abroad and accompanying them, she still completed assembling the shelves.
>
> May the true and peaceful God of the obedient children bless her and her family.

In the spring of 2016, retired professor Dr. Willard Swartley packed up thirty-six boxes of his library, and along with three more boxes donated by retired professor Dr. Wilbert Shenk, took them to Grand Rapids, MI, to be sent with another shipment by Theological Books Network. These arrived in Ethiopia and were delivered to the college in the fall.

And the books kept coming. On September 3rd, 2016, Dr. Helen Walker, a retired professor, brought a van load of twenty boxes of books from the Messiah College library to my house in Virginia.

During our 2017 winter visit to Ethiopia, Vera again put her energy into library work. There were still thousands of books to be sorted, processed, entered into the computer, and put on shelves. Vera, with help from the library workers, divided the surplus books into twenty piles of boxes for the other colleges. There were still extra books, some of them of less quality or importance. These, they put out on tables and sold to the students at nominal prices like fifty cents down to five cents each. The students were happy. Altogether, the library staff sold over $1,000 worth of these books. The library work area looked a lot cleaner after the sale. There were still more boxes of books on the way or waiting to be sorted.

The Addis Ababa MK College extension campus was able to move to its permanent location on the fourth floor of the MKC Head Office building in 2017. Vera arranged for the pickup to transport over 4,000 books, selected and labeled for the new Addis campus library, along with the necessary shelving. After assembling the shelves, she arranged the books in place. At the close of 2017, the number of volumes in the college library exceeded 35,000.

Again, in the summer of 2018, Dr. Tesfaye Haile, a pastor in the Washington area, brought a load of eleven large boxes of his personal library to our home in Virginia to be sent to the MK College Addis Campus. These were added to fifty other boxes that were shipped in August. The container full of beds and chairs, along with the books, arrived in Bishoftu in October 2018.

CHAPTER 25

Experimenting with A Graduate Program

The idea of launching a graduate seminary degree program was incubated in the minds of Dr. John Miller, retired professor and guest lecturer from Pennsylvania, and Woudineh Endayelalu, who had recently graduated from MBBS in Fresno. That was back in Kotebe in the summer of 2006, when John returned to teach a few courses.

John got acquainted with, and developed respect for, the ambitious young scholar. From their conversations, the two creative minds began envisioning how to launch a master's level program. It would alleviate some of the faculty shortages in the areas where Anabaptist-oriented training was highly desired. John shared this need and vision with Dr. Ervin Stutzman, Dean of Eastern Mennonite Seminary, and others.

This led to a drawn-out exchange between EMS and the administration of the college. Two years went by as the officials worked out the details of the many questions related to feasibility, programs, curriculum, accreditation, teaching faculty, scheduling, and funding.

With the change in leadership at the college in 2007, the new president, Negash Kebede, continued the correspondence with EMS, hammering out the details of a master's program plan.

EMS found that its participation was limited by its accrediting association restrictions. This restriction meant that, at most, EMS could give a post-graduate certificate upon completion of twenty-nine credit hours, but not a full degree.

To complete a full master's degree, Negash Kebede of MK College, and Sara Wenger Shenk representing EMS, negotiated a tripartite agreement with EGST in 2009, assuring that EGST would honor the twenty-nine credits a student earned from EMS, if the student wanted to take the rest of a degree from EGST. This was less than desirable, but the best that could be negotiated under the circumstances.

Finally, the two parties agreed upon a Memorandum of Understanding. EMS would send some teachers each year and the college would find other teachers to keep the program going. It was an attractive idea considering it costs over $30,000 to keep one student in school for one year in Virginia, but only about $1,500 at Bishoftu. That is something like twenty for the price of one.

Launching the Program:

The graduate program got underway on June 16, 2008, when a cohort of thirty came for six weeks, taking two graduate courses taught by Dr. Calvin Shenk of EMS.

The program moved ahead nicely for three years. Each summer, three professors came from EMS to teach three courses. In addition, the students took one distance education course during the year. They accumulated twelve credit hours per year. Students were able to continue their regular employment, utilizing their annual leave to take the nine-week summer program.

Of the thirty students who began to take the master's level courses, twenty-four returned in the summer of 2010. This program continued until eighteen students earned twenty-nine credit hours or a half of a degree over three summers. Then arrangements were made for them to complete their work at EGST.

Outcomes: Evaluation

In January 2016, eight years after launching the program, the eleven remaining students took the last two required courses. A professor from EGST taught the first three-week course, and a teacher from Fresno

Pacific University came for the second three-week course. Then the only requirement remaining was for them to turn in an acceptable thesis before they could graduate in May.

However, a year later, most of them were still struggling with completing their papers. Their busy daily working hours and distance from a good library made this goal hard to reach. Two of them went ahead and completed their programs and graduated from EGST. Two more were still taking courses at EGST. One completed his degree in a European university. Two more dropped out. However, in May 2017, the last of them graduated.

It was time to evaluate and make decisions whether this program should be continued, modified, expanded, or terminated. On the positive side, the program, over an eight-year period, upgraded sixteen MKC leaders to the qualification level of a master's degree. The others who began, but for various reasons were unable to complete the program, were also upgraded in significant ways.

While eight years is a prolonged period, this upgrading was accomplished without displacing the leaders from their homes, families, church communities, and places of employment, which would not have been true if they had gone abroad or entered full-time studies.

This was achieved at a low financial cost. Without including those who benefited but failed to complete the program, sixteen leaders were upgraded to MA level at a cost of less than $60,000, a small amount compared to the over $700,000 it would cost if they all studied in the USA.

Next Steps

This graduate program was an experiment. For the participants it was an eight-year ordeal, a nightmare. Most of them would not repeat the process, but all of them encouraged the college to establish a full-time master's program.

During this lengthy period, there was a change of leadership. Kiros Teka Haddis replaced Negash Kebede as president, and Gishu Jebecha was installed as academic dean of the college.

In evaluating this experiment, both the new president and the dean expressed dissatisfaction with the arrangement with EGST. They felt that developing and offering our own MA program would be better and was doable. Kiros advanced his view that Mennonites are known for their emphasis on peace, so our graduate school and our nation should have a Bible and peace studies program.

The board agreed with President Kiros that, since we were a part of the Anabaptist/Mennonite family, rather than seeking outside partner institutions, we ought to cultivate partner relationships with other Anabaptist/Mennonite institutions of higher learning. Further, MKC, as a growing church, had a growing interest in having its leaders educated to the master's level. Its ever-growing body of over 2,000 alumni was pressing for this to happen. Further, there were tens of thousands of MKC young people graduating from the thirty-four secular universities in Ethiopia. Many of them would like to enhance their education with some religious studies.

In 2016, the board of trustees approved in principle and requested President Kiros to bring a proposal for an MA program curriculum. Kiros and Gishu undertook research to assess the current need and resources. They also began to explore the possibilities of developing an affiliate relationship with one of the Anabaptist seminaries that could lead to a full-blown MA degree level program.

In summary, a vision was emerging that the college should negotiate a relationship with a sister seminary in the USA or Canada. MK College would not seek to use their accreditation but issue its own degree. The partner would help with advice, encouragement, curriculum development, and by sharing a teacher or two as possible. Other expat teachers would be recruited, as would be available from other sister institutions as well.

In line with that vision, came the need to strengthen our faculty by encouraging our teachers to get PhD level training at appropriate recommended schools and by hiring people with that level of qualification.

CHAPTER 26

Personal Transition

Vera and I were having problems meeting the financial expectations of our Mission. While part of my job was to raise funds for the college, we found it harder to raise funds for our own support. Our sponsoring agency began reminding us of the fact that our personal support level was below the required minimum to keep us in Ethiopia. We kept getting these subtle warnings that we may have to be recalled home. While we did not anticipate that would happen, it became a real irritant. We believed God had enough resources out there that we should not be withdrawn from our work before he saw fit. We chose not to pressure our loyal Missionary Support Team (MST) to raise more funds, but it was a nagging problem.

In the spring of 2010, we made the big decision to terminate our relationship with EMM after thirty-two years of serving under their provision and supervision. We decided we would try going on our own. We appealed to our supporters to continue with their support by sending their funds directly to us. Most of them did.

Vera and I departed Ethiopia for a two and one-half month home leave that summer. We arrived in time to visit our daughter Cindy's family before they returned on another mission assignment to Peru. We travelled, visiting supporters and friends along the way to Alberta and back, and to Ontario and back. In Alberta, we had a mini-Hansen family reunion to celebrate my mother's 90th birthday.

In July, we attended an Old Timer's Retreat in Lancaster,

Pennsylvania. This was for former missionaries who had served in Ethiopia and for the few Ethiopians of the diaspora who had known them. We returned to Ethiopia in September, where I taught for the semester. We led an Experience Ethiopia Tour in February.

As Vera approached her 70th birthday, and I was only eight months behind, we began to give thoughtful consideration as to our future relationship with the college. It was time for a change—not exactly to retire, but to change the way we worked supporting the college.

Fifteen years had passed since we returned to Ethiopia to assist in developing the college. During those years, our lives had been deeply enriched by working in partnership with visionary and dedicated church leaders. We felt the deep bonds of love and common purpose between our fellow staff members and ourselves. I was inspired by the outstanding commitment shown in the lives of our student-evangelists. I felt empowered when teaching such eager learners. Also, the task of developing the institution challenged my entrepreneurial spirit. These memories would always be with us.

At the same time, although we appreciated the progress made in those fifteen years, we were disappointed by our failure to see the vision realized. In fact, the vision seemed less clear than it did at the beginning.

We were not sure that the board even had a vision anymore. They had reached a plateau. We did not see concern over the fact that, instead of growing, student enrollment had declined by 30% from what it was a few years prior. The board showed a lack of interest or action in local fundraising for the college. Also, there were serious internal problems and a lack of team spirit within the administration and teaching faculty. There was a leadership problem, but the Board seemed unaware or unconcerned.

In weighing that situation, Vera and I felt that, although we immensely enjoyed our work in Ethiopia, our time had passed. We made our contribution. There was nothing further we could do. Accordingly, I submitted a letter of resignation, effective March 12th, 2011, to the chair of the Board.

Vera and I began making final preparations for our departure. This was a time of emotional turmoil. I realized that the giving and correcting of final exams in January marked the end of my teaching career. What an awful thought. I loved teaching, and I loved the students. What would we do next? Yes, I could use a few months of rest, but then what? However, upon reaching our "three score years and ten," we knew the time had come for us to wind up our affairs and depart. What would be the next phase of our pilgrimage here on this beautiful earth? As in all phases of our lives, we chose to trust our God to lead us, one step at a time, into his purpose for our future.

However, before departing Ethiopia, I agreed to continue promoting the college in North America as an "ambassador" and as a volunteer fundraiser under the title of "Director of College Advancement."

On Saturday afternoon, March 5, 2011, the administration put on a farewell celebration in Vera's and my honor. A crowd of several hundred people attended, some of them our former students, some even from our Bible Academy days, forty-one years earlier.

There were the expected flowery speeches. Some of what was said was true, and some appropriately exaggerated, as is the custom. Anyway, it made us feel good to get so much attention, and I found myself wanting to believe what was said. They made me feel guilty for leaving them at this time, while we were "still healthy and strong." They also presented us with nice gifts, tokens of appreciation, to stir our memories.

After the ceremony, President Negash invited everybody to follow him out around to the front of the academic building. There, he asked Vera and I to cut a ribbon to "open" a sign with these words: "Hansen Library." This ceremony was followed by a feast for all.

Hansen Library - 2011

Into Retirement

After being surprised by a lavish farewell celebration and saying our final goodbyes to so many friends, we took our leave on March 12. On our way, we stopped in Israel for eight days, visiting some friends and seeing the sights. We arrived at our retirement home in Harrisonburg, Virginia on March 21, 2011.

After spending three days getting Vera settled into our house in Virginia, I flew to Alberta, Canada, for a meeting with Negash Kebede. He had come as the keynote speaker at the annual convention of the Northwest Mennonite Conference (NWMC). After visiting briefly in Alberta, I went on to British Columbia to do some fund-raising. Thus began, for us, what some call "retirement."

On July 17, the Harrisonburg Mennonite Church, the congregation in which Vera and I are members in Virginia, had a special service to celebrate our forty-one years of ministry. Dr. Paul T. Yoder (former missionary to Ethiopia) gave a summary of our ministry. Our daughters Karen and Sheryl each gave a nice tribute, and Pastor Craig Mavin gave the shortest sermon ever, read a verse that ended, "Go thou and do likewise!" They gave us a gift and a reception afterwards in which they showed a running slide show of our lives. Then there was a potluck lunch which capped the event. We felt very honored.

In the fall, the NWMC Board requested that I, although officially retired, should continue making annual visits to Ethiopia. To meet the requirements of the Canadian Revenue Agency (CRA), they needed someone on site to check, making sure the money sent from NWMC was used according to the Agency Agreement. Since I was a Canadian citizen still bearing the title, Director of College Advancement, I was qualified to fit that role. This meant I would visit Ethiopia every year and continue to produce the semi-annual reports for the conference as required by the CRA. They also stressed the importance of the college, showing a clear vision and plan, and an explanation of what, why, and how those plans will be implemented.

CHAPTER 27

A Crisis in Leadership

Accountability.

While Darrell Jantzi led the MK College Link (Canada) efforts in fundraising in the Mennonite Church Canada constituency, I undertook the same responsibility in the USA and in the NWMC in Alberta, Canada.

We both were frustrated by the failure of the college administration to provide regular and timely financial reports. In fact, we had received no auditor reports for several years, and the financial reports we received were often incomplete and difficult to understand. Promised reports seldom materialized.

This weakness in accountability was due, in part, to poorly trained or incompetent people carrying the responsibility in the finance office. I, keeping watch on the growth and development of the college, felt that the funds were properly used, but the accountability factor made us uneasy.

Turbulence

At the beginning of the spring semester of 2012, the college had only five full-time faculty and sixteen part-time teachers. Several of the full-time teachers were disillusioned and had quit and moved on to more amenable challenges. The college had only 155 students yet was offering forty-three courses. The economics of such a spread was seriously questionable. However, the dean took delight in offering many options.

President Negash was having a hard time building and keeping a strong team spirit among some of the staff who resented his leadership style. He had served one year beyond his four-year term, but the board had taken no steps towards doing an evaluation, extending it for another term, nor for his possible replacement. They seemed oblivious to any brewing problem.

The dean, Belihu Delelegn, had been teaching for twelve years and needed a break. He had been accepted and offered free tuition for a doctoral program in The Netherlands. He lacked funds for personal travel and living expenses. It would have been mostly a distance learning situation, but he would have to do some of the work in the Netherlands. The president was unwilling to assist with finances or even help with a positive reference. Belihu was very discouraged. Also, he had negotiated a promising arrangement with EMU and James Madison University in Virginia but was blocked by a lack of endorsement from the president.

. Discouraged, Belihu resigned his position as academic dean. His resignation was promptly accepted. He continued as a teacher. A new dean and a new finance head had not been appointed, so the president carried the load himself.

The campus showed signs of general neglect. The lawn mower had broken down, and no one repaired it, so the grass looked rather "natural." The vegetable plots looked untended or unproductive. However, the many Grevillea trees were growing beautifully.

The same malaise was affecting many of the departments. Tigist Alamirew had returned in the fall of 2011, from two-and-one-half years of medical leave in the USA and had resumed her work in the library. She found the interpersonal relationships between some of the library staff had diminished effectiveness in their work. There seemed to be a need for a change in leadership at the top.

Presidential Leadership Transition

Things eventually came to a head when a petition was signed by staff and handed to the chair of the board of trustees. This awakened the board from its complacency. They began an investigative evaluation process which led to a transition in leadership which took place in June 2012. After five-and-one-half years of service, outgoing President Negash Kebede handed over responsibility to the new incoming president, Kiros Teka Haddis. Kiros was a forty-seven-year-old father of four, with over twenty years of experience in higher educational administration in various governmental institutions.

The Church's formal installation of Kiros as the president of the college took place on September 19, 2012. The event was celebrated in the presence of local government authorities, church leaders, members of the board of trustees, members of the community, and the college. Tewodros Beyene, president of MKC, led in a dedicatory prayer for the new president and his wife, Azeb Tsegaye.

The ceremony gave the new president psychological and spiritual support. It was the church's way of confirming the call of God and the anointing of the Holy Spirit upon Kiros for this heavy sacred task of leadership. The ceremony also symbolized the unity of the college leadership with its church. It was a testimony, signifying that the college was an integral part of the community and of the nation, seeking the wellbeing, development, and prosperity of all.

Kiros Teka Haddis, President 2012-2018

Under New Leadership

As he launched his presidency, Kiros demonstrated a serious commitment to improving the quality of order and accountability in the administrative processes. He accepted the challenge of establishing more efficient systems, work habits, and heal broken relationships. He was a good role model in combining a deep spiritual commitment with meticulous organization in his personal work, which gave him moral authority to demand the same from his staff.

A lot of fresh faces replaced the staff who had left. He hired those replacements from the local community of Bishoftu as much as possible. He put together a stronger accounting department and administrative team. He hired an agriculturist to make better use of the land and water resources for self-sustainability. He was committed to lead towards the realization of the original vision to develop the institution as a Christian liberal arts college.

Enrollment climbed to around 180 students in the regular undergraduate programs. The number of female students increased slightly. The graduate program, held in cooperation with EMS and the

EGST, had twenty-four of the college alumni enrolled on a part-time basis.

Construction on the proposed women's dormitory was delayed due to the disruption of leadership transition and change of key staff. At the same time, energy and limited resources were focused on constructing the fourth floor of the Meserete Kristos Church Head Office building to be used as an extension campus in Addis Ababa.

The new administration added more staff until the ratio of staff to students seemed excessively high. Efficiency was lacking. Does a small college really need three drivers for instance? What were they doing when they were not driving? Why was there such a large cleaning staff? Why were there so many workers sitting in idleness while the yard looked so untidy and so much maintenance work remained undone? Could these excess workers not be more efficiently utilized to keep the buildings and compound tidy and attractive, and the electrical and plumbing systems in better working order? How many guards should be sitting at the gate? Why could not some of them be watering some of the flowers in front? Why could staff and students not be trained to pick up and dispose of trash as they see it?

Strict job descriptions and division of labor are good and necessary in government institutions. However, in a Christian environment, workers should be encouraged and expected to "go the second mile" in service and willingly accept to do extra tasks outside their job descriptions. In the eyes of this outsider, the staff needed to be trained in the meaning of a Christian work ethic. It is a Christian duty to work willingly together "as to the Lord," not just according to rule or for the paycheck.

Apart from that, there was also a problem of motivation. Salaries remained a mere pittance, even after many years of faithful service. And with little recognition for their work, service staff tended to become tired and unresponsive to the challenges.

The original vision of making this Christian college strongly rooted in an Anabaptist theological perspective had been weakened by the departure of many of the teachers who were trained in Anabaptist seminaries. Their replacement with new teachers who were only trained in ETC or EGST (schools which follow the Protestant Calvinist theological perspective) diminished the likelihood of students getting a solid biblical and theological training in the Anabaptist perspective.

Patience, a Key to a Successful Journey

Tigist, meaning "patience" in the Amharic language, played a quiet, but significant role in the history of MK College. Her story is worth including in this narrative.

Tigist Alamirew began her life in humble circumstances in a conservative Orthodox community in the northern province of Gojam in the town of Fenota Selam. She was introduced to Jesus Christ through high school friends at age seventeen. Through Jesus, she surrendered her life to God completely. Her Orthodox family opposed her bitterly as she followed her new faith. She literally "passed through the fire" of persecution.

She sought refuge at her aunt's house. However, in their effort to save her for Orthodoxy, her relatives and a group including an Orthodox priest, demanded that she recant. To reinforce their demand, they forced her face into the charcoal cooking fire. Tigist fainted. The damage was irreversible. Caring relatives took her to a hospital where she slowly recovered from the deep burns. Later operations did little to remove the ugly scars burned into her beautiful face.

After she healed a bit, Tigist moved to Addis Ababa, and, with the help of Christian friends, was given a place to work in the Meserete Kristos Church head office. While working, she was able to study accounting and bookkeeping at a vocational school. In time, her radiant testimony of faith in Jesus Christ and her loving forgiveness towards her family resulted in most of them coming to faith as well. That is another story.

After Tigist completed a six-week basic library training, she was transferred to the new Meserete Kristos College to work as cashier, secretary, and to assist Vera in developing the library. She also committed herself to a local congregation, where she became a strong prayer coordinator, and recently, an elder.

Having been saved from dead orthodoxy through her initial dedication to Christ, and then being saved from the fire, Tigist felt called for a purpose, a ministry yet to be revealed. As she studied the Bible and communed with her God, she offered herself, and all she was, to serve as he would lead. In working among the students, Tigist sensed God showing her that now was the time to prepare, to study Bible and theology and get ready for his call.

When the first evening extension course was offered in January 1998, Tigist joined it. A year later, when the college moved to Kotebe, the hassles of rush-hour transportation and attending evening classes became too much. Tigist asked for permission to take courses in the day program, alongside her work. The management committee decided employees could take a maximum of one course per semester. Therefore, besides taking one course per semester, she used her annual leave to take three three-week block courses during the summer.

By 2004, Tigist was able to graduate with a two-year associate degree in Bible and Christian Ministry. Then she continued working on a BA degree in Peace and Conflict Resolution.

In 2006, before Tigist completed her degree, a "good Samaritan" arranged all expenses and accommodation for her to travel to the USA for plastic surgery on her disfigured face. That process took two years. During her stay in the USA, besides improving her appearance, she improved her English and gained a broadening experience of the larger world.

When she returned in 2008, Tigist resumed her work at the college, which had been moved to Bishoftu. She also resumed studying alongside her work. She was able to graduate with a BA degree in May 2011. It was a long road, fourteen years since she sat in her first evening class.

In January 2013, Tigist was appointed to a new role as Distance Education Coordinator. The Distance Education Program was developed to provide learning opportunities for the hundreds of full-time lay ministers in the hinterlands who were unable to join MK College's regular programs.

Learning, designing, and implementing such a program was a huge challenge. Modules needed to be prepared on time. Communication in remote areas was difficult where roads shrank to mere trails and then fizzled out into mule and foot paths. Mailing addresses or post offices were very distant or nonexistent, and phone service was often unavailable. Then, there were budget challenges. Some participants in the countryside lived in a subsistence, hand-to-mouth, agricultural economy. Ministers who struggled to feed their families found the fees, even as low as three dollars per course, to be prohibitive.

The demand for the program in the outlying regions was remarkably high. One region alone, out of the thirty-two regions, had seventy-eight applicants. The college accepted only 150 for this first trial run. Imagine what joy Tigist felt when three years later, of those who first registered, 124 completed requirements for the diploma and graduated. Of those remaining, some found the pressing needs of their ministries too demanding of their time, or they did not have the funds, so they dropped out of the program. For these busy servants of God, to graduate was a remarkable feat of perseverance.

A significant byproduct of the distance education program was that it introduced the college to a much wider range of congregations. The exposure to systematic biblical study motivated some to become full-time students in the degree program at the college. The next year 106 new participants registered for the distance education program.

It took Tigist a long time to reach the point of being a coordinator, but nothing could stop her now. Despite her busy schedule, she enrolled in a master's program at EGST in the evenings. In the spring of 2016, she graduated with a master's degree in developmental studies. Today she serves as a lecturer in the MK Seminary.

CHAPTER 28

More Fundraising

Once again, the quest for funds took Vera and me on another journey to Ontario, Canada, in October 2012. These journeys were often repetitive, tiring, and disappointing. Occasionally, we would strike a "mother lode" that made the journey exhilarating and rewarding.

On one such morning, we drove to Burlington with Darrell and Florence Jantzi and Ken Frey to keep an eleven o'clock appointment with Harry Voortman, the elderly founder, owner, and CEO of Voortman Cookies, Inc. Darrell came with carefully presented proposals for assistance in building the top floor of the MKC Head Office in Addis, to be used as an extension campus for the college and for student scholarships. The interview started with the elderly Harry Voortman coming with question after question, often leading the conversation away from what we carefully planned to present.

Finally, Darrell was able to direct the flow of conversation to the task at hand. We managed to show our eleven-minute DVD, then presented something of our plan for the Extension Campus. Too soon the hour was up, and we never got to emphasize the need for scholarship support as well. Mr. Voortman thanked us for the good explanations and took his leave of us at the end of the hour. Darrell managed to leave several handouts in his hands. We left with mixed feelings, leaving the outcome to Harry and to the Lord.

The next day, Mr. Voortman phoned Darrell to inform him that he would contribute $100,000 for the Addis Campus Extension project. What encouragement!

A Fraternal North America Visit

The following spring, after the installation of Kiros, the Link Board and Mennonite Church Canada invited him and the board chairperson, Kelbessa Muleta Demina, to North America for a fraternal visit. They invited me to organize and lead the tour. This became a six-week, get acquainted, learning, public relations, fund raising, meeting-our-partners trip that lasted from April 16 through May 30, 2013.

Our itinerary began in Harrisonburg and took us to the New York Mennonite Conference meeting at Seneca Falls in upstate New York. We had meetings with friends and supporters in Lancaster, Pennsylvania; Goshen, Elkhart, and Indianapolis in Indiana; and Bluffton and West Liberty in Ohio.

We flew to Minneapolis, Minnesota, then on to Calgary, Alberta, where we visited my home church and family in the Brooks area, in time for Mother's Day weekend.

In Calgary, we found Shemsudin Abdo and brought him to the conference minister's home for a fellowship meal. We enjoyed sharing stories with Shemsudin, the first Ethiopian to serve as General Secretary of MKC back in 1969, and prisoner for four-and-one-half years during the Dergue days. He later, because of involvement in human rights issues, incurred the displeasure of the EPRDF government and went into exile. As a refugee, he translated the whole Bible into the Kotu dialect of Oromo. At age seventy-eight years and half blind, he was busy making a one-volume Bible commentary in that language. We were delighted to have this opportunity to fellowship with this historic person.

We met with members of the NWMC Board. After getting to know each other and clearing up some questions, we finalized an updated schedule for the Agency Agreement between the conference and the college.

Then we flew to Winnipeg, Manitoba, to meet Mennonite Church Canada officials and the Canadian Mennonite University (CMU).

We spent the last eleven days of our trip in Ontario, where Darrell Jantzi and the MK College Link Canada had planned a full schedule to meet friends and supporters.

In Burlington, along with Darrell Jantzi, we met with Mr. Harry Voortman again. As we entered the corporate office and said a prayer to our God, whose interests we represented, Mr. Voortman met us in the lobby. We introduced our guests to Harry who welcomed us to go up to the boardroom on the sixth floor. Since it was a national holiday, the offices were empty, and Mr. Voortman gave us full attention for two hours. He asked many good questions, and we gave answers.

Finally, he summed up the interview by asking, "In light of your plans to open a liberal arts program and your need for scholarship assistance, if I were to give you $200,000, how would you allocate it? We responded by saying we could use some of it for the necessary expenses of opening the liberal arts wing, but would use some of it for scholarships to enable students to continue in our present theological program as well.

The next morning, we were in Darrell's house discussing the itinerary for the day, when Ken Frey, Mr. Voortman's financial advisor, phoned. He suggested we prepare a careful proposal for how we would use the $200,000, provided Harry agrees to support us. Moments later, he called again and informed me that Harry had just called and informed him that he had decided to support our college to the tune of $200,000 per year, for five years! This was a high moment for all of us.

At the conclusion of the tour, we took time to think about the impact of our fraternal visit. Kelbessa remarked that it was "a unique tour experience, unique from my three-year AMBS experience." The brothers remarked that this was a huge continent. They were amazed at the number of contacts, persons, and organizations backing the church and college in Ethiopia. They remarked about the number of Ethiopian contacts they made during the tour. They were surprised at how the Ethiopian diaspora in Ontario was reaching out to the Mennonites.

A New Service Bus

Moved by the tales of frequent breakdowns, stranded staff, and consequent absenteeism in their workplace, not to mention the late-night returns to their homes, an anonymous philanthropist donated $85,000 to purchase a new bus. The administration promptly ordered a new thirty-two passenger, Toyota Coaster bus, to be shipped from the factory in Japan. It arrived in November 2014 and has been giving dependable service ever since. God bless the donor with a long, happy life!

CHAPTER 29

Building the Campus Continued

Developments in the Fall of 2013

John Peters returned to Ethiopia in June 2013, to teach for three weeks. In September, Jim and Peg Engle and I returned to Ethiopia to teach for the fall semester. Vera came a month later. I brought along our grandson, Justus Payne, an eighteen-year-old first-year student. He became the second American to come as a regular student for one year.

A Revised Master Plan

One of the consequences of the Negash presidency was the fallout from his disregard for legal building codes and requirements. Back in 2003, Bedru submitted the architectural designs and the campus master plan to the Bishoftu Municipality for official approval. He paid good money for a building permit.

Negash, having grown up in a former time when codes and building permits were ignored, if they even existed, simply ignored both the campus master plan and the approved architectural designs. He freely chose to place the buildings wherever he thought best and made changes to the designs as he saw fit.

The consequences were felt when Kiros sought a permit to construct a women's dormitory. The municipality sent out engineers to inspect the campus. They found, except for the academic building, all the other buildings were "illegal." They were not in the positions specified in the master plan, and they did not conform to the architectural designs. Also, the building permits had expired. A new day had new code requirements. The buildings were illegal and could be condemned and destroyed.

However, the officials had mercy. Ethiopia is a poor country. Its citizens do not all know the law. The buildings were of superior quality and excellent value. So, grace could be extended, if the college would pay for their engineers and architects to draw up a new campus master plan and alter the architectural designs to reflect the reality on the ground. That way, everything would become legal. The college had no choice. This exercise was undertaken and completed after several months, at considerable extra cost.

A Dorm for Women

As mentioned earlier, women played major leadership roles in the underground cell church movement during the years of persecution under the Dergue regime. They led Bible studies, preached, taught, evangelized, and discipled new believers. Women comforted and encouraged those who suffered.

However, with the restoration of religious freedom, men emerged out of hiding and assumed most of the public leadership roles. Females continued as respected leaders in the less conspicuous helping roles. Officially, the church recognized there was no gender barrier to any leadership position or role. However, in practice, deep seated Ethiopian culture still impacted the church. Very few females held key positions, and almost none of the delegates, elected by the members and sent to the annual General Assembly, were female. With that cultural reality, it was no surprise that about 95% of the college's students were male, and that the men's dorm took priority.

However, most male leaders recognized there was much potential talent and gifting in women who constitute at least 50% of the church's members. Most of these women were less educated with fewer opportunities to exercise and develop their gifts. From its inception, the founding fathers of the college intended that females would, or at least should, be given equal opportunity for admission along with their male counterparts. A few females took advantage, enrolled, and graduated. Their contribution to the church and society has been significant.

In 2019, four of the twelve full-time faculty were females, all of whom held master's degrees. One of them was coordinating the college's Distance Education program, educating 271 church leaders. A female graduate was heading up the ministry to female prisoners in fifty prisons. Several had started unique ministries to rehabilitate destitute street women. One was editing another denomination's magazine. Several were serving as evangelists in their congregations. At least two had been ordained as pastors. Several were holding key positions in different para church organizations. A few were doing graduate studies on the master's level, with future contribution yet unknown. Others were working with congregations in compassion ministries, assisting children of destitute families.

While these women were engaged in their critical careers, they were also better equipped to serve their congregations as Sunday school teachers, youth workers, Bible teachers, deacons, office workers, and elders. Their education also contributed quality to their domestic lives as wives, mothers, and homemakers, as well as members in their communities. These were some of the ministries in which our female graduates were engaging. So much more could be done, were more of our female members capacitated through education.

Having completed construction of the dorm for men in early 2012, we fully expected to continue construction of a women's dorm. The few female students roomed in the same undesirable conditions in the top floor classrooms vacated by the men. There seemed to be a problem of vision and leadership between the administration, the board, and the church. While they all agreed the college needed to have a boarding facility for women, they could not decide on the size, nor the urgency of constructing one. They did not show enthusiasm for the project. It did not help that all the decision makers were males! We fundraisers were disappointed.

The donors were ahead of the decision makers. In 2010, we were given an anonymous grant of $100,000 towards the construction of a women's dorm. The donor requested a progress report every six months. We had their money, but for a full five years, had nothing to report. I was embarrassed.

Groundbreaking

As dawn broke on February 25, 2015, the sudden roar of earth-moving equipment shook us awake. At the building site, they began moving topsoil. A few hours later, officials, guests, and staff began assembling under an acacia tree, shaded from the hot mid-morning sun. This was the hour for the long-delayed official ground-breaking ceremony. At a signal from the contractor, the digging machine and the trucks, busy moving one-and-one-half meters of topsoil, paused, and engines shut off. In the silence that followed, the dust settled, and then the ceremony commenced.

Representing the architects, Daniel Assefa gave a brief report on their work. The contractor confirmed his promises. President Kiros spoke briefly about the master plan and vision for campus development over the next twenty years. He invited Tewodros Beyene, General Secretary of MKC, to make appropriate remarks and lead in a dedicatory prayer. Following this short program, the crowd moved to the cooler chapel, while the engines roared back to life and to their task at hand.

In the chapel, all joined a service of worship and thanksgiving, led entirely by the female students. This was a long-anticipated, historic moment, three years following the completion of the men's dorm.

Construction

What was agreed upon in the signed contract bore little resemblance to what transpired in real time. From the beginning, the project was plagued with setbacks. Blame for delays was placed on shortages of building supplies, shortages of skilled labor, and the escalation of wages.

However, the performances of three separate contractors and the college administrators were not without fault. Three years and two months after the groundbreaking, after the failure of two broken contracts, the third contractor completed the job.

The final product was a beautiful piece of art. Inside, all the ceilings and walls were carefully painted. Vinyl flooring covered the bedroom floors. Ceramic tile covering the hallways and bathrooms gave a neat, clean finish. The outside walls were painted in attractive, two-tone colors, and appropriate paver-block skirting completed the building.

A dormitory for women - 2018

Finally, on May 12, 2018, following the annual graduation ceremony, the guests were invited to go to the site of the newly completed women's dormitory. There, they participated in a dedication and ribbon cutting ceremony. As the ribbon blocking the entrance fell away, the guests moved inside to inspect the marvelous, modern facility. At four persons per room, this facility could house up to 258 women. It provided two large communal bathrooms on each of the four floors. There were also three lounge areas with three kitchenettes, and a large meeting room, enabling it to be used as a retreat center for outside groups who might want to rent space for special meetings.

To equip the new dormitory was a big challenge. In the spring of 2018, we collected and shipped another container of used equipment from Harrisonburg, Virginia. The shipment included 170 used dorm beds, eighty wooden chairs, 127 metal dining room chairs mostly donated by James Madison University, plus 320 folding chairs. To this, we added ten large round tables and forty-nine boxes of used books.

Besides what we could stuff in that container, we had enough extra collected in storage to fill another container which was shipped two years later.

Funding the Dorm

The overall projected cost was set at US $910,000 (18.2 million birr). Following that first gift of $100,000 in 2010 over a five-year period, funds slowly trickled in. The goal was finally reached when an anonymous Canadian couple offered a matching gift challenge in the spring of 2016. They would match, dollar for dollar, any funds we could raise, up to Cdn. $200,000 between May 3rd and September 30th. The outcome of this four-month, matching grant challenge was a success beyond our expectations. We received over 300 responses, which with the grant netted well over US $500,000. We thanked God and his generous donors!

Life in Bishoftu Revisited in 2015

Mid-January 2015 found Vera and I back in Ethiopia for another two-month visit. This time we brought our granddaughter Desta Hansen with us. Since we arrived after midnight, and there was no one to meet us, we hired a taxi to deliver us and our luggage to the Bishoftu campus.

Imagine, a tiny yellow taxi with the driver and three oversized passengers crammed inside along with carry-on luggage. Picture nine, large, bulging suitcases, stacked three high, in three rows, strapped to the roof. Now, visualize that little taxi creeping out in the dead of night, on a poorly lit, potholed highway, for a forty-five km journey. How comforting our relief then, when the driver turned onto a brand new, six-lane expressway, and whizzed us to our destination in minutes! What a road! With limited access and toll gates, we realized that Ethiopia had truly entered the modern era!

After awaking the unsuspecting guards at the campus gate, we entered, only to find our reserved room in the guesthouse securely locked. The key was with the host, fast asleep in her home, half a km away. By the time the guard ran, retrieved the key, and welcomed us in, it was close to three a.m. Imagine how comforting it felt to once again be home!

An Administrator's Residence, a Gift

Peter and Heleen Stam Stuurman, managers of the Dutch owned Alfa Dairy Farm across the road from the college, wanted to assist the college in some meaningful way. They sent an application to their church in The Netherlands to raise funds for and have a group of Dutch volunteers come to construct an administrator's residence. That church raised 17,000 Euros, not enough to complete the house, but to get a good start. Peter oversaw the project, using his tractor to level the building site. He purchased the necessary supplies and had some masons prepare the foundation.

In mid-April 2015, a team of twelve, eight men and four women, from the *Hervormde Gemeente Nieuw-Lekkerland Dorp* congregation arrived. They came with just one assignment: construction of a 1,500 ft² administrator's residence. Since the foundation was already prepared, the group started with the above groundwork of steel and blocks.

They began the work each morning promptly at 6.00 a.m. The four women took care of the catering. Whether it was coffee or tea for a small break, or potatoes and cauliflower for dinner, they made sure the men could do their job properly. Several of the men prepared steel for the roof construction in the workshop. The rest installed steel frames for the walls and laid blocks in the spaces between. The daily work stopped at 6.00 p.m. After dinner, they enjoyed a Bible study each evening.

After two weeks, the basic building was in place, but their time had expired, and so did the funds to complete it. At a farewell chapel worship service, amid expressions of appreciation, love, and prayers, they handed the keys to the college administrator. The team went back to The Netherlands as ambassadors, telling others about the college, their ministry, and the hospitality which they experienced.

The students and staff were deeply impressed by what they saw in the lives of these strangers, now become brothers and sisters. Their eagerness to work together continuously, for twelve hours a day, their diligence, punctuality, and faithfulness, were exemplary for the college community to witness.

It took the Dutch team only two weeks to pour the floor pad, erect the walls, place the roof, and rough in the plumbing. However, it took the college another two years to raise the needed $24,000 to finish the plastering and painting, installing doors and windows, fixing lighting, and plumbing, and installing cupboards.

One of the problems, besides funding, was the lack of cooperation by contractors. The first one, realizing his bid was too low, withdrew from the project. The next one started it but failed to complete it as he moved to America. He wrote a release document, excusing the college from any payment owed to him in exchange for releasing him from his contract obligations. The third contractor took a year longer than the contract stipulated. Finally, in March 2018, President Kiros, Azeb, and their family moved into a lovely new home.

A Diesel Generator

The electric house was built in 2007 to house the campus transformer and a diesel generator. However, we delayed the purchase of the generator due to a shortage of funds. We hoped that the government's electric services would improve. That turned out to be a vain hope. For eight years the college endured frequent blackouts during office hours, as well as during the dark nights when students needed to study. With its patience exhausted, in the fall of 2014, the college finally purchased a diesel generator for about $25,000. It was delivered and installed in February of 2015.

Since then, it has been used during those frequent, lengthy, electric outages for office computers and the computer labs. However, the generator is still not used during the many dark evening hours. The prohibitive cost of fuel was the reason it was not considered necessary for student use.

In recent years, with the availability of modern cell phones with light capabilities, students have adapted. Ambitious students can study, even in the darkest of those nights.

Internet and Wi-Fi Service

Intermittent internet and email service as well as unreliable land line telephone service caused much frustration and consequential complaining. After eight years of patient, and not so patient, endurance, the college was finally able to pay for and persuade Ethio Telecom to dig a kilometer-long trench and install a fiber-optic broadband cable to the campus in 2015. This was an especially important improvement, considering the growing need in modern education to have internet access.

This marked the dawn of the digital age, when computers, or tablets, and smart phones have become essential requirements for any student who wishes to succeed. The entire world was being connected. Even the community youth would sit on the ditch bank along the road, outside the academic building, tapping into the college's wi-fi with their smart phones. However, even this broadband service proved to be sporadic and unreliable, much less than what we expected.

Abundant Life-Giving Water

A shortage of rain in 2015 reduced the water table. The second well failed at the beginning of 2016. So, once again the growing crops had to be abandoned to their waterless fate, incurring loss for the college. More alarming, this put the college in a very precarious position depending upon the first well for basic human needs.

Recognizing the need for water security, Kiros consulted the Department of Water Resources. They recommended drilling a 130-meter-deep well. The projected cost, with pump, was set at US$50,000, so an appeal was made for funding.

Hearing this need, a widow, Martha Clymer, offered a matching grant of up to $25,000 in loving memory of her deceased husband, the late Dr. David Clymer. This encouraged supporters in the USA and Canada to respond generously, and the appeal was more than matched. As a result, the well was drilled, yielding an abundant supply of water. The legally required water use permit certified it was potable and of good enough quality to be bottled for commercial use.

Besides guaranteeing the daily needs of humans, poultry, and cattle, this well enables the irrigation of the whole compound, including producing vegetables for cafeteria use and for sale.

Volunteerism and Short-Term Missions

Volunteerism is all about self-giving. Jesus, who voluntarily came to show us the way to life, is the best example. Volunteerism ought to be a central characteristic of every one of his followers. A true disciple will emulate Jesus by willingly giving up his own interests, giving his/her time, energies, and resources to help others in need.

MK College could not exist without volunteers. A missionary is a volunteer. Any underpaid teacher, administrator, or worker who works for less than he/she could earn elsewhere is in some respects a volunteer. And those who travel out of their way, leave their comfort zone, donate their time, are also volunteers, whether it be short term for a few days, a few weeks, or long term for years. Donors who lay down their wealth or a portion of their wealth, to serve their fellow humans are volunteers.

The group of twelve Dutch men and women who came and built an administrator's house were not the only volunteers who contributed to the growth and success of the college. From time to time, individuals or small groups of volunteers from outside Ethiopia made their way to MK College where they helped in unique ways, being a blessing and in turn receiving a blessing, a learning experience they would treasure for the rest of their lives. It is always "more blessed to give than to receive."

While the Experience Ethiopia Tour appealed to the older more affluent set who were pleased to do the "tourist" things, a younger group of ten from Bethel Mennonite Church in Ontario visited the college for three weeks. They were more interested in helping around the campus and working in the community. They helped clear the brush from a football field, installed a ceiling in the chapel, made a little meditation garden in the inner triangle of the men's dorm, as well as some other small projects that made the campus more complete. They also worked with children in the neighborhood. They gave some time to help in an orphanage in Adama. They were all excited about what they learned and what they could contribute. It was a life-changing experience for them.

Then there was Paul Wytenbroek, a recently retired shop teacher from Abbotsford, British Columbia, who came as a volunteer for seven weeks in March and April 2010. Having a shop teacher background, he was the right man to teach our maintenance people in the use of tools, making and setting up worktables and supply racks, making a bolt and screw cupboard, installing the used machinery sent by Equipping the Saints some years earlier. As a departing gesture, Paul slung his work boots up on a rafter in the shop where, to this day, all can see and remember, a cool volunteer!

Lois Nafziger never forgot Ethiopia. She had taught in the Nazareth Bible Academy back in the 1970's. She had adopted and raised an Ethiopian daughter while she practiced law back in Pennsylvania. Then, in 2000, she survived a bout with colon cancer. Since she was healed, she took up biking with passion.

When she retired, Lois wanted to do something special to help the Meserete Kristos Church teach its leaders. She dreamed up a "Lois Rides" challenge to raise funds. She rode her bicycle 3,100 miles from San Diego, CA to Jacksonville, FL between March 4 to April 30th, 2010. Her goal was to raise money to be split between her local church's Timberline Transitional Housing Project and Meserete Kristos College. Her heroic effort raised over $30,000 for the college. Lois was a life-long volunteer.

In November 2010, three of the older German volunteers, those who came the previous year to help build the chicken house, returned for two weeks to assist in gardening. They really did an amazing amount of work, leaving behind a patch of sprouting alfalfa and another of sprouting sweet corn, and a larger patch ready to be seeded. Although the man was eighty and his wife and friend were not much younger, they were still tough, hardworking, and a notable example of joyful volunteerism.

Low-paid Staff also Volunteers

Wondimu Hundesa was the first person to be hired when the land at Bishoftu was allotted for a college back in the year 2000. An unemployed ex-army officer, he was recommended by his church and was hired to be a guard while the first fence was being constructed twenty-three years ago. He remembered a time when the campus was a wild overgrown area, a place where trucks emptied their loads of the city's septic tank sewage, spreading the black, stinking mess on the field. It was a garbage-strewn, forsaken place, where hyenas prowled around scavenging in the night.

He felt a great pride and ownership for this campus because he sacrificed many years of his life in helping develop the land. The bushy thorn trees that reinforce the surrounding fence were planted and watered by Wondimu's hands.

In the early days, Wondimu and his team of gardeners grew tomatoes, cabbages, hot peppers, onions, Chinese cabbages, lettuce, garlic, local cabbages, carrots, red beets, cauliflowers, and even sweet corn. While much of the food grown went directly to feeding the students, cash was earned through the sale of any surplus.

Even though the position was never highly paid, Wondimu was always thankful for the work. It was his way of serving God. He believed God would bless him for his efforts, and he was prepared to serve to the end of his working career.

After he commented many times about sacrifice and hard work, I asked him why he stayed. His answer was one which should challenge us all. Wondimu said, "I have five children of my own. I am doing this for the next generation." Wondimu saw hope and opportunity for the youth and children of Ethiopia in this school. Graduates were doing many wonderful things, and every year, more and more were graduating and expanding God's kingdom, making a positive impact on the Ethiopian society.

CHAPTER 30

A Christian Liberal Arts University: An Illusion?

Our Dilemma: A Question of Integrity

The vision of its founding fathers was that the MK College should have liberal arts programs along with its Bible and Theology program. Realizing this vision was much more challenging than expected. Much time, hard work, and funds have been expended to establish a strong Bible and Theology department, refine an administration system, and build the campus. This was accomplished while raising enough funds to maintain ongoing programs, equipping hundreds of graduates for their various ministries. Still the vision has not been fulfilled.

While Negash's gradualist approach, introduced fourteen years earlier, was still functioning, it had stagnated. The church and its college have not taken further steps forward to implement the vision. Many of the members of the church, especially those whose hopes were dashed for sending their children to their own college, were asking "Why not?" And many of the long-term donors and supporters across North America and Europe were also wondering why the college remained only a theological college, and not a multi-disciplined Christian college.

We fund-raisers, attempting to bridge the vast chasm between the foreign donors and the Ethiopian church and its college, felt frustrated and embarrassed. We had made promises and collected funds from generous donors who believed our message, trusted our sincerity, and felt the Ethiopians' pain. Then we had to keep reporting, year after year, that launching the liberal arts programs was delayed. Our integrity was in question.

Historical Overview: Steps in the Formation of the Vision

In the years immediately following the fall of the Dergue Government and the granting of religious freedom in 1991, MKC leaders sensed a need for an educational institution for the training of evangelists and pastors as well as educating their youth.

In their deliberations, the leaders envisioned establishing a Bible college that would grow to become a full Christian university. It would have a biblical seminary and a liberal arts college. With that vision, they pooled their extremely limited resources and launched their little Meserete Kristos Church Bible Institute in January 1994.

It was their vision that attracted and persuaded Vera and me to accept their invitation for us to return to Ethiopia, to teach, and to assist as consultant in their newly formed institute. In interviews with the leaders, I was very clearly informed that the vision was to establish, "not only a Bible college like so many others," but to create a "Christian liberal arts college, like Daystar."

Since I was then teaching at Daystar, I understood what this vision meant. The vision agreed with my sense of call. An important part of my job description was to also serve as a "consultant" to the church as it developed its vision for the college.

The vision was clearly stated in the college's constitution, adopted on August 16, 1997:

Article V, Vision, Section 1 states: "While the college began as a small Bible institute, it is growing into a baccalaureate degree-level college. It envisions becoming a full "Christian university," offering a broad range of undergraduate and graduate programs designed to meet the training needs of the growing Christian communities in the Ethiopian cultural, socio-economic, and spiritual context."

Article VII, sets forth the strategy: "For the fulfillment of its purpose, mission and vision, the college shall provide residential and extension programs in the liberal arts, beginning with theology, leadership, management, community development, entrepreneurship, business administration and teacher training, in accordance with the needs of the Christian community in Ethiopia."

In the year 2000, the sixty-six-page project proposal and application for land, which the General Secretary of MKC signed, and we submitted to the Oromia Regional Government, was entitled "A Project Proposal for the Establishment of the Meserete Kristos College as a Multi-disciplined Institution of Tertiary Level Education in the Liberal Arts Tradition." This request for land resulted in the college being granted the 60,000 m² at Bishoftu, upon which the campus was being built.

In 2002, the MKC Executive Committee, in its restructuring of their college, reaffirmed and provided for the establishment of two wings in the college, a seminary and a liberal arts or science wing.

When construction started in July of 2004, the architectural designs called for a campus with a capacity to accommodate 2,000 students, assuming a liberal arts campus. The current buildings were designed in partial preparation for that eventuality.

Again, in April 2006, the board hired Ethiopian Educational Consultants (ETEC) to develop the plans required to guide the college in setting up and seeking pre-accreditation from the Ministry of Education.

ETEC produced its final documents required to proceed immediately with implementation, having all the relevant information in place. However, in the following month, the newly installed president, upon receiving the documents, dismissed the exercise as premature. He preferred taking a slow gradualist approach to developing a liberal arts program. The trustees agreed with him. The costly and time-consuming process was wasted, and no further action was taken at that time, nor in the sixteen years since.

President Negash was reluctant to move ahead immediately because the campus was not yet developed to accommodate an influx of more students and a multiplication of programs. There was no extra dormitory space, and the kitchen/dining facility was only temporary. However, they could have developed the programs while the construction of these buildings was in progress. That way, they would have been ready to launch as soon as the facilities were in place. This was not pursued.

The men's dorm was completed in February 2011, with space to accommodate 384 men. Yet, no effort was made to launch a liberal arts program. Both dorms remain to this day underutilized.

Thirty years have passed, and millions of dollars have been raised and invested in the buildings of the current campus. All these steps have been taken, and yet, the vision of having "a Daystar in Ethiopia" has not been realized. Why not?

The main reason is the lack of long-term visionary leadership. One of the disadvantages of frequent changes in leadership is the lack of people on the decision-making board who know its history, who really understand why their predecessors made long-range decisions with future implications. Such was the case with the long-range goal of making the MK College a Christian liberal arts college.

Building the campus took more than a decade longer than we expected. When they made the decision to build a large dormitory for 258 women, there were less than twenty female students in the Bible and Christian Ministries programs. The then current leaders had to wrestle with the wisdom or even desirability of making this investment unless the college offered programs that would attract women. The questions, "to build or not to build?" and "how large?" could only be answered after they decided an answer to the question, "Do we really want our college to become a Christian multi-disciplined university or not?" The fact that the building was built, implies that their answer was "Yes."

Deeper than the lack of long-term visionary leadership, it has become apparent that the real issue is the lack of consensus among the church's leadership. Although the leaders gave verbal assent, they were aware of lingering opposition from a substantial portion of the church's leadership who were hesitant to push ahead with the project. This hesitancy had several reasons, valid or invalid.

One reason had to do with a general suspicion of anything connected to the term "liberal." Some members were not sure that liberal arts would be good for the church. This uneasiness arose from deep concern that the church might adopt liberal theology in the future. Repeatedly, they referred to early American colleges, like Harvard and Yale, which started as theological schools but grew, and, over a two-hundred-year period, became secular institutions.

Further, no one in the then current leadership had experience attending any Christian liberal arts college or university. They did not see the value. The impact of the Harvard and Yale stories cancelled out all the hundreds of examples of good Christian liberal arts institutions existing in the world.

The term "liberal" is a good word and fits well into what an ideal Christian should become. It has to do with openness, accepting others, kindness, generosity, abundance, progress, as well as liberation or setting the oppressed free, hence liberty and freedom. Jesus Christ was the true liberal, the true liberator. Popular politics notwithstanding, let us not see that word as a dirty word.

Definition of the Term, "Liberal Arts" (with some help from WikiLeaks)

The ancient Greeks were the first to make a distinction between the "liberal arts" and the "practical arts." Plato and Aristotle defined the "**liberal arts**" as those subjects that were suitable for the development of intellectual and moral excellence. The practical arts were simply useful. Plato, who established informal education through his "Academy" around 387 BC, based education on the principles of philosophy. He held that knowledge and understanding should be acquired through scientific discovery, critical thinking, and the questioning of accepted assumptions.

Today, modern colleges and universities offer undergraduate courses that combine a broad mixture of educational objectives. Modern liberal arts programs retain Plato's promotion of critical thinking, and the advancement of knowledge through analysis and scientific research. They also include Isocrates's concerns for developing moral and intellectual excellence through literary and rhetorical studies. There is a consensus that liberal arts education should span a broad range of academic fields.

Currently, "liberal arts" studies are distinguished from pre-professional or pre-vocational studies which are intended to prepare the student for specific kinds of employment. In contrast, "liberal arts" refers to the unspecialized, nonscientific studies pursued in an undergraduate college. It can also more broadly refer to all undergraduate studies in the arts and sciences, including subjects like literature, history, political science, sociology, and anthropology.

While there is growing emphasis on the "practical" pre-professional and pre-vocational courses of study in most universities and colleges, there are still a strong minority where the liberal arts approach is valued. Where the pre-professional and pre-vocational programs prepare the student for a career, it is felt that liberal arts education better prepares the student for life.

A broad-based, non-specialized education prepares the graduate for a variety of experiences and occupations he/she can expect to pursue over his/her lifetime. It provides a broader, stronger, more wholesome base upon which to develop one's total life perspective and experience. In a Christian college, the addition of Biblical and theological subjects and the teaching of the liberal arts from a Christian perspective enriches the whole educational experience immensely.

Current Precedents of Liberal Arts Education.

Most current Christian colleges and universities in North America follow a liberal arts curriculum to some extent. Also, the Mennonite-related schools offer a well-rounded education with emphasis on a chosen field, but also make one more aware of the larger social, psychological, economic, political, and historical environment in which the student lives and will serve.

Most early Mennonite missionaries who founded the Meserete Kristos Church and left their imprint on the kind of church it is today had graduated from one of our Christian liberal arts colleges. They were able to serve as doctors, nurses, teachers, administrators, businesspeople, and development workers because their education provided them with the spiritual and biblical foundations plus the practical skills that made them so effective in their work. So, in a sense, whether we recognize it or not, MKC carries in its genes some qualities that were imparted through that earlier liberal arts education.

In Summary:

MKC leaders made the decision to launch a Christian liberal arts college thirty years ago, re-affirmed that decision many times since, and made many slow but important steps toward that goal during subsequent years. They have not yet reached that goal; however, the road already travelled is long; the goal is close. It would be difficult to turn back now.

Recent developments in the educational field and in government requirements have provoked new questions and misgivings. However, if we believe God led us to start down this road, and he has provided step by step as much as we were able to implement, then we must move forward, adjust, find solutions to the problems, and make a way. If it is God's vision, there will be provision. If it is his will, there will be a way. Obstacles there will be, but with his help, they will be overcome!

However, in looking back over the thirty-year history of failure to implement the original vision, one can now see there has been a quiet, scarcely spoken resistance to the vision from the beginning. There has never been consensus or unanimity among the leaders. There have always been those who felt the funds used to implement the vision would be better used to fund the priority task of evangelism. And, especially during the conflict between the church and the college leadership of 2001-2003, this unhappiness contributed to the opposition, even though at that time the college was 100% focused on training evangelists and pastors for the church. It was a long-range vision, which the opposition feared and resisted.

Fifteen years later and under a new generation of leaders, that resistance remains. Hence the campus is being built, but the new programs are not being developed and implemented. While there seems to be unanimity in the decision to upgrade the college to the level of a seminary, it seems best to the leaders to refrain from moving ahead with the multi-disciplined university vision, unless or until, there is consensus within the church to do so.

CHAPTER 31

Sustainability and External Support

The Challenge of Sustainability

At the turn of the century in Ethiopia, there were dozens of private colleges springing up with the main driving motive behind them— profit. MK College is a non-profit church- owned college. Once the large outlays of capital investment in the campus are complete, the college could be self-sustainable. However, to become sustainable, it will have to charge fees to cover operating expenses. If it provides quality programs that are in demand, it could outperform many of the for-profit colleges.

However, seeing how colleges and universities operate in other countries, it would be presumptuous to say it would no longer need help. There will always be a need for scholarship assistance for the youths of the poor. Whether scholarship support originates from outside or from within the country is another matter.

President Kiros Teka deserves credit for trying to push towards achieving financial self-sustainability. In the seven years of his administration, he consistently pushed the college administration to be more self-sustaining. He challenged the community, the board, the church leaders, and the congregations to financially support the college. As a result, the college was able to lower the rate of out-of-country subsidy for operations from 95% to 72%. Yet almost all the funds for building the campus were raised outside of Ethiopia.

Local Efforts Towards Sustainability

Back in the beginning, in 1994, the MKC Head Office provided the small figure of 55,000 birr (about $5,000) to support its Bible Institute. However, as gifts began to trickle in from outside, even that small budget figure was no longer available. Those were tough times, and some congregations were not sending in their dues which were set at 15% of contributions. So, the budget could not be met. At that time, thirty years ago, the annual per capita GDP of Ethiopia was around $100.

In the decades following, there was always a shortage of scholarship funds, as this fast-growing church had many more emerging leaders who desired to be trained. The college's financial situation set limits on the number who could attend. It was not only giving generous scholarships, but it was also building a campus, one block at a time. The church simply did not have the money.

Was the 100% subsidy given to students a mistake? People from other Christian colleges, accused MKC of "purchasing students," which meant some students were coming to MK College because it was free, not because they liked the education or that the quality was better, or that they felt called.

To move toward self-sustainability, the administration began requiring each student to bring $30 as a "cost sharing fee." They raised it to $40, then $50, then $110, then $180. In 2021 the cost sharing fee was raised to $370, which was about 14% of the actual cost, which was above $2,800 to provide one student with tuition, room, and board for a full year. The doubling of the fee to $370 provoked consternation among students. Most, backed by their congregations or families, were able to overcome this hurdle. In some cases, a grace period enabled the neediest to continue to study while making appeals to their acquaintances for assistance. For them, this was a difficult hurdle to overcome. Some fell into arrears and had to drop out of school.

Again, the students saw this as a huge challenge to their limited capacity. Many still do not understand what the actual costs of operating a boarding college are. To those who do understand, the very existence of

Meserete Kristos College is viewed as a miracle, brought into existence, and operated by the generous assistance of international partners. The gifts, given down through the years, have taken on a life of their own through the graduates, ever growing and blessing more people, building the Kingdom of God. Scholarships are "gifts that keep on giving"!

In 2021, local income from tuition fees, facility rents, congregational offerings, bank interest, dividend income, and agricultural activities generated the equivalent of $218,200 which was equivalent to about 31% of the total expenditure budget of about $700,000. Seminary administrators were very aware that being dependent upon outside sources for 69% of funding was a serious weakness.

They tried to economize while finding ways to increase self-sustainability. By requiring full-time teachers to teach the equivalent of four courses or twelve credit hours per semester, they reduced the number of hired part-time teachers. Previously, a full load for a teacher was only three courses or nine credit hours.

Today, MK College is still dependent upon the charity of outside donors for about 95% of its building costs and 69% of its operating costs. While most educational institutions depend upon outside subsidies to balance their budgets, the administration and the board realize that the current rate of dependence is much too high. Besides praying, steps are being taken to correct this.

The college community makes prayer and fasting a priority. Included in their daily prayers and chapels, the students and staff ask God for provision and direction in solving the problems of the college as it seeks to grow.

Campus facilities such as classrooms, men's and women's dormitories, chapel, guesthouse, and other facilities, when not in use, are rented to groups for prayer, congregational, or small group retreats; for short term training, or conferences; or for weddings. Such uses generate income.

Good arable land and a water well are another resource that the college uses for growing vegetables and fruit. A dairy barn was built, and five Friesian dairy cows were purchased. These cows are kept inside, in a zero-grazing mode. The college no longer has to purchase milk for the students.

A cattle-fattening project has turned out to be profitable. Lean steers are purchased in the countryside, where the prices are much lower. After feeding these animals nutritious teff straw for several months until they are fattened, one by one, they are butchered to enhance the diet of the students with good cheap protein. Besides providing food for the students, surplus vegetables, milk, and eggs are sold on the market.

On March 16, 2019, a special fundraising event took place on the top floor of the new MKC Head Office building in Addis. The purpose was to raise funds for the construction of the much-needed kitchen and multi-purpose dining hall. The aim was to begin the process of raising at least 10% of the projected cost of $869,000 needed for this large project. The outcome was a contribution of $8,715 in cash and pledges, equivalent to 1% of the projected cost.

Through the past three decades, the economy in Ethiopia has been improving. In 2022, although the annual GDP indicator had risen to be above $1,028 per capita, it remained among the poorest in the world.

As the church grows and the economy improves, the potential for achieving self-sustainability also grows. However, the college's public relations office is underperforming its potential to produce and promote schemes to raise funds locally. It could aggressively arrange fundraising activities, contact certain people for contributions, and prepare a local address database and send out information to the congregations. Also, the recently formed Alumni Association has the potential to assist the college in generating local support.

External Support for MK College

Over the span of twenty-three years, I participated in twenty-five fundraising trips within North America. The aim was three-fold: to increase awareness in North America of the existence and growth of the Meserete Kristos Church; to encourage fraternal relationships between Christians in North America and their brothers and sisters in Ethiopia; and to encourage those who have abundance to share with a church in need as it seeks to train its leaders to strengthen its people in this "global Kingdom of God."

MK College Link and Resource Generation

In the USA, the MK College Link Board appointed Tilahun Beyene to work as a Resource Generator. He was hired on a one-half time basis to work at fund raising and prayer support for the college. He divides the remainder of his time between coordinating the work of the International Missions Association (IMA) and pastoral work.

Tilahun began work on July 1, 2014. Tilahun was well qualified for this work. This native Ethiopian came to faith through the Meserete Kristos Church and served in various capacities including on the Executive Committee of the Church. His business experience included working for Ethiopian Airlines for many years. He and his wife, Heywet, along with their children moved to the United States in the 1990's. He had served as a member of MK College Link Board since its beginning in 2001.

Tilahun has helped to set up an endowment fund for scholarship support through the MK College Link in the USA. He also helped to establish several local chapters of "Friends of MK College," groups that undertake fundraising activities in their localities. He has also collaborated with me on some fundraising trips.

Our External Partners

Over the past thirty years, many kind and generous people and organizations have become our external partners. While many have made a onetime contribution, others have become faithful supporters in prayer, in volunteer service, and in financial sharing. Who are these external partners? And how were they motivated to become partners?

Through the years, our external partners have been over 2,000 individuals or couples in Canada, the USA, and Europe, 124 congregations, forty-one business organizations and foundations, and eight estate bequests. Altogether these have contributed well over $10,000,000 in cash, plus at least $1,800,000 worth of services and support.

Our external partners include fifteen full-time expatriate professors who gave a year or even many years in teaching, fifty-four volunteer professors who have come to teach for short block courses, plus eighteen professors in the master's programs,

Our external partners include the many volunteers who have given significant amounts of time, energy, and resources to benefit the college in some way. For example, in donating, collecting, and sending books, in organizing and establishing library book systems, in setting up computer systems, in packing containers, organizing fund drives, in doing fundraising projects, in participating in work teams and so on.

Our external partners include non-government organizations such as Eastern Mennonite Missions, Mennonite Central Committee, TEARFUND UK, Virginia Mennonite Missions, Mennonite Church Canada, four Mennonite universities and/or seminaries, Northwest Mennonite Conference, MK College link, MK College Link Canada, Equipping the Saints, and Crossroads International, Hong Kong. These have supported MK College with consultation, funding, sending personnel, training teachers, or contributing material or technical support.

Public Relations Officers Appointed

The public relations office remained dormant from the beginning of 2007 until the fall of 2013 when Pastor Teku Kebede was appointed as Public Relations Officer. In addition to his teaching load, Teku was to focus on creating awareness and building up financial support for the college within the Ethiopian Christian community.

Teku assumed this assignment along with his teaching load, after having served for thirty-seven years in various ministries such as child educator, evangelist, pastor, church leader/elder, teacher, conference speaker, trainer of trainees, author of books and articles for magazines and newspapers both secular and Christian, and as a member on different church committees, including the college's board of trustees.

Henok Tamirat, a graduate of the class of 2016, was employed to assist Pastor Teku Kebede in the Public Relations Office. Because of his expertise with computers and cameras, Tamirat assisted with photographing and producing the MK College Newsletter, videos, and other promotional materials. He was the technically responsible person to manage the college's website as well as the Facebook account and the use of YouTube for PR purposes. After many years of neglect, the website was updated.

The college's public relations officers and the administration worked together, making slow progress towards creating awareness and ownership among the church constituency. There was also a general increase in financial capacity among the congregations, especially in established urban congregations. Together, there was a slow measurable improvement with the church in assuming responsibility for its college.

However, in 2022, Teku was transferred to the role of student dean, and Henok resigned and found employment elsewhere. The office remains empty.

Other Developments in 2015-2017

In January 2017, Jewel and Richard Showalter brought thirteen students from Rosedale Bible College in Ohio for a six-week learning tour. The students boarded at the college while the Showalters taught Introduction to Missions for three weeks, and their son, Matt, Dean of Students at RBC, taught Introduction to Islam for the second three weeks. MK College helpfully supplied guides and chauffeurs for a variety of field trips.

After spending thirteen years studying and working in Fresno, California, Emebet Mekonen returned in September 2016 to join the teaching faculty. She was known as the "mother" of the college, having worked since its founding in 1994. During her time in California, Emebet went through a painful divorce and educated her four sons, plus earned several master's degrees and one PhD. As her sons grew up and were on their own, Emebet felt free to return to teaching in the college at Bishoftu in the fall of 2017.

Observations on the Negative Side

During this period, there were noticeable signs of decline. The excellent facilities were underutilized with only 193 students enrolled on a campus that could accommodate 600.

After twenty-three years, the anticipated liberal arts programs seemed no nearer to becoming a reality. The church leadership preferred to advance the seminary. There was no consensus to permit the college administration to move ahead with the earlier vision.

Measured against modern acceptable standards of effectiveness and efficiency, the work ethic on campus, including teaching faculty, management, and staff was low and in need of improvement. Weak general service management resulted in underutilization and under supervision of laborers. Tardiness and long breaks cut the efficiency of each employee. A sense of ownership and commitment to teamwork seemed to be lacking.

As time went on, a big problem for the president was the sense of entitlement the older staff exhibited. The socialist principles of the labor laws made it almost impossible to discipline or fire unproductive labor once hired. The long-term result was too many unproductive, inefficient, and unhappy workers on the payroll.

The negligence of the general service manager was most evident in the lack of general maintenance of the buildings, the grounds, and equipment. Leaking roofs, peeling paint, and broken tables, chairs, and desks carelessly discarded, could have easily been repaired. Broken window hinges and locks in the academic building left windows hanging precariously open and in danger of falling or further damage. Broken glass allowed birds to get in and mess up the rooms. The administration was incapable of motivating the workers.

Trees, shrubs, grass, and weeds needed constant attention. Only one gardener was assigned. He, being distracted by anyone who called him to other "go for" duties, could not keep up with the whole compound. The college needed another resolute, knowledgeable gardener to help in this area. Obviously, another leadership crisis was brewing.

Inaugurating the MKC Head Office Building

Back in 1996, a veteran founder of Meserete Kristos Church, Million Belete, presented a well-thought-out plan to construct a large multi-storied building that would serve the Church as its head office, with plenty of extra space that would be rented out to earn the income necessary to pay for the building, and to supplement church income in the decades ahead. The leadership of that time rejected his plan as untimely.

A decade passed, and new leadership assumed the challenge, and began laying the foundation. However, costs had escalated, and Million's plans for financing the project were overlooked. Another decade passed while the skeleton slowly took shape as funds became available. Construction stalled at the seventh level. Then, in 2012, members of MK College Link in the USA and Link Canada joined forces to raise funds to get the job done, with the understanding that space on the fourth floor would be reserved for the College to use as its Addis extension campus. Even with that help, it took another five years to complete. In the summer of 2017, the process of moving church offices into the new building began.

At last, on the afternoon of February 10, 2018, a grand opening ceremony celebrated the dedication this significant edifice for the glory of God and the enhancement of His kingdom work. As guests gathered outside, the Addis Ababa MKC Choir led them in song. Twenty-two years after first suggesting his vision, the now elderly Million Belete shuffled forward to cut the ribbon and lead the guests up the six flights of stairs to a large assembly room at the top. Experience Ethiopia Tour guests followed along with the other guests.

Meserete Kristos Church Chairperson, Birru Robele welcomed the guests. The choir sang more songs. Abiyot Lemma, one of our graduates, preached a fiery, challenging sermon. Short speeches were given by key people including Tewodros Beyene, Million Belete, Mamo Dula, and Darrell Jantzi. A prayer of dedication closed the ceremony, after which all enjoyed a light lunch.

When the long-awaited fourth floor became available as a permanent campus, the College began accepting applications for its degree program taught in the Amharic language. Classes began in September 2017 with only ten students. Students paid thirteen dollars per course.

Today, the building is fully occupied. Several Christian NGO's rent all the extra space, providing a good income that benefits the vital ministries of the church, Million's vision has become reality! That assembly room bears the name of Million Belete Hall, and a portrait of this saint adorns a pillar at the entrance.

CHAPTER 32

Challenges of 2018

The Ethiopian Federal Governments' expressed goal was to bring this country up to become a "middle-income country by 2025"! With a lot of help from China, they built a light rail metro system through Addis Ababa, built a new, limited access expressway between Addis and Adama, and built a new, high speed, electric railroad from Djibouti to Addis (the old one was 100 years old and out of use). They were working on what would become the largest hydroelectric generating dam in Africa, the Renaissance Dam on the Blue Nile River, expected to generate up to 6,000 megawatts. They established the second largest wind farm in Africa. They were expecting to export surplus electric power to Djibouti, Kenya, and Sudan. They launched a plan to bring electrification to the rural areas throughout all of Ethiopia. They built thousands of kms of highways and secondary feeder roads, opening the country to development and commerce. Hospitals, elementary schools, and universities were being constructed in all the regions of the country. Whereas about 45% of elementary school aged children were in school in 1996, that number had doubled to over 90%. With the performance of previous governments, one could never have dreamed of seeing this much development in his/her lifetime.

Political Unrest and Change

As foreigners returning to Ethiopia, with our eyes, we could not help but notice evidence of growing prosperity reflected in the continuing building boom. New, massive, high-rise construction projects dominated the skylines over the cities.

However, our ears heard of unhappiness with the government over the ever-widening gap between the rich and the poor. We heard of a myriad of corrupt and oppressive actions that further impoverished the poor and benefited the rich. These rumors, coming from the mouths of the poor, were reinforced by snatches of news about widespread student uprisings and the brutal and deadly suppression of the same.

Widespread spontaneous protests that sometimes turned violent and destructive marked the fall of 2015. How else could the voices of citizens be heard when the ruling party controlled the media, claimed a 100% win in the last election, and had all the guns (and prisons) to prove it? Protests by mobs, including peasants, laborers, university and high school students, were broken up by the military. Thousands were shot with live ammunition. There were reports of 600 killed and thousands injured. Besides these, uncounted others were arrested, incarcerated, tortured, and traumatized without trial. These brutal acts only triggered more and angrier protests.

The immediate pretext for these uprisings was disapproval of the government's plans for expropriating Oromo land for its ambitious urbanization schemes, and for the sale of huge tracts in the countryside to foreign investors. These actions stirred memories of a thousand injustices the people had experienced in the past. Adding to these grievances, a pervasive famine conjured up memories of the last days of the Haile Selassie regime. It looked scary.

To complicate matters, Oromo agitators, who wanted to throw out the government and establish an independent Oromo nation, stirred up the students and the peasants so that a violent mob spirit took over. Rumors about confrontations in other areas spread as well. Most of this did not get into the western press.

State of Emergency

Responding to this crisis, in October of 2016, the beleaguered government resolutely declared a "state of emergency," suspending the right to protest. This locked the whole country down for six months. A feeling of uneasy anger, yet calm, prevailed, and life and commerce went on as usual on the surface. It was in this atmosphere of calm that we returned and led our Tour in 2017. Although we did not feel it personally, nor did we have any problem in expediting the Tour, the environment around us was tense with social unrest.

The "six months" turned out to be ten months. That gave the government time to investigate and arrest the leaders one by one, interrogate and torture them, and possibly disappear them without recourse to legal procedures. It seemed like a drastic way to deal with the unrest, rather than listen to the grievances of the people. Arresting more and more people and filling the jails with the nations' best and bravest citizens, is not a long-term solution.

The government's use of brutal, lethal force stopped the destruction and violence for the time being. However, principal issues of justice and human rights were covered up, and the wounds only festered and grew.

An angry, educated citizen explained that the people wanted more than superhighways, railroads, and buildings. They wanted to be respected as human beings. This government seemed to think that, if they provided material signs of progress, such as hospitals, schools, and factories, the people would not mind if their opinions and rights were trampled in the dust. Families were mourning their dead and remembering their members being tortured in prison. The anger only deepened.

When the authorities ended the state of emergency ten months later, the spontaneous demonstrations resumed. In October 2017, an annual traditional Oromo ceremony, *irrecha*, was held at its usual site at Hora Lake, about two kms from the college. This was a pre-Christian thanksgiving celebration, held just after the end of the rainy season and the beginning of harvest. It is said that up to four million Oromos visit this "holy" site each year.

That year, during the ceremony, a tightly packed crowd, estimated at over a million people, was standing, listening to the President of Oromia addressing them. A few protesters began shouting, interrupting the speaker. The police opened fire with rubber bullets and teargas into the densely packed crowd. In the stampede that ensued, many people were trampled to death. The official number of those who died was fifty-five. But local witnesses claim the real number was one-hundred and seventy-eight.

A Facebook video showed the terrified masses panicking to escape the bullets and teargas, pushing, and shoving and falling into a very deep drainage ditch, from which they could not get out, while others fell on top of them. Those below suffocated. I saw the video. It was horrible.

The following spring, while we were leading the 2018 Experience Ethiopia Tour, popular agitators declared what they called "three days of rage." Spontaneous mobs armed with rocks and sticks made sure all roads leading to Addis Ababa were closed.

Our tour group was in Adama on Saturday night and Sunday. On Monday morning we took the group to Asella to learn about the amazing evangelistic work the church was doing with the local Muslim population. The congregation was building a large new worship center.

On Tuesday, while eating lunch in the Durartu hotel, we received urgent phone calls from the MKC Head Office urging us to get back to Addis as fast as possible. Trouble was brewing. Fifteen minutes after we left Asella, a major riot broke out in that town. God protected us, and we missed the action. On the way, though, as we were going through a smaller town, a mob stopped us. Addisu, our bus driver, spoke nicely to them in Oromifa, and they let us pass. From there, we drove all the way to Addis without any problem. It was an additional unplanned experience for our Experience Ethiopia Tour participants. However, we had to cancel the next day's planned visit to a project near Holletta, a hot spot for protesting.

With the demonstrations resuming in various places. EPRDF, the ruling party, was alarmed and confused as to what to do next. The prime minister apologized to the people for the high-handed dictatorial attitude and corruption of some officials, the main cause of the spontaneous protests over the past two years. He promised to release political prisoners and turn one of their notorious jails into a museum. The government also took back much of the land around Addis, which had been divided out to cronies and family members of the regime.

However, these promises were too late. By late February, the beleaguered government felt it had to re-instate a state of emergency for another six months to maintain order. The EPRDF leadership held a closed-door meeting that lasted over two weeks, trying to decide how they could satisfy the demands of the citizenry and restore confidence in their government. They still wanted to keep hold of the reins of power at the same time. In this process, the prime minister resigned. The party then had to select a new leader.

Finally, after much haggling and acrimony, they appointed Dr. Abiy Ahmed as the new prime minister. The people were ecstatic. This forty-two-year-old educated man, holding a doctorate in conflict and peace studies, seemed to have the confidence of a substantial portion of the population, and this appointment would bring some stability, while the people give him time to make a difference.

On Building a Kitchen and Dining Hall

Health inspectors from the Ministry of Public Health visited the campus in the fall of 2017. They informed the college administrators that its food services were inadequate and below standard. The current kitchen and dining hall had been constructed in 2007 as temporary emergency facilities to enable the little college to begin its operations on the new campus. It had never been intended that they should meet governmental health and building codes. The "temporary" status had persisted for eleven years. The time had come, the college had to upgrade or replace the kitchen and dining hall, or it would be closed.

This ultimatum stimulated the launching of a fundraising campaign among international friends and supporters. With the board's approval, Kiros Teka and Kelbessa Muleta undertook a five-week fraternal visit to raise funds for this project.

They left Ethiopia immediately following graduation on May 12, 2018, and arrived in Ontario, Canada, the next day. Their itinerary took them from there to Virginia, Pennsylvania, Indiana, and Ohio. They completed their tour by attending a four-day Ethiopian MKC Diaspora Conference near Washington DC. As they went, they shared information and updates with church officials, congregations, colleges, and seminaries, and visited friends and supporters.

When the building fund reached $440,000, and with architectural designs in place, contract worth $458,188 was signed with a builder to construct a new kitchen and multipurpose dining facility. The builder was to complete it within 450 days.

Ground-breaking and construction started on March 16th, 2020, just before the COVID-19 pandemic closed the schools. Despite the shutdown of much of the economy, construction went on. Unfortunately, inflation and shortages of materials escalated the costs way over budget and delayed building progress. In July 2021, an urgent appeal was sent out to raise an additional $220,000 to complete this construction.

On August 26, 2022, international guests, Doug Klassen, representing Mennonite Church Canada, and Carl E. Hansen, representing the Northwest Mennonite Conference, joined Meserete Kristos Church chairperson Biru Robele and President Desalegn Abebe in a ribbon-cutting ceremony. The church's General Assembly held its 91st meeting in that new hall.

Completion of this project provided a permanent facility large enough to accommodate up to 1,000 people. It would serve and safeguard the health of a growing campus community. In addition, church organizations, NGOs, and families will benefit periodically from this modern facility by using the campus as a venue for large conferences, educational seminars, workshops, weddings, and other activities. This additional use will provide a source of income for the College as well. In a real sense, it helps to fulfill the early vision of including a conference center on campus.

New kitchen and multipurpose/dining hall

91ˢᵗ General Assembly of Meserete Kristos
Delegates Meeting, 2023

CHAPTER 33

Another Leadership Transition

Summary and Ending of a Presidency

Kiros was a strong, industrious, hard-working person. He was supported by Azeb, his faithful companion, a woman of prayer. Spiritually, he was a man of prayer and action, very committed to fusing the secular and spiritual as one whole way of life. He sacrificed the security of his government job for the rough and tumble of working with the church.

For the first three years, Kiros worked enthusiastically. He set a good example and challenged every worker to accomplish the goal, mission, and vision of the college.

Some of the workers had developed very disinterested and self-serving work ethics, wasted time, and demanded more money for less work. When Kiros tried to admonish or correct them, his approach was counterproductive. The workers felt that his blaming, scolding, and threatening diminished them. Also, workers felt a sense of entitlement. In this church institution, grace should abound, and policies could be ignored.

Coming from a government background, Kiros tended to be strict, demanding adherence to business procedures and policies. He tried to create a more productive work environment. To avoid temptation or corruption, and to reduce chaos, Kiros made and implemented policies that some felt were too bureaucratic and inefficient. Dissatisfaction among those workers began to escalate.

The condition deteriorated. Disgruntled workers and students refused to attend the chapel services. Those students protested that they did not speak or understand Amharic, the national language. After threatening the students, Kiros relented and allowed chapel to be conducted in both Amharic and Oromo languages.

Government labor laws made it difficult to fire unproductive workers. Kiros did what he could to block the unethical or unproductive practices. Consequentially, disgruntled workers turned against him and stirred up sympathy among some students and faculty.

It was also a time when the national sentiment was turning against its Tigrean dominated government. For some, Kiros' ethnicity as a Tigrean was an underlying source of suspicion, rumors, and gossip.

At one point, with feelings running high, the dissatisfied workers formed a labor union, registering with the government. However, representatives of the church head office came to the college and challenged them. If they were Christians, their issues must be seen and judged by the church. They accepted and cancelled the labor union membership. The church leadership, now made aware of the conflict, began to investigate the issues. The investigation was drawn out for a period of almost three years.

Further, there were weaknesses in the governance provided by the Board of Trustees. Since trustees were serving the church voluntarily, it was difficult to gather a quorum to deal with urgent issues. Members often failed to show up, even though they had agreed upon a meeting date. When there was a lack of quorum, decisions could be delayed for months. This had always been a challenge under past administrations as well.

Kiros tried to keep a positive spirit of oneness and enthusiasm among the staff. However, too many lengthy delays in making decisions and implementing them led to growing resentment. Caught between the management committee and the board, Kiros struggled.

The issues raised involved decisions made where there were no rules in place. Kiros, exasperated by repeated failures in getting the board to meet, began to make policies and implement them without the board's decision. The management committee and president felt they needed to go ahead and do what they felt was necessary, and that they should not be blamed. Others argued the opposite. Such disagreement changed the atmosphere negatively. Kiros questioned why he could be held accountable as an offender rather than being blessed by what he did for the good of the college.

This investigation went on. For at least five separate times, church representatives came to the college and spent until midnight discussing the issues with the college's management committee. As the discussions went on, the spirit of the relationships also deteriorated.

While this was going on, Kiros asked for a vacation. His health was not good, and his wife was bedridden with chronic back pain. He was exhausted. He pleaded with the chairperson of the board that he had been unable to have a break for the last four years. The chairperson agreed verbally, but not with board approval.

Therefore, before the last meeting with the church representatives, Kiros, stressed to the point of breaking, went ahead and took vacation without the formal approval of the board. He assigned Teku Kebede to fill in for him while he was gone. This appointment was irregular. According to the protocol, that assignment belonged to the academic dean.

The chairperson notified Kiros that he should be in the meeting before taking his leave. Kiros responded that he was unable to attend, as he needed to have a break for the sake of his health. When the meeting took place, the representatives were informed that Kiros was outside Ethiopia. They were not happy.

Two weeks later, the board concluded that Kiros had abandoned his job. They ordered him to be back within three days. He did not report. Later, they received word that Kiros had written a letter of resignation and had gone to Canada. Today, Kiros lives in Toronto with his wife and younger children.

Under New Leadership

With the untimely resignation and departure of President Kiros Teka Hadis on July 1, 2019, the church leadership appointed Gishu Jebecha

Ebissa, the academic dean to assume the role of acting president. Almost two years later, on May 6, 2021, when restructuring the college as "Meserete Kristos Seminary," they confirmed Gishu as the principal.

Gishu came to this position after a long history of service in the church. In 1996, he began his ministry as an evangelist in his local Misrak Adama Meserete Kristos Church. After four years of service, he enrolled as a student at MK College. In 2004, he graduated at the top of his class and returned to serve God's people, as before, in his home congregation.

After another five years of service, Gishu went back to academia. He earned a Master of Arts in Theology degree, from Radboud University in 2011. He further proceeded to gain his second Erasmus Mundus Master of Bioethics, from Radboud University and University of Padova, awarded in 2012.

Upon his return to Ethiopia, Gishu found employment as a lecturer at MK College. There he became the academic dean. Further, while working, Gishu earned an LLB, Bachelor of Laws, from Oromia State University, School of Law, awarded in 2019.

Gishu is a member of Global Associates for Transformational Education (GATE) and responsible for leading faculty development workshops in how to teach transformational learning. He has also worked as a member of the ACTEA Visitation Team, responsible for enabling an educational institution to come to a clear analysis of itself in relation to accepted quality standards. He was a member of the executive committee of the Adama MKC Region. Gishu and his wife, Frehiwote Bekele Mengistu, are the parents of four children.

Principal Gishu Jebecha Ebissa, 2019

International Outreach to Kenya

Through a generous donor, the college was able to offer five full scholarships to the Kenya Mennonite Church, allowing them to select five qualified persons for degree level studies in Bishoftu. Four men and one woman began the program in August 2019. One of the men dropped out after his first year for personal reasons. Four of the Kenyans did very well in their studies and graduated. Unlike Tanzanians and others, Kenyans were welcome into Ethiopia without requiring visas.

Kenyan students from left to right: Ellon Maura Okach, Omondi Elvis Otieno, Grace Leah Otieno, Victor Okoth Oloo and Nyangore Christopher – 2019

Guest lecturer, John Thacker & class 2019

Green Legacy

Ethiopia with its endemic famines is a noted example of a nation where unchecked deforestation, and consequential land degradation, has worked havoc with the climate and food production.

The new Prime Minister, Abiy Ahmed, challenged the citizenry to participate in his government's radical "Green Legacy Tree Planting" reforestation program. The goal was to plant 4.7 billion trees by October 2019.

Progressive Ethiopians rallied to the challenge. According to reports, on one day, July 29th, over 350 million saplings were planted. No doubt a world record!

At Bishoftu, college staff, instructors, and the few remaining summer students joined local citizens, estimated at 1,000 people, to plant trees on the hillside above the college before noon. Among them, the Bishoftu Medical College soldier-trainees, wearing their uniforms, accompanied the planting program with their slogan song that says, "*We have one country! It is Ethiopia!*"

Four years later, the beautiful green foliage of an emerging forest once again covers the barren hillside. A few scattered concrete outcroppings of partially built foundations mar the uniformity of the emerald canopy.

Launching an MA in Theology and Global Anabaptism (MATGA)

Back in the summer of 2018, while visiting Anabaptist Mennonite Biblical Seminary (AMBS) in Elkhart, Indiana, Kelbessa Muleta and Kiros Teka Haddis suggested the possibility of a partnership between AMBS and MK College. This initiated a dialogue between the presidents of the two schools.

As a follow-up, Dr. Sara Wenger Shenk, President of AMBS, accompanied by her husband, Dr. Gerald Shenk, visited the college in March 2019. Kiros, Kelbessa, and the college management team, negotiated with Sara to offer an Ethiopia specific version of AMBS's new MA in Theology and Global Anabaptism (MATGA) degree to qualified Ethiopian graduate students.

MATGA was a fully accredited, online degree program available to other AMBS students anywhere in the world, effectively making Anabaptist theological education accessible wherever there was a high-speed internet connection.

Out of the discussion, an agreement emerged in which a version of MATGA would be adapted for the Ethiopian graduate students. It would include AMBS professors teaching three courses on the campus in Bishoftu each summer. Students would take the remainder of the courses online. The curriculum, contextualized for the Ethiopia setting, would include a particular concentration of peace studies.

A month later, April 2019, upon the approval of the church, the board, and the college leadership, the agreement took immediate effect. On the Ethiopian side, the college assigned Dr. Emebet Mekonnen to serve as the coordinator of this MA program She immediately sent out announcements to the graduate constituency.

On the USA side, AMBS appointed Henok Mekonin, an MK College alum, and a senior student at AMBS, to assist with communication and intercultural aspects of the MATGA Ethiopia program. Henok continues in 2024, as a global leadership collaborative specialist working for AMBS. He provides specialized expertise for the MATGA Ethiopia partnership.

In Ethiopia, the MATGA program, a cohort of nine students, was launched in the fall of 2019. By 2023, fifteen students had graduated and twenty-nine were enrolled.

At the beginning, this online program presented many challenges. The major challenge was the intermittently functioning internet. Access to dependable electric power, in an environment plagued by perpetual unannounced blackouts, was another. Students who were less familiar with digital technology needed coaching. Many had financial difficulties. American instructors needed to make the courses relevant to the Ethiopian context. Another major challenge was keeping to the time schedule with 7,500 miles and eight time zones separating students from instructors.

The program consisted of sixteen courses with a total of forty-six credit hours to be completed in three years. Assuming the student was a full-time employee, the program was prepared to fit a students' busy schedule. It is also assumed the student would use nine weeks of his/her summer vacation to attend the intensive courses offered on campus each summer.

This version of MATGA provided master's-level programs in Bible, theology, and peace studies from an Anabaptist perspective. It was tailored specifically to educate leaders for the Meserete Kristos Church who expressed a need for trained leaders and other professionals capable of defending the faith, promoting peace by interfaith dialogue, advocating for human rights, and supporting interethnic peacebuilding.

The purpose of offering an MA in Theology and Global Anabaptism was to "prepare scholars, teachers, pastors, and leaders to integrate the knowledge of and formation in the Anabaptist tradition with service in their current and future communities." The need to train leaders with a strong peace emphasis was urgent as they prepared to work for God's kingdom in their country, troubled by war, ethnic strife, bigotry, and corruption,

There were several other reasons this online MATGA program fit well. It was less costly, more time-efficient, and was distance friendly. Students could take the courses from anywhere in the country as long as they had a computer, electric power, and internet access. They received quality education from well-known teachers. They could complete the entire program from Ethiopia, without family separation, obtaining a student visa, or incurring the expense and hassle of travel to Elkhart, Indiana.

AMBS President, Dr. David Boshart
with MATGA participants 2022

Facing Unsettling Challenges, Spring 2020

It is always a pleasure to report on glowing successes and new milestones reached. However, in the year 2020, dark clouds hovered over Ethiopia. The universal spread of the COVID-19 pandemic, the rise of the fratricidal war with the Tigrean Peoples Liberation Front (TPLF), and the disturbing ethnic unrest in other parts of the nation, all left a strong negative impact on the economy, sense of security, and optimism for a better future. The hope of becoming a middle-income country faded behind those clouds. Yet, regardless of appearances, behind these dark clouds, the sun was still there, somewhere, shining.

It was with this confidence that the leaders of the church moved ahead, evaluating the present and re-imagining the college's future, renaming it "Meserete Kristos Seminary." It was in this faith that administration and staff continued with their mission, training leaders for the churches and societies of Ethiopia!

The Year of COVID-19

It was early March that the spreading rumors of a global COVID-19 pandemic reached us in Ethiopia. The news media was fixated on it. Nations were closing their borders, issuing banning orders against large gatherings of all kinds, closing schools, churches, and sporting events. As international air travel was being banned, volunteers Brian Dyck and Lynell Bergen, living at the guesthouse, got orders that they should return to Canada immediately. Vera and I were enjoying our working winter vacation and were not ready to leave just yet.

Then on March 17, 2020, Prime Minister, Abiy Ahmed, issued a directive ordering all elementary schools, high schools, colleges, and universities to close their doors. Responding to the directive, the college administration agreed to suspend classes and send the students home "for at least two weeks, a period to be monitored and extended if conditions recommend doing so."

This all happened because "four foreigners and their Ethiopian driver were tested and found to be positive with this virus." We were suspicious there may have been many more cases that the government did not want the public to know about. Better to blame a few foreigners.

Shockingly, throughout the entire world, the normal patterns of human economic, social, and spiritual intercourse were suddenly and drastically altered by the power of that one little invisible, but deadly virus! So much for the superiority of man!

It took a week for the students to vacate the campus. Only the four Kenyan students, Vera, and I were left, quarantined on the empty campus, along with a dozen hungry cats, which were dependent upon what they could snatch from the now locked kitchen.

Our self-isolation at the Bishoftu campus was getting old, and the picture of the worldwide pandemic was worsening, making a total shut down of international travel a likelihood. Therefore, responding to the concerns of our family members, Vera and I decided to ask Lufthansa to transfer our tickets to Ethiopian Airlines, which was the only remaining airline working out of Addis to Washington,. Ethiopian agreed and gave us seats for Friday night.

Our Ethiopian friends could not understand. Were we not fools? What kind of wisdom would drive us to leave the relative safety of Ethiopia, where less than a dozen had succumbed to the dreaded virus. Why would we deliberately expose ourselves to the probability of infection in the USA? There, hundreds of thousands jammed their suffering or semi-conscious loved ones into the overcrowded hospitals, or, God forbid, deposited their corpses into the standby refrigerated trailer-morgues? This was what they witnessed on television every evening. With this potential destiny in mind, our farewells triggered deep concern, and prayers.

We packed all our things, left the eleven hungry cats to the tender mercy of our lonely Kenyan friends, and took a sad leave of the few remaining staff and friends available. Accompanied by his lovely wife, Mercy, Henok delivered us to the airport on April 11.

In Dulles, as we dismounted and went through immigration, we handed in the health questionnaire we had filled out. On the questionnaire, there was space for them to record our temperature. However, the officers did not bother. Their only question was whether we had visited China or Iran. They did not check us nor ask about visiting countries in Europe. What does that say about the American tendency to politicize everything, even the pandemic?

In Ethiopia, the "two weeks" became five months while the pandemic took its toll on humanity and the economies of the world. By this time, Ethiopia had adjusted to the shock and learned to live with precautions.

The pandemic had an impact upon the college. Graduation was postponed, summer courses were cancelled. On October 12th, the college was cautiously re-opened, inviting only the senior students to re-assemble using all the recommended safety procedures. The eighty-four students, who should have graduated in May, received their credentials on November 14th.

After the seniors graduated, the first, second, and third-year students returned to complete the interrupted spring courses for the next six weeks. New students joined them in January for the 2021 spring semester.

Excessive increases in the prices of food and construction materials reflected stresses in the economy due to the epidemic. However, construction of the kitchen and dining hall did not stop.

The online MATGA program also continued without disruption, with the exception that the guest lecturers from AMBS could not be present to teach the anticipated summer block courses.

MA Level Theological Education that is Culturally Sensitive and Practical

One of the primary goals of the MK Seminary's strategic plan was to provide theological education programs that were distinctively within the Anabaptist tradition and that were contextually appropriate.

While the MATGA program was moving ahead, the seminary, based on its needs assessment, revised, or developed its own curricula for undergraduate and graduate programs that would better serve Ethiopian churches of all denominations.

For example, surveys showed that there was a need for and interest in mission studies. Therefore, besides its *Bachelor of Arts in Bible and Theology*, the seminary added, a *Bachelor of Arts in Mission and Intercultural Studies*.

There are more than eighty different language and cultural groups in Ethiopia. It was inevitable for congregations to develop using their own mother tongues. There were leaders who were not conversant in English nor in Amharic. These leaders would benefit in their ministries by having some basic theological and biblical study programs in their mother tongues. Beginning to remedy this, the seminary introduced undergraduate programs in the Amharic and Oromo languages. These programs were offered from diploma level up to undergraduate degree level in the branch campuses.

Further, the survey pointed out the need for providing continuing educational opportunities for its former graduates to refresh themselves and to sharpen their skills. Post-graduate programs would enable students to cultivate deeper roots in biblical and theological traditions of Christianity, engage in critical reflections on the application of the Bible and Christian theology in diverse cultural contexts, and to serve in various Christian ministries more effectively.

As a result, in November 2022, MK Seminary launched the *Master of Arts in Biblical and Theological Studies* taught in the English language at its main campus in Bishoftu. To be more inclusive, due to lack of proficiency in the English language of some of the graduates, it also launched a *Master of Arts in Practical Theology* program taught in Amharic at its Adama campus in December.

This was an innovation as there were no other recognized theological institutions in Ethiopia that offered a master's degree in theology taught in local languages. This bold step was approved by the church leadership based upon the conviction that these church ministers must have the opportunity to pursue graduate studies in theology.

One of the challenges of teaching theology in the local languages was the shortage of reference books and textbooks suitable for this level. Administrators are addressing this challenge by investing in developing tailored course materials for the programs.

Forty-nine students were accepted into the first program. It was scheduled in such a way that the students could pursue their studies while continuing their regular work or private business.

Canadian Missionaries

Back in 2018, the Holyrood Mennonite Church in Edmonton, Alberta, granted their pastor, Werner DeJong, a sabbatical leave to teach in Ethiopia for a semester. Werner and his wife, Joanne, spent that fall as guests at MK College. Their lives were touched.

What they learned and experienced that semester made it easier to respond positively to an invitation to return to MKS, for a three-year teaching term in January 2022. They enjoy living on campus interacting with students, sharing meals, and having meaningful conversations while walking, or drinking coffee. Their presence reflected the growing partnership between Meserete Kristos Church and Mennonite Church Canada.

With these eighty-four graduating in 2024, the number of MK College graduates increased to 2,357.

EvaSUE, a Nationwide Reach

Evangelical Students' Union of Ethiopia (EvaSUE) has been serving students and graduates in Ethiopia (and Eritrea) for more than fifty years through evangelism, discipleship training, missions, and leadership development. Every summer, EvaSUE holds yearly conferences for student leaders representing all the university and college campuses in the whole nation. In recent years, these conferences have been held at the MK Seminary campus.

Again, in August 2023, 620 student leaders gathered for the annual EvaSUE ten days of conferences for a leadership group and a mission's group. Each group was involved for five days packed with prayer, worship, meetings, training, group discussions, and other activities.

They were hosted in the new seminary multipurpose hall, dormitories, and guesthouse. Their positive experience has served the seminary as an advertisement, attracting students from the secular campuses. After they graduate, some enroll in the seminary to pursue Bible and theological studies.

Evangelical Students Union (EvaSUE)
leaders conference, 2023

CHAPTER 34

The Meserete Kristos Seminary Today

At the close of its first thirty years, it is appropriate to evaluate the Meserete Kristos Seminary. What is its present condition? What are its achievements, its shortcomings, its failures? Is it meeting the expectations and needs of its founders and current owners? How can it be improved? What should be its goals and strategies for the future? To answer these questions, it is appropriate to keep in mind the need and condition of the church.

In the year 2023, the Meserete Kristos Church baptized 27,008 new members, an average of seventy-four per day. It counted 567,000 baptized members in a faith community of over 950,000 who worship in 1,462 congregations and 992 church planting centers. Over 4,000 ministers served these people,

The church seeks to be faithful to its mandate to care for orphans and widows, victims of famine, refugees displaced by violence and war, and the destitute who have lost hope. Through its MKC Development Commission (MKC-DC), the church is implementing child sponsorship programs with direct benefits to 34,581 needy children and indirect benefits to 155,405 family members. With a budget of $5,585,545, supported by MCC, the Canadian Food Grains Bank, and five other donor agencies, it has also been deeply involved in famine relief, food security, health, HIV AIDS, and peace building programs.

The church's Prison Ministry is carrying on a wholistic program of meeting prisoners' needs in fifty of the nation's 132 prisons. In twenty-eight prisons, it provides male or female chaplains who give full-time service in preaching, teaching, and counseling. It fosters hope through supplying Bibles and helpful Christian literature, and by building simple worship shelters in the prison compound. It reduces suffering by distributing used clothing and by building latrines and water tanks. Prisoners are hungry for the Gospel, and active congregations are growing in most of the prisons.

Together, all these programs and the congregations require solid trained leaders. Whereas, thirty years ago, there were almost no MKC leaders trained to the baccalaureate level in Bible or theology, as of 2024, a total of 2,357 persons have graduated from one of the colleges' certificate, diploma, or degree programs, and are providing much of that required leadership.

Meserete Kristos Seminary Campus in 2024

Campus arial view, 2024

Reorganizing Theological Education

The continuous influx of new believers creates a hunger for biblical and theological knowledge and the desire to sharpen skills for ministry. To feed that growing appetite, spontaneously, Bible schools sprang up in congregations throughout the country. As these "Bible schools," "Bible institutes," or "Bible colleges" popped up, the MKC Executive Committee, in 2020, reorganized all its theological institutions, establishing a system of accountability and accreditation.

From College to Seminary

The Meserete Kristos College was renamed *Meserete Kristos Seminary* (MKS). The title of the commanding executive officer was changed from *president* to *principal*. The seminary is headquartered on its main campus at Bishoftu. It administers two branch campuses, one in Addis Ababa, and the other in Adama.

At Bishoftu, the seminary offers undergraduate, and graduate (masters) programs taught in the English language. Its programs are in theology, leadership, peace building, and community development. It seeks to prepare ministers, leaders, and peace and development ambassadors who can serve the church and society at a higher level.

On its branch campuses, these courses are offered in Amharic and Oromo languages. Currently, in the spring of 2024, enrollment in all the seminary programs was 348 students. This included twenty-three students in the MATGA program administered jointly with AMBS in the USA.

In addition, the seminary has supervisory responsibility over regional Bible colleges and local Bible schools that offer degree and diploma programs in either Amharic or Oromo languages. These had a combined enrollment of 872 learners. At that time, including those in the seminary, a combined total of 1,220 individuals were registered in one of the theological education programs of the whole church.

Regional Bible Colleges and Bible Schools

As of the spring of 2024, twenty-one regional Bible colleges and local congregational Bible schools were operating under the regional offices or congregations of MKC. They receive comprehensive academic guidance from the central MK Seminary regarding curriculum matters and teacher qualifications. All of these instruct their students in a local vernacular such as Amharic or Oromo.

These schools usually start with a simple certificate level program, but soon upgrade to diploma level. Some of them, like the Wollega Bible College in Nekempte or the one at Adama, offered diploma and degree programs taught in Oromo, the local vernacular. This was uncharted territory as there was a scarcity of books and reference works in that language.

These regional Bible colleges and Bible schools operate on different, locally determined bases. There is no boarding provision. Each student must pay the specified fee per course, which may vary from three dollars to twelve dollars, depending on location. Collectively, the fees cover the cost of paying the teachers' salaries and other expenses. The classes usually meet in rooms provided by a church in the area. Outside subsidies are not needed.

The students include evangelists, pastors, elders, lay leaders, and men and women from all levels of society. The majority are members of MKC, but some belong to other denominations. Classes meet on weekends, like Friday evening, Saturday, and sometimes, Sunday. Some schools offer classes on weekday evenings. Thus, students may pursue their livelihood careers and still advance their knowledge of the Bible and Christian theology. This is proving to be a remarkably effective and self-sustaining approach.

Usually, instructors in the regional Bible schools have their undergraduate degrees from the central MK College, and most of them have at least some post-graduate credits from EGST or EMS. Most of them are employed in other church work, so tuition costs are minimal.

The training has become popular, meeting a need felt by those who desired to grow in their knowledge of the Bible and Christian ministries. God alone knows how much raising the general knowledge of the Bible on the grass roots level, did, and will impact the moral, social, economic, and political environment in those local communities and in the nation.

Its Teaching Faculty

Apart from an occasional guest lecturer from outside, all the instructors are Ethiopian nationals, and mostly members of the Meserete Kristos Church. Currently three of the nine full-time instructors and several part-time instructors at the Bishoftu Campus hold master's degrees from Anabaptist seminaries in North America. Four more have had graduate training through the extension program from EMS topped off with additional courses from EGST. Two other full-time instructors have their master's from EGST. Two are PhD candidates.

MK Seminary faculty & staff, 2024

Leading Through Purposeful Planning Strategically

In September 2021, volunteer consultant, Kebede Bekere, initiated a year-long strategic planning process. He led the seminary's staff and faculty in examining every aspect of college life and administration, noting the strengths and weaknesses. They then formulated priorities and set goals.

The outcome was the adoption of a five-year Strategic Plan which set out eleven goals. The highlights included a renewed commitment to excellence, more Anabaptist-focused education and staff, and financial sustainability through creative income-generating projects. The school would continue to recruit students from across East Africa. It would build a strong, newly streamlined theological program in English. It would introduce new graduate programs in English at the main campus while limiting programs in local languages to the satellite campuses. New short-term training opportunities would be made available for church leaders and ministers.

To be effective, the strategies and plans must be put into action. To enable that to happen, they must be a regular topic of discussion, often reviewed, and progress monitored periodically. Goals must be adjusted annually based on progress. Strategy must be linked to budgeting. Employees must be encouraged.

CHAPTER 35

Impact: an Ever-Widening Stream

Thirty years after its founding in 1994, we might ask "What impact has the college had on the church and the societies of Ethiopia?" Seminary training broadens and deepens better understanding of the Bible, theological concepts, and the human response. This assists graduates in effective decision-making, teaching, counseling, attracting others to Christ, promoting doctrinal soundness, and inspiring godly living. All of which contributes to the growth of churches and strengthens the moral fiber within the nation.

Graduates are serving as pastors, teachers, and evangelists in local churches and church planting centers. Some of them get promoted to larger responsibilities. For example, the president of MK Church and the heads of the departments at the church head office are all graduates of the seminary. Leaders of forty-seven of the fifty-three MKC regional offices are graduates.

Many are serving in various departments, directing mission programs that reach the unreached, translating materials into vernacular languages, designing study and teaching materials, serving in prison ministries, and leading in peacemaking interventions in bloody ethnic conflict zones.

A few have gone on to graduate schools. Several of our current teachers and the principal, academic dean, and student dean are all graduates of MK College who have completed master's level degrees in graduate schools.

Graduates, scattered throughout the nation, have spawned regional Bible schools. They are passing on the college's teaching to hundreds of lay leaders from MK congregations, and other denominations. The biblical knowledge and moral values gained, are moving out in an ever-widening circle, blessing the churches, communities, and families in the regions, thus transforming the societies of Ethiopia.

Other graduates have been called to national level ministries. Two are heading radio ministries. Others are working in prison ministries. Several are heading Compassion projects. One is head of the Horn of Africa Project. Another is a peace coordinator in the Inter-Religious Council of Ethiopia. Others are in peace and reconciliation ministries. A few are serving in key positions in the Ethiopian Evangelical Church's fellowship. Others are coordinating para-church organizations.

Also, many of our students, coming from sister denominations, are now serving as pastors, teachers, and missionaries in those churches. Several are leading in various Orthodox renewal movements. Beyond national borders, many are giving leadership in churches among the Ethiopian diasporas on several continents.

The sacrifice of time, energy, and resources invested by so many in this educational enterprise over the past thirty years has already brought huge changes, and the story has only begun. Those influences will multiply and transform the lives and communities of generations who are still unborn and will have an unfathomable impact on incalculable multitudes in eternity. A scholarship is a "gift that keeps on giving."

A Ministry of Reconciliation

Evangelist Adane Dechasa Teshale served his congregation as an evangelist for some years before attending MK College. After graduation, he returned to serve his church for more years. At the time of this writing, he was serving as Director of the Peace Building Department in Ethiopia's Inter-Religious Council where he shares his expertise in peace building and theology. His motto is from Matthew 5:9, "Blessed are the peacemakers." To further his expertise, Adane earned an MA from EGST in 2016 in peace and related issues and is currently pursuing another MA at Addis Ababa University with emphasis on peace and security in Africa. He also earned various certificates in the areas of transformational leadership, conflict transformation, peace building, restorative justice, mediation and dialogue, and common values and golden rules for inter-faith leaders.

Adane provides short training workshops both within and outside Ethiopia. He teaches publicly on peace building, tolerance, and coexistence. As an evangelist, in addition to his formal work, Adane serves as the chairperson of his local church, as secretary of the Addis Ababa Region MKC Executive Committee and as a member of the Mission Board.

Adane regards MK College as the springboard for his educational and ministerial life, the foundation where he was encouraged and equipped to serve with competence and confidence.

A 21st Century Martyr

The Meserete Kristos Church was deeply saddened by hearing of the death of Pastor Tesfaye Seyoum in Eritrea in the spring of 2023. Tesfaye was among the first batch of the Associate of Arts degree in Theology program of the MK College in the late 1990s. He was a founder of MKC in Eritrea and a pastor in the underground church in Asmara.

Being a conscript of Jesus, called to a ministry of peace and reconciliation, Tesfaye could not surrender himself to the government for conscription into the military. Like Menno Simons, he evaded the arresting authorities for many years, while leading the congregation clandestinely. However, the time came when he was discovered, arrested, and imprisoned for practicing and propagating an illegal religion. Along with a few other believers, he was imprisoned in a steel shipping container, out in the desert heat by day, and the cold at night, with severely limited water, food, and bedding.

Broken in health after ten torturous years in prison, Tesfaye was released to a hospital, where he went to be with the Lord—another

Anabaptist martyr. "Precious in the sight of the Lord is the death of his saints!" (Ps.116:15 NIV)

MKC is one of the churches not allowed to practice their faith in Eritrea. The family, his wife and one daughter, was further persecuted by the authorities refusing them their right to bury their beloved for over one month. A life of following the Jesus way, can be costly. It can lead to a "cross"! However, it also assuredly leads to a reunion with the persecuted, murdered, and resurrected Lord!

A Full Gospel Bible College in Adama

Another of our graduates, Assefa Abraham, a pastor in the Full Gospel denomination was appointed to head up a new Full Gospel Bible College in Adama. As principal, he wanted my advice and blessing. He arranged for my visit in March of 2015. We found a small school in rented quarters offering diploma courses. It reminded me of our Haya Hulet Mazoria campus twenty years earlier. The board members planned to expand the programs to the degree level. We noticed that they did not have a single reference book in English in their library, yet they wanted to open a degree program in the English language! I thought, "May God help them!"

Three years later, I visited them again. This time they had rented a larger campus and had more students and teachers. Their denomination had gotten behind them with more finances, and the institution was growing. Another of our graduates was working there as a part-time lecturer.

Orthodox Renewal Movements – Ethiopian Emmanuel United Church

In 1974, Getahun Tadesse was born into a rural Orthodox family near Welenchiti, thirty kms east of Adama, Ethiopia. In growing up, he and his adolescent friends were very committed to the St. George Orthodox Church in their town. They would get up before dawn to attend mass.

They avidly studied Orthodox books with their legends and traditions. As they grew in their knowledge and enthusiasm for the things of God, they were attracted to the Bible, which they "studied aggressively." They took a two-month certificate level training and began leading and teaching in their Sunday children's classes, participating in the ceremonies. They were noted as serious young people.

As these youth approached adulthood, they began to introduce new songs and sang the old songs to faster tunes. They added prayers and asked new questions. The priests began to complain against them, accusing them of becoming *pente* or "heretics." But these loyal youth had no intention or interest in the imported Protestant "heresies." They loved their Orthodox Church and only wanted to make it better.

Yet, in 1993, tensions built up and the church officials decided to excommunicate them. They brought a letter of excommunication, but the youths refused to accept it. Instead, they demanded that the elders call a congregational meeting to explain all their reasons.

The meeting took place at St. George's Church on Monday with about 400 people attending. The elders explained their reasons for excommunication, then gave Getahun, who was the leader of the youth, ten minutes to explain their position. The people became divided, and many shouted against the chairperson of the congregation.

When the meeting was dismissed, the youth stood at the three doorways and announced to the people, as they went out, that they were invited to a meeting the next night at the house of Tefera Folea, a businessperson. About 200 people showed up on Tuesday night. Most of them decided to form a new church. In the months and years that followed, persecution from the traditionalists was very harsh. Some of the members returned to St. George's Church. The rest remained steadfast in the new church.

For the first year, the new group refused to be excommunicated. That is, they kept the customs and rules of the Orthodox Church. They kept the fasts, women wore the *natala* on their heads in worship, leaders functioned as priests and dressed in the priestly gowns. They thought of themselves as "reformed Orthodox."

Without their knowledge, similar movements developed in many other towns and cities spontaneously between 1993 and 1995. From the beginning, they all wanted to remain Ethiopian Orthodox. They did not want to join the Protestants. However, harsh persecution made them change their strategy. They adopted the preaching style of the *pentes*. Two years later, they adopted adult baptism. Five of the leaders from Welenchiti were baptized by the renewal group leaders in Adama, then they went home and led all their members down to the Awash River and baptized over 300 there. Without knowing it, they had become Anabaptists!

They needed a burial place, as the Orthodox would not allow them the use of their own hallowed burial ground. In 1994, the leaders from these various renewal groups met in Adama and decided to organize a church to get a license from the government. They chose to call their denomination "Emmanuel United Church of Ethiopia." "Emmanuel," because they had no one besides God with them. "United," because they came from many different cities, but were all united in one common faith and vision. That year they got their license. Four years later, they were recognized and accepted as a separate indigenous denomination by the Ethiopian Evangelical Churches Fellowship.

Getahun remembers at the beginning of 1993, they had little knowledge or experience to guide this emerging church. They had no trained leaders and no written documents to define or guide them. Therefore, they accepted it as God's generous providence when MKC Pastor Siyum Gebretsadik arranged for the new Meserete Kristos Church Bible Institute to offer their group two scholarships in 1996. The first two scholarships were given to Fasika Wondimu and Zacharyas Boogale. Mezgebu Tesemru and Getahun Tadesse accepted scholarships the following year. After two years of study, these young brothers gave full-time service in leading their new denomination. In the years following, MK College continued to provide two scholarships per year to the Emmanuel United Church.

Following his graduation, Getahun Tadessa pastored a church in Shashemene for two years, then returned to MK College for two more years, in which he earned a degree. Following that, he shepherded a strong church in Markato, Addis Ababa for seven years. In June of 2013, his denomination elected him as president.

In 2014, I was privileged to visit Getahun in their head office. He admitted that Emmanuel United Church in many ways was shaped by MK College. First, his wife and partner, Selamawit, who worked as program producer preparing two programs every week for Living Hope Christian Radio, was also a graduate of 2008. Fasika Wondimu, who also returned to earn a degree, was heading up the evangelism department at their head office. Getahun Abebe was heading up the pastoral department. Tesfaye Shiberu was serving as coordinator of their college and preparing the curriculum for the education department. Mezgebu was pastor of their congregation near their head office in the vicinity of the Africa Union headquarters.

Overall, thirty-five out of thirty-six of their top leaders were graduates of MK College. In other words, the top leadership of the Emmanuel United Church is MK College trained! What they learned in our college had enabled them to write their many training manuals, prepare training materials, write books, and produce radio programs.

They had also started a "mobile college" which offered a diploma program taught in Amharic. It had 500 part-time servants as students and had graduated around 300. All their teachers were our graduates who worked as full-time leaders for the church and taught block courses on a part-time basis. Getahun, himself had written two books in Amharic, one on "Conflict Management and Resolution" and the other on "Church Planting and Evangelism."

As of 2022, twenty-nine years since its founding, the Emmanuel United Church had 544,000 members (including children) who met in 680 congregations scattered all over Ethiopia and in some overseas countries. Truly, the MK College scholarships given to leaders of the Emmanuel United Church were an investment that is still paying off in amazing dividends!

Alumni Impacting Diverse Ethnic Groups

Each of Ethiopia's eighty-two ethnic groups, has its unique world view, belief system, cultural practices, and language or dialect. Evangelists face many challenges as they cross those cultural boundaries bringing the gospel to a people for the first time.

How should one introduce the gospel into a unique culture? What are the commonalities that make a good starting point? How much separation should there be from the influence of the Ethiopian Orthodox Church, or from the Muslim faith, or from the different pagan gods and cultic practices? How much change should one expect on the cultural level? What cultural practices should be abolished? Which modified? Which maintained? Which embellished with added Christian value?

Worship may be organized following the indigenous fashion, but the dominant practices of the larger MKC will be introduced, and will gradually be adapted, especially in the hymnody and style of praying.

MKC Thrives in Southern Ethiopia

The Meserete Kristos Church has experienced phenomenal growth in southern Ethiopia. Many of the college's students originated from there, and many of its graduates serve in the churches there.

In 2012, in the growing city of Awassa, the MKC Regional Office was housed in the main church compound. This congregation carried a ministry to thousands of students from the nearby Debub University campus. In the town of Shone, the Shone MKC Regional Office oversaw thirty-six congregations and sixty-four church planting centers which had more than 20,000 members.

For Easter break of that year, Ernie and Lois Hess, and Vera and I, drove 460 kms south to the town of Arba Minch (*forty springs*). Woza Buea, one of our students, an evangelist from there, had come with us to visit his family. He helped us find lodging for the night. We spent Saturday checking out the tourist sites, visiting the forty springs and a crocodile ranch. We found only one MKC congregation in that town, but it was large. They ran a Compassion project that helped 280 poor children attend school.

After two nights, we left Arba Minch and started our return journey. We reached the town of Hossana in the afternoon and found a hotel, then hunted for an MK Church. We found the Debub Hossana MKC building and talked to the guard. He was delighted to show us around. The building was still under construction, but it could seat close to 1,500. He informed us that up to 2,000 people attended there on Thursday evening services.

The guard led us to Legesse Teka's home. He was one of our earlier graduates. He and his wife welcomed us warmly and fed us Easter supper. Legesse served as the executive secretary of the Hossana Region of MKC. He informed us that the original MKC congregation in the area began only seventeen years earlier. The region had just divided, leaving a new region with seventeen congregations and the mother region with twenty-one congregations. They still had 11,000 members in their region. The new region had about the same. A remarkable growth in so few years!

The next morning, another of our early graduates, Elsae Helebo, came to our hotel and took us to the regional office. He oversaw the HIV AIDS program, did the work of an evangelist, taught at their Bible college (Yes, they also had a Bible college), and was studying part time for a degree in community development and leadership at a local private college.

Elsae showed us the church's college "campus." It consisted of one small classroom of about a twenty-seat capacity, and a library consisting of four shelves of books in the church office. Students paid fifty birr ($3.75) per month, and teachers earned their living in other church jobs.

Six of our graduates were teaching part time at their Bible college. They had their first graduation with eighteen receiving certificates the previous September. At the time, they had two programs running with thirty-eight students. (Note: That was in 2012. As I was writing this in 2024, I received notice that the college in Hossana currently has seventy-nine students, including thirty in a new master's program!)

There were three large MKC congregational worship centers in

Hossana and more church planting centers. Elsae took us to the second one. It was a bit smaller and could only seat about a thousand.

Upon reaching home that evening, we were all impressed with the little glimpse of what we got to see of the churches and especially with the role our graduates were playing in the steady numerical and qualitative growth of Christianity in those parts. It was heartening to realize that the small sacrifices made through the years in the interest of training church leaders were paying off big time.

Revisiting Hararge with the Evangelium Mission

Thanks to the foresight of the late Emperor, Haile Selassie I, Eastern Mennonite Board of Missions and Charities (EMBMC), now EMM, was granted permission to do mission work in Harrar Province. Responding to the vision of Orie Miller and the pioneering leadership of Dorsa and Mary Mishler, Daniel and Blanch Sensenig launched a medical work in Deder in 1949. A dresser school and primary school quickly followed. The Mission launched a clinic and primary school in Bedeno in 1950. Other primary schools and clinics soon followed in the nearby valleys. These brave souls were pioneering in uncharted waters, following a vision for a string of churches stretching from Addis Ababa, following the Franco-Ethiopian railroad line, all the way east to Djibouti.

Twenty-two years later, between 1972 and 1975, it was Vera's and my privilege to work at Bedeno and Deder, directing a rural community development project for three years (See my memoir: *Into Abyssinia: The Odyssey of a Family*). At that time, the Mennonite Mission and MKC had established work in Addis Ababa, Adama, Wonji/Shoa, Metahara, Abadir, Dire Dawa, Deder, and Bedeno—a mere skeleton of that envisioned line.

Since our return to Ethiopia in 1996, it has been our privilege to make several visits to that Hararge Region. It is hard to describe my feelings as we revisited this part of God's creation. My mind kept going back to our previous life when this was our home territory. For so many times we and our children traveled through those magnificent

Ahmar mountains, clothed in various shades of color throughout the seasons. How often we marveled at their long steep slopes, covered with a patchwork of tiny fields, populated with tiny huts, yards, and scattered trees perched on the edges of deep ravines. And how familiar the unending flow of traffic in donkeys, cattle, sheep, goats, and humans carrying their heavy loads to or from the markets, in a never-ending line.

Poverty still looked the same. The clothing and fashions looked the same. The people looked and acted the same. The mosques were the same, however there were many more of them. Only these days, the road was paved, and many more vehicles were on the road, and the towns were much larger with new schools and public buildings. The population had doubled, and one wondered how they could all be fed from the same over-farmed, eroded hillsides.

Of particular interest to us was the small, yet growing presence of Meserete Kristos Churches in most of the towns and villages we passed through. It is not possible to talk about church growth in the Hararge regions, without reference to the influence and support of Shimeles and Jutta Retta and the Evangelium Mission of Germany.

Shimeles Retta was born in the 1950's and raised as a Catholic in a rural village in Hararge Province. As a university student, he had escaped from the Dergue government, spent years in a refugee camp in Sudan, then made his way to Germany. There, he went to university and met Jutta, a German woman, who became his life-long companion. After being converted to Christ, they both were discipled by Mennonites who had migrated from Russia in the 1990's.

Together with the Brotherhood of Mennonites, they formed the Evangelium Mission, a Germany based support network. With this support, Shimeles and Jutta started to work in the Hararge Region of Ethiopia in 1995 in cooperation with MKC. On several occasions, I was privileged to travel into Hararge with this amazing couple. Let me recount some of those experiences.

When we travelled with Shimeles and Jutta in 2012, their work was focusing on eight of the MKC regions in Ethiopia, namely in Eastern and Western Hararge, Awash Sheleko, Adama, Arsi Bale, Meta Robi,

Wolisso, and Jimma. These regions cover the wide east/west Islamic belt across the country. The mission was supporting 460 evangelists working in church planting centers and local congregations in the countryside. The mission provided salaries, training, and guidance in collaboration with the local church elders and regional representatives. To cope with the growth of the churches, the mission also supported construction of meeting houses as resources allowed.

A second evangelistic project was ministry to children. Noting that congregations often neglected children, the Rettas launched a program to train Sunday school teachers and supported four kindergartens in different areas. They also had a charity project which supported destitute people, needy students, and a prison ministry.

In Adama, the Evangelium Mission subsidized the rent for a new office building for the Adama MKC Regional Office. This office building included two very adequate classrooms for the regional Adama MK Bible College. The college had about seventy-five students coming in for classes on Fridays and Saturdays.

While traveling east past Welenchiti, Jutta told me the amazing story of the church in Ruketi Chelle, a pagan community where their evangelist planted the first church in 2006 with 120 members. At this time, 2012, it had 4,008 members thriving in three congregations and several church planting centers among seven villages within a radius of sixteen kms.

East of the town of Asebot, we made a right turn onto a gravel road that wound around in the desert and gradually climbed towards the little village of Kemona, about twenty-five kms from the asphalt. There, the mission had supported an evangelist for nine years, who planted the Kemona MK Church in this predominantly Muslim area. The believers had sacrificed and suffered a lot to get started. However, they had recently completed the requirements for full status as a local congregation, having four elders and fifty-seven adult baptized members. They were renting a meeting room for worship from a Muslim merchant.

The believers were ecstatic to report that the local government had given them a 750 m² plot on the top of a hill, to build a house of worship. They had already built a fence and leveled the land. They were very eager to show it to us. So, we climbed the hill and paused for a group prayer of thanksgiving, dedication, and commitment. It was getting dark as we drove out of Kemona to return to the highway. Sometime later, I received a photo of the completed Kemona MKC building.

In Asebe Teferi, also called by its Oromo name, "Chiro," we visited the Mahal Asebe Teferi church. This congregation built its first building in 1979, only to have it confiscated and closed by the Dergue government in 1982. For seven years, the congregation ceased to exist. However, in 1989, leaders started a house church movement. The new government returned the property to the church in December 1991. Tewodros Desta was serving as the pastor. Girma Gelaye worked as an evangelist. They both had been our students in the early days of MK College. The German Brotherhood had helped them build a large worship house. It stood beside the smaller, older building. This congregation planted five daughter congregations, two in the town and five in the outlying towns at Bedessa, Gelemso, Kemona, Boke, and Boke Tiko.

A separate building was being constructed behind that older church building for the Western Hararge Region's head office. The region had ten congregations and twenty-five church planting centers. Another former student, Wondwesson, oversaw regional education and Girma Gelaye became the general secretary.

The Hirna MKC was the first church planted by the Evangelium Mission. It, in turn, had planted several daughter churches. Zewdu Benberu was serving as an evangelist. Another evangelist, Tesfaye Godana, was in training at MK College. The congregation was meeting in an orange plastic shelter. It had 180 members plus children. Outside was a large concrete foundation, laid some years back, upon which the elders hoped to erect a permanent worship center, pending funds to complete it.

In Deder the original mission hospital, taken by the Ministry of Health, was still serving the growing population. A new hospital was under construction on the premises. The original MK congregation had planted many daughter churches in the hills and valleys around.

At Chelenko we met the evangelist, Fekadu Demeke, another MK College alum. This congregation was founded by the Deder

MKC in 1998. The church had ninety-nine baptized members. The Evangelium Mission was assisting them in running a kindergarten for the community.

An ancient wall, built in 1560, surrounds the historic core of the much older city of Harar, at one time considered the fourth most holy Islamic city next to Mecca, Jerusalem, and Medina. This core still stands much as it was, a "holy" city with ninety-nine mosques, a place frequented by pilgrims and tourists. Outside the wall, the modern city spreads for miles around. It is a seat of government, the capital of the Hararge Administrative Region. It has military training institutions, schools, universities, hospitals, and hotels.

To have a thriving Meserete Kristos congregation in this environment was quite amazing. The first fellowship began meeting in rented quarters in 1990. Persecution led them to change locations often. Twenty years later, in this fourth most holy city, the church had more than 500 members in its main congregation, and several daughter congregations in various parts of the city. The main congregation had constructed its worship center that could seat 1,500 and had a three-level office/classroom extension at the back. They had a major ministry to hundreds of university students.

Girma Seramola, an early graduate of our college, was serving as the pastor. Under his leadership, this Harar MKC started outreach points in places like Bedeno, where they bought a building, and Grawa where they built a worship hall and offices and hired full-time evangelists.

Alemwork, one of our female graduate evangelists, arranged for us to watch a man feeding hyenas after dark. While the rest of us took photos, a few courageous ones among us hand-fed the hungry beasts, holding a small slab of meat on a short stick and letting a hyena pick it off and eat it! Most amazing to me was the communal self-discipline shown by this pack of wild, ferocious, hungry animals. They all congregated in the shadows while each took a turn, one by one, coming up to the human holding the stick, taking the meat, and quickly retreating into the dark. Then the next one came forward taking his/her turn. Had they been pigs, as I knew them, the whole mob would have rushed out of the bushes, overpowered us humans, and gobbled up the tasty morsels in a moment. The weaker ones would have been left out. Taking turns? —The unfathomable social life of the hated, feared, and little understood hyena!

In 2018, we visited Harar again. This time, another of our graduates, Akeya Zeleke, a young pastor, showed us the site which the church had just purchased to build a second permanent MKC building. To legally acquire this property for a church meeting house was a major victory and answer to prayer because the Muslim population strongly resisted the encroachment of evangelical Christians into their holy city. When a property would come up for sale and a deal about to be struck, Muslim money would pop up from somewhere and offer a much higher price, or the seller would suddenly reconsider, and the property would no longer be for sale.

The city of Dire Dawa had grown immensely. It had spread out in the desert to the west and north for several miles with modern new buildings set in wide modern boulevards. Its university had 10,000 students. The city's population had grown to over 300,000. I was impressed that, despite the nation's poverty, it was certainly experiencing economic growth, unprecedented in its long history.

Back in the 1970's, we used to worship with about fifty young people in the small chapel on the Mennonite Mission compound. Now, in that former chapel, we found someone giving instructions in discipleship to thirty-six young people. The mission buildings served as offices for the church's various ministries. The rest of the compound was covered with a huge worship center for the Mehal Dire Dawa MKC, a building capable of accommodating up to 2,000 people.

This was only one of four large congregations in Dire Dawa. It had more than 2,100 members and 550 children, including those in its church planting centers. The congregation had also opened a Bible college that was teaching forty-six parttime students. The teachers were graduates from our college.

Mekonnen Asfaw, the General Secretary of the region, showed us the original documentation that missionary Daniel Sensenig signed, agreeing to a thirty-year lease for the mission property in 1956, for which he paid a total of 20,000 birr, a hefty sum in those days. Today that would cover about one month's rent.

West Dire Dawa MKC (Sabian) had about 1,300 members including 350 children. Being near Dire Dawa University, this congregation had a special ministry for over 700 students. Misrak Dire Dawa MKC, located in the Muslim eastern part of the city, had two church planting centers, both started with the help of the Evangelium Mission. Both used rented halls. Being in a Muslim area, growth was difficult.

Just across the street from this church, Evangelium Mission built a spacious four-floor office and training center. Its 3,000 m² floor space accommodates the mission's head office, a training center for about 120 persons, and guest rooms. Temporarily, it was serving as the East Hararge MKC Regional Office and home of its Bible college.

This regional office gave oversight to twelve congregations and several church planting centers. Two of our graduates were working there. Alemayhu Legesse was coordinator of Outreach Ministries, and Girma Haile, was coordinator for the region's education department and head of the Bible college.

Among the few places that we visited; it was very gratifying to me to note that our graduates were giving leadership in all these churches. They were doing magnificent work. Seeds planted were bearing fruit!

An Old Timers' Retreat

Shimeles and Jutta Retta of the Evangelium Mission sponsored a special old timers' retreat on March 8-11, 2012. Somehow, somebody thought Vera and I qualified and invited us. Without looking in the mirror, Vera and I decided to accept the invitation. It would be a wonderful reunion to meet all those elderly folks we once knew and worked with. Who would be there?

Shimeles raised the question, "How can we older persons pass on to the next generation what we have learned in our walk with the Holy Spirit in our lifetime?" It was his purpose to challenge the older people to pray for the church and its mission. As Aaron and Hur held up the arms of Moses in the Biblical story (Ex. 17:12), older people can hold up the hands of those who are actively leading and ministering in the church through prayer.

The invitees started gathering in time for dinner, on Thursday evening, at the Peniel Guesthouse in Adama. By the next morning, these saints, about forty in number, assembled for breakfast in the original North Nazareth (Semien) Church, built in 1970-71. There they were, in various stages of advancing age, all old timers, remnants from the missionary era, people who knew and worked with the missionaries. These were the heroes of faith, the fathers and mothers of the church, who knew suffering and persevered through persecution in the early days. We had known many of them at one time or another. Some we had not seen for forty years.

The program began with introductions. After a sermon and some songs, a major part of the program over the next two days was telling stories of God's faithfulness. In every culture, storytelling is the old persons' prerogative.

On Sunday morning, the group had breakfast at the guesthouse and made their way to the church. They sat in a group near the front during the two-and-one-half hour service. The old timers were recognized and honored. This was the sixty-first year since the baptism of the first ten believers, which marked the formation of MKC.

Sitting there during that Sunday morning service, surrounded by a packed auditorium of about 1,500 worshippers, I tried to imagine what this scene would mean to the pioneers. What would it mean to those missionaries who prayerfully, patiently, painfully, and faithfully planted seeds, one by one, in the barren desert soil so many years ago. What were they thinking, feeling, and expecting when it took six years of prayerful, self-giving service, before they could see the first "ten trees planted"?

Could they even have imagined what we were experiencing today? Could they imagine 2,400 thriving congregations and church planting centers ministering to 950,000 followers of Jesus, spread out from Djibouti in the east, to the Sudan in the west, and from Moyale in the south, to Asmara in the north?

Surely "seed planting" in the Kingdom of God is a very worthwhile activity. It may take time and patience to see the results. It may also involve sacrifices and suffering, and yet there is a harvest! The pioneers held the words of the psalmist as a promise:

> *Those who sow in tears will reap with songs of joy. He who goes out weeping, carrying seed to sow, will return with songs of joy, carrying sheaves with him. Ps. 126:5,6 (NIV).*

CONCLUSION

Expert physicists say, considering the laws of gravity and aerodynamics, the bumble bee's body weight, shape, and structure, would never allow it to fly. However, the humble bumble bee, being unaware of all those scientific *facts*, flies! Stepping out in faith, facing the impossibilities, opens God's door to success!

Over the past thirty years, we have witnessed this college emerge from its first thirteen students, squeezed into one small compound at Haya Hulet Mazoria, to become a seminary with a nationwide network of over thirty Bible colleges, with over 1,220 under instruction. This was accomplished with a huge amount of faith. Its leaders have dared to step forward into the unknown, against the concerned advice of negative thinking pragmatists, with little more than a firm belief that God wills it and will provide.

Recognizing that "We are fellow workers with God" I Co. 3:9 (JB), we have seen the Lord's partnership in the struggle. By his grace we have seen prayers answered. By his intervention we have seen obstacles overcome. By his provision, we have seen the college grow. By his blessing, we have seen it bless the thousands of students who came, learned, and moved on in service. We have seen them go on to bless their families, bless their congregations, and bless the organizations in which they work. As a result, the church and the nation are also blessed. Already there has been a profound impact, and the work of the college has only begun!

Yes, we have been highly privileged to be "fellow workers with God." Together with him, this story has been a triumph of faith in an uneasy odyssey!

FINALLY, A CHALLENGE
TO YOU, THE READER

In this third decade of the 21ˢᵗ century, Ethiopia continues to face troubled times. Amid political and ethnic tensions, poverty and natural disasters, the people continue to suffer. In this needy and troubled milieu, God has called his church to minister in Jesus' name, to be as light and salt, calling people to a better way, to be reconciled to God, to live in peace with each other, and to share His love and peace.

Behind that challenge are the leaders. To equip and encourage the leaders, stands the Meserete Kristos Seminary and its related colleges. That seminary continues to make, a significant impact on the quality of leadership and the resulting growth of God's "salt of the earth" people. Through its alumni, it spreads its unique influence in the struggling nation. And behind this seminary stand its faithful partners and supporters. Without them, this influence would have been impossible!

If you feel moved, remember this institution with your prayers, encouragement, and support! Join them as partners by sending your inquiries, comments, and contributions. For tax deductible receipts, in the USA, write your check payable to "MK College Link," and send to MK College Link Board, 1890 Windy Hill, Lancaster, PA 17602, USA.

In Canada, write your check to "Mennonite Church Eastern Canada," attention "Meserete Kristos Seminary" send to 201-50 Kent Ave, Kitchener, Ontario, N2G 3R1, Canada, or to "Northwest Mennonite Conference," attn. "Meserete Kristos Seminary," and send to Box 1316, Didsbury, Alberta, TOM OWO, Canada.

Otherwise wire funds directly to Bank of Abyssinia, Bole Branch, Addis Ababa, SWIFT Code ABYSETAA, to Meserete Kristos College Account #31976.

Or you may be interested in supporting the *Meserete Kristos Church Founders Endowment Fund*. This fund, in honor of the early church founders, will provide a stable long-term source of tuition scholarship assistance for worthy students.

The MK College Link Board invites you to join them in building this endowment fund. Send your gifts (marked Endowment Fund) to: MK College Link Board, 1890 Windy Hill, Lancaster, PA 17602, USA.

May God's Kingdom come! May God's will be done! And may God bless you!

Other Books by the Author

This is the author's fifth book. Previously, he published four books in his *The Odyssey of a Family* series. In *Pilgrims Searching for a Home*, he recounts the life story of his grandparents who escaped the horrors of the Bolshevik revolution in Russia with their family, only to settle in western Canada in time to face the hardships, disappointments, and trauma of the Great Depression and the "dirty thirties."

In his second book, *Shaping of a Servant*, the author begins by telling the story of his pioneer parents and their cross-cultural marriage. He continues in an autobiographical form, remembering his growing years in rural Canada. He notes and evaluates the circumstances and events that God used to shape him and prepare him for a life of service. It is the story of the formation of a young man growing in self-awareness, struggling with a sense of divine call. It leads to a romance in which he finds his significant other.

In his third book, *Into Abyssinia*, the author gives an informative and lively account of the first eight years of his and his family's living and serving in pre-revolutionary feudal Ethiopia. It is a story of adventure as a novice missionary couple learns and adapts to a vastly different culture, amid social upheaval, while raising a family in the less developed hinterlands.

In his *Reconciliation in Trans Mara*, the author recounts how his family, with two teenaged daughters, leave their comfortable home in Canada and live as missionaries among the Maasai people in Kenya for six years. Through land demarcation and settlement, and the introduction of elementary schools, health clinics, planting churches, agricultural development, and better animal husbandry techniques, a nomadic people's way of life is transformed. Through wholistic community development, enemy tribes are reconciled and learn to live in peace. It is a story of cross-cultural shock, homesickness, and danger, but more than compensated by adventure, new learning experiences, cross-cultural friendships, and the satisfaction of seeing development and the wholistic transformation of a society.

These books are available at www.westbowpress.com/bookstore.

Printed in the United States
by Baker & Taylor Publisher Services